MUMBAI

Praise for *Mumbai*

'This book embodies a skilful narrative that constructs a trajectory in the making of Mumbai, seamlessly weaving the stories of past with the present. In the process, Sidharth Bhatia takes us to places that don't register in our everyday lives in Mumbai, and makes us comprehend events that laid the ground for the city's present aspirations. He provocatively juxtaposes the perceived upgradation of the city with an incisive analysis of the harsh daily reality of its citizens. This kaleidoscopic reading and documentation of both the immediate past as well as the forces today that are shaping the city is a critical piece of work for future historians.'

—Rahul Mehrotra, architect and professor of urban design and planning at Harvard Graduate School of Design in Cambridge, Massachusetts

'I've been working with slum dwellers in Mumbai for over forty years now and know from experience that they would rather pay taxes to the government than to the slumlords. But they live in slums, which are considered "illegal". This denies them a life of dignity.

Sidharth Bhatia's timely book brings them and their lives into the public eye. As we watch luxury apartments being built around us, millions of citizens live without basic amenities including running water. And many of them have been shifted to the peripheries of the city, making them further invisible to policymakers and the city at large.'

—Shabana Azmi, actor and housing rights activist

'"Mumbai abhors a vacuum," writes Sidharth Bhatia in *Mumbai: A Million Islands*, noting that empty spaces in India's commercial capital are soon occupied, turning land into slums or space under staircases into tiny tailoring shops. More than a history of failed housing policies, this deeply researched new book reads like a tender love letter to a disappearing city, written with the intimacy of someone who wants its stories told before they are lost for good. Masterfully weaving together the human tapestry behind his city's dramatic transformation, from the rooftops of Queen's Mansion to newer luxury towers that dot the skyline, Bhatia has achieved something genuinely impressive: a book replete with personal drama but also an important contribution to understanding our planet's complex urban future.'

—James Crabtree, author of *The Billionaire Raj* and former Mumbai bureau chief of the *Financial Times*

MUMBAI

A MILLION ISLANDS

SIDHARTH BHATIA

HarperCollins *Publishers* India

First published in India by HarperCollins *Publishers* 2025
HarperCollins *Publishers* India, Cyber City, Building 10-A,
Gurugram, Haryana – 122002, India
www.harpercollins.co.in

2 4 6 8 10 9 7 5 3 1

P-ISBN: 978-93-6989-341-6
E-ISBN: 978-93-6989-596-0

Typeset in 12/16.2 Aldine401 BT
by HarperCollins *Publishers* India Pvt. Ltd

Printed and bound at
Thomson Press (India) Ltd

FSC
www.fsc.org
MIX
Paper | Supporting responsible forestry
FSC® C010615

This book is produced from independently certified FSC® paper
to ensure responsible forest management.

HarperCollins Publishers, Macken House, 39/40 Mayor Street Upper,
Dublin 1, D01 C9W8, Ireland

To
Almona, Aliya and Rhea, who love this frustrating city
as much as I do

Aaj ki raat bahut garm hawa chalti hai
Aaj ki raat na footpaaath pey neend aayegi
Sab utho main bhi ugoon tum bhi utho tum bhi utho
Koi khidki issi deewar mein khul jayegi

('It is a hot wind that blows tonight.
Sleep will not come tonight on the footpath.
Let us rise; me and you, and you as well.
In this walled space a window will surely open.')

—Kaifi Azmi, 'Makan'

'But look what we have built ... This is not the rebuilding of cities. This is the sacking of cities.'

—Jane Jacobs (journalist and urban activist),
Introduction, *The Death and Life of Great American Cities*

CONTENTS

1

INTRODUCTION

'Mumbai is Upgrading' is painted on billboards all along the southern part of the Mumbai Metro-3 construction, hiding the work going on behind them. Is it a bold claim or a myth?

Let's look at some examples.

For six years, the work on the longest metro line—running from Cuffe Parade in the southernmost tip of the city and to Andheri in the northern suburb—has been going on, falling behind schedules, beset with problems ranging from the pandemic lockdown, political battles, funding issues and much more.

Interestingly, the lockdown did not stop the continuous construction of the Coastal Road—another 'upgrading' project—connecting Marine Drive in the south to Kandivali in the northern suburbs. The road runs almost parallel to the metro, the western railway suburban services and the roads; while many experts warned it would be a white elephant.

Many citizens, especially vehicle owners, were happy when some part of it was inaugurated, due to the sheer convenience of avoiding the usual traffic jams. That was till some inherent problems surfaced—flooding inside the tunnels during the usual rains and traffic jams at both entry and exit points. The irony is that even after the whole stretch becomes operational, it will serve only a tiny percentage of the total number of private vehicles in the city.

And then there is the 22-kilometres-long (approx.) trans-harbour link (officially known as the Atal Bihari Vajpayee Sewri-Nhava Sheva Atal Setu), which connects the eastern part of Mumbai to the Indian mainland across the water. This makes travelling easier to Navi Mumbai and Pune, but it is nowhere near meeting its estimated traffic.[1]

Both the Coastal Road and the Atal Setu have been made at huge costs—₹20,000 crores for the former and ₹17,800 crores for the latter—and for the benefit only of a small number of cars. A fraction of that money to upgrade public transport would have benefited a much larger populace.

Do we need more proof of Mumbai being upgraded? Look around at the skyscrapers that are being constructed. The city is full of high-rise buildings coming up rapidly, each more exclusive, expensive and targeted at the 'elite'. It can be a high-end, sea-facing apartment in Walkeshwar, near tony Malabar Hill, priced at over ₹3 billion or a more modest ₹20 million-flat in the very distant suburbs. Both promise attractive amenities—gym, swimming pool, club, walking tracks—and a gated life, where the rest of the city wouldn't intrude and the miseries and chaos of Mumbai city would be far away.

These pockets of upgrades are like new islands in themselves, emerging over 300 years after the British company—the East India Company—weaved seven islands together and created a new, whole city—Bombay. They wanted mobility between the islands and towards the Indian hinterland—for their goods, people, administrators and, if needed, the armed forces. The East India Company knew that more land would mean more trade and, therefore, more profits.

The project of connecting the seven chosen islands was an experiment. When the experiment was very successful, the policy of reclaiming land from the sea became the template for successive British governors and, after Independence, for the Indian government. This reclamation continued non-stop, but post-1947, the emphasis changed.

But how did the experiment start? The first big step in this project under the Britishers was to connect Bombay Island (Bombay was the name of the biggest island among the seven islands) with Worli Island in the north by filling the Worli creek that flooded other parts of the city during high tide and constructing a road. The experimental project was the brainchild of then Bombay Governor William Hornby and was started in 1782.

Hornby wrote to the company directors in the UK for permission, but started the construction regardless. One year later, the missive arrived from England rejecting his proposal, but the project was complete and he was, consequently, sacked.[2]

Legend has it that every attempt by the East India Company to fill the creek and construct the road between the two islands failed till the 1780s. Then a native engineer called Ramji Shivji Prabhu stepped in and told the governor about a dream he had about the goddess Mahalaxmi. In the dream, the goddess told Prabhu that her idol lay in the creek and if they could find a home for her on land, she would give her blessings to the project. Interestingly, an idol of the goddess was found in the creek and the construction went ahead smoothly. A temple dedicated to the goddess was built in the 1830s, which stands till this date at the southern end of the Vellard. This is the story of the Mahalaxmi Temple, overlooking the linking road.

Whether the legend is true or not, the success of constructing that road set off many other projects to connect various islands by filling up the water in between them.

One such was the Mahim Causeway, between Mahim (effectively the last island on the western side between Bombay and Salsette, another big island) which was connected to the Indian mainland. There was a big swamp between Mahim and the mainland, which was dangerous during high tide and the rainy season, prohibiting people from crossing over to the other side. The East India Company refused to pay for any reclamation, till Lady Jamsetjee Jejeebhoy stepped in with a donation to fund it on the condition that no toll would be charged on it.

Much of the earlier reclamation was for utilitarian purposes—to create roadways, for example—till the early twentieth century. In the post-plague years (meaning, in the final years of the nineteenth century), when the Bombay administration decided to demolish old houses in the congested parts of the native towns for their project, a decision was taken to create new land in various parts of the island to accommodate those who were affected. One such resettlement area was the Backbay Reclamation, which involved filling up the sea in the western parts of the city, specifically in South Bombay.

A whole new shore was created, beginning from Chowpatty and ending at Colaba as a continuous stretch. But before the project was completed, the money ran out and the project at the Colaba end was left out (though, Colaba got its own reclamation). The Kennedy Sea-Face (famously commemorated by a lamp post in Chowpatty) was, finally, completed in 1920.

The land, which was to be for recreational purposes, such as garden areas, was eventually auctioned off, plot by plot. The richer sections of the city found the sea-facing views of this new precinct much too tempting and bought the plots, constructing modern buildings on them—later to be called 'Art Deco'—which eventually became the posh area of the city. 'The Backbay Reclamation Project symbolized a major shift in the spirit of the city from Victorian to an International city,' write Mehrotra and Dwiwedi.[3]

As mentioned before, the idea of reclamation did not stop post-Independence. The goal was to create new land, which mainly benefited builders and was targeted towards the richer sections of society.

One shining example is Nariman Point, which swallowed the sea beyond Marine Drive, and was developed to create a new business district for the corporate world. This is a classic example of a precinct that emerged with no proper planning for wide roads, to handle the additional traffic or ancillary services like transport and reasonably priced restaurants for the hundreds of staff that thronged the area daily.

In some time, the inevitable happened—traffic became a mess. The condition was exacerbated by the scores of food vendors that set up shops to cater to a ready-made clientele; in addition, the buildings did not have enough parking space, which led to the parked cars clogging up the streets.

Ironically, this situation repeated itself over three decades later at the Bandra Kurla Complex. It is a new office district created by filling up marshland, where companies rushed to set up offices. The roads looked wide and well maintained, but getting out of the area in the evenings has turned into a nightmare.

None of these grandiose projects have given a thought to the plight of the common citizen, especially those who do not have cars of their own. Indeed, as has become apparent, even car owners feel frustrated. Consider the example of the Bandra-Worli Sea Link, which opened to the public in June 2009. Buses avoid it because of the toll and two wheelers are not allowed. Similarly, two wheelers are not allowed on the Coastal Road, even though there is no toll here.

As for the hundreds of construction projects all over the city, all part of the 'upgradation' of Mumbai to Shanghai, Singapore, New York, take your pick, they are all expensive and unaffordable for a normal middle-class family. Swimming pools, gyms, gardens and security measures don't come cheap and neither does land. Slums are cleared to get the land, and those who lived there before have to be given homes in situ, which adds to the cost of the buyer of the new apartments.

But the new homes for the erstwhile slum dwellers turn into almost 'vertical slums', barren and dark and, very soon, dirty. Most such buildings are constructed close to each other, leaving no room for sunlight, ventilation and hygiene. The construction is shoddy, in stark contrast to the magnificent towers built on the land where they used to live. The states' and the builders' argument is that the slums were illegal constructions on private land and now each former resident has been given a flat, completely free of any cost. So, what do they expect? The same argument has been advanced in many cases, where buildings have been constructed in places far away from the main Mumbai city to settle the slum dwellers—even when their new homes are in the middle of nowhere, the places have become disease pits and are of poor quality. The counter is always the same—at least they have a proper home.

Housing has been a problem in Mumbai for a long time, especially since the mid-nineteenth century when waves of new migrants came, attracted by employment opportunities in the growing and prosperous city, generated by the newly opened mills.

Most newcomers settled in and around the Parel area, including Chinchpokli and Lalbaug, where the mills were, and in the absence of proper housing, lived in makeshift housing wherever they could find it. Parel began to change.

In the late eighteenth century, the governor's residence had shifted from Fort, the seat of Bombay power, to Parel, to a magnificent new home, which was once a Jesuit monastery.

It was soon named Sans Pareil (without parallel) and became the centre of the upper crust of Bombay society, which gathered at the governor's parties.

The arrival of the mills changed all that. The air became noxious, mainly because of the chimneys that continuously spewed out fumes; and the water quality deteriorated because of the crowded houses in the area, with their poor sanitation facilities. The result was an increase in the air- and water-borne diseases in the area. But that was not true for the British officials.[4] In 1883, Lady Ferguson died of cholera, and the residence officially shifted to Malabar Point, where it stands to this day, in magnificent isolation, gazing upon the Arabian Sea and Marine Drive back bay.

The governor could get away, the masses could not. The masses continued to live in squalor and the authorities could do very little to help. The mill-owners were persuaded to create some housing for workers, which they did. Yet, Bombay continued to grow, with little planning for its housing needs.

In 1896, a plague hit the city and the British administration squarely blamed the poor sanitation in the houses of the 'natives'. Drastic measures were taken to fight it, including razing down those homes—many of them slum clusters—which angered the Indians. 'To deal with the crisis caused by the bubonic plague, a new, supra-municipal body known as the Bombay City Improvement Trust was established on 9 November 1898,' writes Mariam Dossal in her book *Theatre of Conflict, City of Hope: Mumbai 1660 to Present Times*.[5]

The Bombay City Improvement Trust (BCIT) undertook many road expansion and housing projects. A decade or so after the BCIT was set up, a review was undertaken.

The then governor, Sydenham Clarke praised the Trust but said that he 'believed that it had been undertaken without "a cohesive plan".'[6]

On an earlier occasion, Governor Sydenham Clarke had admitted, 'In the absence of any definite policy in the past, Bombay has been permitted to grow up almost haphazard and this has added to our present difficulties.'

In his lecture 'The Housing Question in Bombay' to the Royal Society of Arts, London, which was published in 1910, G. Owen W. Dunn had said, 'The slender means of the working-classes necessitate their residing in as close proximity as possible to their work; their habits and customs lead them to congregate in communities of race, religion, and caste, and these people have not the most elementary ideas of sanitation.'[7] Dunn had impressive credentials—he had been chief engineer of the Public Works Department and had held the position of not just the commissioner of the Bombay Municipal Corporation but also the Bombay City Improvement Trust, giving him an insight into the city's housing, infrastructure and sanitation. The Trust itself had been founded to decongest the city after vast swathes of neighbourhoods were hit by the plague in 1896. The disease-ridden areas were seen as a proof of the unhygienic native ways of living. Yet, more than the cultural aspects, it highlighted that Bombay's biggest problems were congestion and overcrowding. The city's inherent geographical limitations, combined with a rapidly growing population and high property prices, meant that Bombay's residents had no option but to live in cramped conditions, a situation that is familiar even in the shiny, high-rise Mumbai of the early twenty-first century.

'Bombay, like all other large cities, has a very acute housing problem. Not only is it customary for a whole family to live in one room, but this room frequently houses a number of other relations of the family. To meet the needs the Government are now undertaking the erection of a large number of tenement buildings to provide accommodation for 50,000 families. In view of the high price of land it has not been found practicable to provide for the poorer classes in other than blocks of tenement buildings'—wrote D.W. Davidge in his paper 'Development of Bombay', in 1924.[8] It was Davidge who had come up with the proposal for developing the Backbay Reclamation Project as a mixed-use project—with commercial and residential developments and wide-open public spaces.

This did not happen, since it was the rich who took over all the spaces on offer in the reclamation, and built housing for themselves on Marine Drive.

This is something that has happened repeatedly in Mumbai. Every now and then plans are made to help slum dwellers get proper housing but somehow these don't work or make a marginal difference. Almost half the city's population continues to live in 'slums', as defined by UN Habitat in 2003:[9]

> … slums are a multidimensional concept involving aspects of poor housing, overcrowding, lack of services and insecure tenure …

The UN report, which is easily accessible, makes for an interesting read. Though old, it is still relevant as the issues mentioned in the report have remained unaddressed or unsolved over the years. Ask any Mumbai resident, and they would emphatically say that the slum population has only grown. 'My area was so beautiful, till we got slums in the neighbourhood,' said a middle-aged man who grew up in one of the most expensive and tony parts of Mumbai, and it is a sentiment I have often heard from others.

The irony is that Mumbaikars who don't live in slums do not know what a slum is like—they may know their domestic staff comes from there but they may not have seen their homes. Prejudices and assumptions, therefore, are common—slum dwellers don't pay taxes (false—many do); they get subsidized utilities (false—they pay the same rate for electricity and in fact pay much higher for water); they live free on public and private land (but not out of choice), and so on.

On the other hand, what everyone considered a 'slum', may not be always seen by the residents as such. Dharavi, often called Asia's second largest slum, has many diverse micro-colonies. These include the Kumbhars, a community of potters from Gujarat, who were among the earliest settlers. And they object to their community being called 'slum dwellers'.

These nuances escape others. For most Mumbai residents, a slum is a dark and dingy place with a high incidence of crime and is not safe for any 'respectable' person to go.

Articles emphasizing the entrepreneurial culture of Dharavi and regular tours of slum neighbourhoods have somewhat changed these perceptions, but the overall impression is still negative.[10]

Yet, Mumbai is not all about slums, of course. Nor does it consist mainly of buildings, old and new. There are also the chawls, a housing system initially created for labour and, subsequently, for some communities and castes. These occupy a unique place in Mumbai, mainly in the island city, from the 'native towns' of South Mumbai to the textile mills clusters of Parel.

'As late as in 1989, nearly 75 per cent of formal housing stock in Greater Mumbai consisted of chawls. Indeed, the grand topography of the Island City was possible only because 80 per cent of the population were housed in the cramped tenements of chawls over a century,' writes Neera Adarkar in *The Chawls of Mumbai: Galleries of Life.*[11]

Chawls can vary—but, the typical image is of one room tenements facing a common corridor, a few storeys high with community toilets on the ground floor. A lot of wood is used in their construction. In his foreword for *The Chawls of Mumbai*, architect Charles Correa describes them as 'elemental'. He adds, 'The workers in early twentieth century Bombay are not so lucky. The typology of the accommodation that both government and private capital deem are good for them is even more brutal.'

There are other kinds of residential structures too, such as concrete buildings with similar arrangements, built by the Bombay Improvement Trust and Bombay Development Department, both public bodies set up by the government, after the plague of 1896.

Many of these chawls have been demolished and shiny new apartment buildings have come up in the name of redevelopment. It is not for the benefit of the erstwhile residents, who were paid off to move elsewhere, but for free market buyers. The Mumbai chawl is slowly giving way to the luxury apartment tower, and the old textile mill area, with its many chawls, is an attractive proposition for builders to construct skyscrapers. The municipal corporation's own research shows that the most towers—forty storeys and above—were built in that area since 2008.[12]

For chawl residents, whose homes are getting cramped as their families grow, a lucrative offer from a builder is very tempting. The builder wants unencumbered properties—their company offers residents good money to sign off their old homes and leave. This money can come in handy to invest in a new property, even though they may now have to move to the distant northern suburbs, where apartments are more affordable. But at least it's new and their own.

Real estate is a popular topic of conversation in Mumbai and its affordability is a subject that preoccupies people's minds. Despite frequent newspaper articles proving that renting is financially a better option, most people want to ultimately buy their own property for the sake of 'security', not the least because renting too is fraught with obstacles.[13]

The banks are more than willing to lend to buyers, sometimes as much as 80 per cent of the value, which makes it attractive. But with interest rates high, the borrower ends up paying a lot eventually, more so in a city like Mumbai, where properties are more expensive than in other cities.

Additionally, hundreds of real estate projects never get completed, because builders claim they have run out of funds, which means the poor purchaser is left high and dry, having sunk their savings and being burdened with a loan to be paid off. Not only does this affect the middle-class, but even hyper-expensive projects, where the rich have invested, lie incomplete all over Mumbai like a shabby monument to the poor planning and greed of builders. Mumbai leads in this respect.

Trying to get a home in Mumbai therefore is not an easy task. And yet, anyone looking around the city will see only construction sites where newer buildings are coming up. The newspapers carry glossy ads every morning about 'luxury' projects, where the residents will remain in splendid isolation from the messy world outside, and can enjoy the many amenities the housing complex has to offer—the swimming pool, the gym, the yoga room and the walking track. Some come with private theatres to watch films, and even a temple! While visiting an under-construction project and sitting through a presentation of its many attractions—which included Italian marble in the apartment, top-of-the-line bathroom fittings, etc.—we were given the ultimate clincher by the salesman, who thought it would entice us the most: no one from the minority community would be allowed to purchase an apartment in this project. 'We listened to our customers' preferences and we took this decision,' he said, proudly, and adding, 'We have nothing against those people, we will be happy to make a special building for them, if required.'

In all probability, a project like that would be a sell-out. Such prejudices run deep in the Indian society. Similarly, there are buildings that discourage anyone who is not a vegetarian, even as a tenant. Single women—and men—find it very difficult to rent an apartment, much like the people working in the film industry.

When I set out to write this book, I realized that many books on Mumbai, over the years, had not touched upon the subject of housing, especially from the ground-level perspective. Real estate, as a subject, gets a lot of newspaper space, but almost always from the industry point of view. If at all the end user—the buyer—is considered in the narrative, it is in terms of either investment or to highlight the advantages of buying.

But what is it like to actually try to rent or buy a house, live in one with dubious legal status or spend one's life in a slum—these are serious, everyday situations for millions of its citizens that barely get covered by the media or in literature. The slum and the slum dweller are written in abstract terms at best, as a type.

Usually, when a grand plan of 'redevelopment' is announced for slums, say Dharavi for example, to create proper housing for the residents, it follows a certain process. Builders are invited to submit bids, the attraction for them being the vast tracts of land that would become free once the slums are cleared. Almost all these plans come to naught—either because builders find the conditions to be stringent, locals protest vociferously or the required investment is beyond the capacity of most developers.

The more I looked into it, the more it became clear that for an average Mumbai resident, a place to live in was the most important priority. This is true for almost any other city, but Mumbai's unaffordability makes it unique. In 2024, *The Economic Times* reported that the MMR (Mumbai Metropolitan Region), which encompasses Greater Mumbai and its surrounding areas, was the most expensive area in India.[14] And yet, a survey of the country's metropolitan markets, done by the real estate company Knight Frank showed that in 2023 the MMR had the most constructions and also the most sales of all cities:[15]

> The Mumbai real estate market in 2023 exhibited robust growth despite global challenges. It retained its status as the leading market, recording the sale of 86,871 units, marking the highest sales volume in the past eleven years. This upsurge in sales was propelled by a positive economic outlook, increased disposable income among home buyers, a shift in preference for larger homes, and a fear of missing out on purchasing property in the largest real estate market amidst consistent price escalations.

This optimism still excludes millions of people. When the reports are read closely, it is possible to see the social change that this property market reflects. Much of the growth—of construction and sales—is in the far-flung regions of the vast MMR (which includes the northern suburbs, which is outside the range of the Mumbai municipality) and in Navi Mumbai, where land is available in abundance. These are virtually bedroom communities, since a majority of offices and employment opportunities are situated mainly in Mumbai and people have to commute into the city and back.

Yet, new housing complexes are coming up apace in these areas and prices are steadily rising. Any Mumbai resident, prepared to move to far-flung areas for reasonable housing and endure a long ride to work, soon discovers that prices are high there too.

One of the commonly heard grouses is that while the salaried middle-class buy apartments at market rates, those who live in slums get free housing because the politicians want their votes. On the face of it, it is a logical complaint as, periodically and usually before an election, the politicians promise free flats for residents who lived in the slum area till a particular date.

For example, the Slum Rehabilitation Authority had originally promised free housing to slum dwellers who had lived in Mumbai before 1 January 1995. That changed to offering 'discounted' housing to those who built their structures between 2000 and 2011, but the residents had to pay ₹2.5 lakhs for them. Since the growth of slums has not stopped, that still renders large numbers of people as 'illegals'. They too have to be accommodated somewhere.

This does not take into account the sheer indignity of living in slums for generations, mainly because housing is so expensive. Those who move into slums do so because they cannot afford a proper house, not because they like dwelling in slums or hope to get a free flat. They do not get the utilities that others take for granted—water, plumbing, sanitation, for example. They don't get access to medical services or good education for their children. The civic authorities do their best to provide these amenities to slum dwellers but have their own constraints. Just to understand their sincerity, one can look into Mumbai municipal corporation's handling of the Covid crisis in 2021, which was praised for controlling the spread of the disease in an area where sanitation was rudimentary at best and social distancing was simply not possible.

I began researching and writing this book in the pre-Covid period. Even then I realized that writing about a city where changes happen rapidly was never going to be easy. But little did I know that the city would transform so much in three years and at the same time remain the same.

Even while the rest of Mumbai was under a lockdown, work continued on the city's Coastal Road, on the western side, a mega project that a number of citizens had criticized as wasteful. The Brihanmumbai Municipal Corporation, which cannot manage to repair roads around the city, worked round the clock and in 2024, opened the north-south road, with its complicated underwater tunnelling, which serve the needs of a few thousand motorists but has forever ruined the views of the city's bays, for which Mumbai has been justly famous.

I also began to notice that the city's landscape was changing. Mumbai resembled a huge construction site—skyscrapers were springing up where slums existed before. On the eastern side of the city, which had been neglected in the past by developers, entire slum colonies disappeared only to be replaced by gated complexes. Under the government's own Slum Rehabilitation Authority scheme, the builder needed to provide housing to slum dwellers—on the same plot of land, if possible. The builders constructed tenement buildings that were so close to each other that there was no light or circulation of air—'vertical slums', as they have often been called.

In the case of Dharavi, the alternative is even worse. The project was given to the Adani Group, after several previous attempts at getting in a developer. Newspapers reported that the deal had a revenue potential of an astounding ₹22,000 crores and included a number of incentives, which were never given to any previous bidder.

Dharavi is spread over 590 acres, and many of its residents would have to be accommodated within it. But the Adani Group offered a land far away from Dharavi to house its residents—their reasoning was that it won't do to create luxury housing that will have, within its proximity, ugly tenements built for one-time slum dwellers. And the government was happy to oblige—it said that the remaining slum-residents could be shifted to distant Deonar, which has been the city's garbage dump for decades. They were being literally swept away from sight, from their home, while attractive new towers would come up on the same land.

As a native Mumbai resident, the growing number of looming towers and gated complexes replacing old buildings and slum clusters in Mumbai is one of the biggest changes I have seen over the years. Since the 1990s, when builder-friendly laws were first introduced and old defunct mills were razed to be replaced by expensive tower blocks, the pace of transformation has been bewilderingly rapid.

This is particularly noticeable in the Central Mumbai neighbourhoods where old mills once stood—till the 1980s, the landscape, when seen from afar would be filled with smoke billowing from the chimneys. Till the early 2000s, the chimneys stood, even when the mills had fallen silent. By the second decade, however, they had gone and been replaced by skyscrapers, all glass and concrete, glistening in the sun. In just a few years, Mumbai wiped out the legacy of its textile mills, which had contributed so much to its prosperity for more than a century.

And the workers who had toiled for generations to build that prosperity were left with nothing to show for it; the homes that were promises to them as part of the redevelopment schemes on the mill land rarely materialized. All along the former mill areas are old buildings occupied by the families of mill labour interspersed with new 'luxury' towers that sell for half a million dollars or more.

'Luxury' has become the new mantra to advertise real estate, reflecting the aspirations of the consumer. It denotes not just the grand lobby, the clubhouse, the amenities and, implicitly, the others who will inhabit that space and uplift the general profile of the property, but also the aspirations of the customer. After all, no one wants to live next to people with an inferior social status (or, as it turns out, people from the 'wrong' religion or caste).

But the buyer of a luxury apartment too doesn't have it easy. As I found, and have written about, expensive projects are often delayed or worse, come to a dead halt, blocking millions of rupees of prospective buyers who had invested in under-construction properties. This is a country-wide problem and thousands of middle-class buyers, who had taken loans to fund their purchases, find that they have lost their money because the builder has gone bankrupt. In Mumbai, this affliction does not spare even the super rich.

I also realized that the awe-inspiring prices for an apartment—approximately $9 million—which I had come across while researching this book in the pre-Covid days, appeared mundane just five years later. In March 2023, the newspapers reported that an industrialist had shelled out upwards of $30 million for an under-construction property, comprising of three apartments which would presumably be joined together.[16] This figure made it to the papers and private conversations. The fact that the buyers, belonging to the super-rich class, were ready to shell out these kinds of amounts, showed that Mumbai had no dearth of big spenders.

Mumbai has always been home to both the extremely wealthy and extremely poor. The visible inequality has been a Mumbai leitmotif, the clichéd image of the slum and the skyscraper existing side-by-side in the city. Back in the day, the skyscrapers were few and far between. Through much of its history, Bombay had stayed a working-class city, and the super rich were largely discreet. No one could point out a building that stood out and say, 'XYZ industrialist lives here.'

Nor is it only about the super rich. Mumbai has now constructed itself around the needs and lifestyles of the well-off and the privileged, ignoring the wants of the other vast section of the city that makes up its service sector. From entertainment (including restaurants, exclusive clubs) to housing, mobility infrastructure (such as the Coastal Road or the Trans Harbour Bridge), health care sector, education—all new development by the government or private enterprise are aimed at only one segment of the city. Mumbai is now being remade into a version quite unlike what it was before and yet, going back to its own origins and creating new islands of a different kind.

Mumbai was always a tough city. What set it apart was how it offered hope and opportunity to people from all over the country. This was not a city that asked you who your father was and gave you a good shot at success, even though it extracted a brutal cost. Now that cost has gone up.

What I also discovered during my walks around the city was that most residents, dealing with its crumbling infrastructure, expensive housing and rising cost of living, never lose hope. There is always hope that the city will somehow provide a job and income, and perhaps even a better place to stay. It doesn't necessarily work out that way, but the migrants rarely leave Mumbai to return to their hometowns. The daily commute is enervating, the job may pay poorly and the rent is high, but somewhere there is hope of things improving. I met long-time slum dwellers, who were sure that redevelopment would come one day and they would get an apartment—their hope was not unrealistic because over the years, they had seen things improve—one municipal corporation had helped get them a water connection, another had ensured that they got key identification documents. A school and a clinic had opened up nearby some years ago.

Helping them were one of the scores (in hundreds, maybe) of NGOs that were working in the slums. One focused on just getting slum dwellers a water connection—not an easy task if your place of residence is deemed 'illegal'—a second one conducted classes for children, a third provided crèches and a fourth ensured that dwellers got crucial government documents. The good NGOs did not totally replace the authorities, but worked alongside them, ensuring there was no conflict. Grassroot workers from political parties were another important resource. They would secure admission for children in local private schools or put in a word for a job. Most importantly, the much-maligned politician pushed the municipal corporation or the state government for funding for a school or a community centre. Life was never easy, but it was not without hope. A superficial, top-down look at the city misses these granular details.

But will the juggernaut of development roll on, ignoring or even crushing the majority of Mumbai's residents? So far, all the 'upgrading' that has been announced seems to create even more area for entertainment options or expensive apartments. For example, the vast stretch of Dharavi has been handed over to one developer, who has asked for—and is provided with—even more land. The government has its eye on the Sylvan Race Course, which has long been a spot of green area in south Mumbai, where races are held or people take long walks. Why 'waste' such prime space, the government seems to be saying—let's make an entertainment park. It's all to 'beautify' the city and who better to do it than builders and developers?[17]

I got back to all those I had met during my research to see if there was any difference in their lives in the past few years. No one sounded optimistic—access to water was still a problem, the threat of losing their homes still hung over their heads. Their life continued to be precarious. The developments in Dharavi, where almost 600 acres could be handed over to the major industrial house had scared them, said one resident from another part of the city. 'They could one day remove us and then move us far away,' the resident said.

★★★

Decisions taken at a particular time have long lasting impacts. In the late 1700s and early 1800s, the major reclamations that covered the water bodies between the original seven islands created a city that was to become India's economic powerhouse. In the mid-1800s, after decades of thinking about it, the authorities finally decided to bring the walls of the Fort down and opened up vast tracts of land for the development of public and private buildings. To this day, those institutions stand and serve, and have become symbolic of an older, more graceful Bombay. In the early part of the 1900s, the Backbay Reclamation and also the development works in various parts of the city created the most loved precinct of Bombay—Marine Drive.

In most cases, however, the development was on either empty grounds or on freshly created land. In the late 1990s and early 2000s, the turbo-charged construction of new developments has been, for the most part, on lands which were already occupied. And that is how it looks likely to continue. More towers will be built, driven by the notion that in an island city, land is at a premium and the only way to accommodate residents is to build upwards. At the same time, property prices too will go skywards, which makes a mockery of trying to build homes for citizens. More public lands will also disappear, in the name of creating 'infrastructure' for the city. Many slums will also vanish—and so will slum dwellers, placed in far off areas, out of sight of everyone.

The trajectory of Mumbai's future—call it growth, development or upgrading—has been set. I can only hope to have captured a moment, a snapshot of a particular era, but an era that sets the tone for the times to come. Neighbourhoods as they are now—whether in slums, chawls or in old, low level buildings—and the communities they fostered over decades, will disappear, and in their place will come insular, gated complexes which will keep out anyone who doesn't belong. They will have their gardens, their clubs, their swimming pools, while water will become an even more scarce resource for millions. Bridges and tunnels will be built and proudly displayed as a sign of progress, but when the rains come, the roads and railway tracks will be flooded.

Environmentalists will point out that this happens precisely because sewerage lines are getting clogged because of more and more unbridled construction, but that somehow will go unheard. It is the price of change.

It is not as if old areas should not be rebuilt, nor that those who live in poor quality housing should not get to live in better buildings, but the creation of new housing stock almost totally excludes the current residents. When old buildings are demolished or old slum areas are razed, what takes its place are inevitably expensive new towers. Such is the law of the marketplace—the builder will explain. And the space has to be fully exploited—hence the tallest tower that can be built, with 'luxury' specs and views that cost money; the developer has to earn back his investment. That is and will in the coming years, change the city's profile—physically, socially, economically.

Mumbai will always remain Mumbai, and perhaps a shinier, glossier Mumbai will be seen, but what is being witnessed is a monumental shift, a complete overhaul of not just the city's face but also its innards, and, some might say, perhaps also its soul. It is the fundamental remaking of the city.

2

A HOME IS A HOME

It's a nice enough apartment, a bit small at 250 square feet, but has many advantages that make up for its limitations. There is a bathing area, a kitchenette and access to an open terrace area, which is well lit and breezy, and looks out over the low-rise roofs of other buildings. Most of all, it is conveniently located, within walking distance of two major railway stations as well as shops, restaurants, cinemas and even an art gallery.

Over the years, Nainesh Thakkar, in his early forties, has acquired all the mod-cons—a fridge, a washing machine, a flat-screen television and an air conditioner—and now runs a small business, packing and supplying dry fruits to shops in nearby Crawford Market. During the day, his two women employees sit near his home sorting and deseeding dates. In Mumbai, even a home like this is quite a luxury.

There is only one problem with it. The 'flat' is on the roof of a building, the Victorian-era Queen's Mansion on Talwatkar Road—more commonly called Prescott Road—opposite the Fort, in the area that came to be known as Frere Town. The road was originally named after Miss Prescott, who ran a school in the vicinity, and was built in the aftermath of the 'share mania' of the 1860's. The foundation of the Mansion was laid in 1871, according to the book *Bombay Place-Names and Street-Names* (1917) by Samuel T. Sheppard.[1]

The area mainly consists of offices, and the most famous institutions near the building are the Freemasons' Hall, the Cathedral and John Connon School and Siddharth College, which was founded by Dr Ambedkar. The streets here empty out by 6 p.m., like in much of South Bombay, as office employees head to their suburban homes—after 7 p.m., the streets of Frere Town are eerily quiet.

Queen's Mansion itself was once a hotel; the management had given the terrace to a few of its employees, who never left even after the hotel shut down. Over the years, 'apartments', most of them of the same size as Nainesh's, changed hands and now there is a thriving community of about twenty-eight families living in these dwellings. They have all the mandatory and all-important documents to prove their identity and their address.

The terrace is cleaved in the middle by two large, overhead tanks where water is collected and distributed to the other tenants in the building, which include advertising agencies, the cultural space Jnanapravaha and the well-known art gallery, Chemould Prescott. None of these offices has much to do with the denizens of the terrace, who use a separate, winding cast-iron staircase to go to their homes—it is a steep climb and one that can get very difficult for relatively young people, let alone senior citizens.

Appliances, beds and other heavy and large items are lifted up by rope; when someone dies, the body is brought down in a similar way, by tying it to a sturdy rope and slowly lowering it down. Nainesh and the others are used to it—it is home after all, and the convenient location more than makes up for these hardships. And he has lived here since he was born, so he doesn't find it strange at all.

It is a typical Mumbai story, one of not just enterprise and determination, but also of desperation, where each inch of space has possibilities—tailors sit under staircases, workers sleep outside shops and move away early in the morning to get on with their day. Rooftop homes are not unheard of, but this is probably the only community that lives on one.

Not just Nainesh Thakkar but his mother too was born on the terrace. His maternal grandfather Ravji Thakkar began living there in 1950 when there were only four rooms on the rooftop, where originally the cooks of the hotel had stayed. After the hotel had shut down, the staff remained and began 'selling' plots. Ravji Thakkar started his dry fruits business and when his daughter married, she and her husband moved in.

In time, more rooms came up, most of them built by the existing residents. These were sold and now there are twenty-eight of them. Nainesh went to school from there and then to a college in Worli; 'I used to bring all my friends here.' When he got married, his in-laws were not particularly perturbed about where he lived, but worried about how their daughter would climb up and down the staircase.

No owner of the building has succeeded in getting the residents to move out—the previous ones, known among the community only as the 'Birlas' reportedly sold it to an investment firm that collects the rent—₹200 a month—every six months. There is always talk of paying them off to move out, but such speculation goes nowhere. Nainesh dreams of 'selling his place' and with the money, combined with some savings, collecting enough for a bigger, more private apartment, but he hasn't yet found a buyer.

The exact legality of such a sale, or indeed of the structures themselves, is a grey area. Can a space, which is not owned or even legally rented or leased, be transferred for money? That is a question that is not easy to answer in Mumbai—there are many ways in which a property is occupied. One can be in possession of property for years, even generations, and have all the requisite identity documentation, and yet not be a tenant or an owner.

Towards the end of the Art Deco stretch of Marine Drive, closer to the Princess Street flyover, are three buildings that were set up decades ago by the Shri Patan Jain Mandal. The buildings were meant for migrants from Patan in Gujarat, widely known for, among other things, the Patola sari. The sari is a collector's item, exquisitely handwoven by a dying breed of traditional craftsmen and often priced at over ₹5 lakh.

The affable Nikhil Banker is the secretary of the Mandal. His day job is as a diamond broker, but he calls himself a social worker and is the go-to man for problems faced by the residents. It took me weeks to set up a meeting—he was just too busy managing his duties. On Saturdays, for example, he oversees the management of the regular medical camps for members of the community.

When I meet him, it is in his 500-square-foot apartment in building three, one of the forty-eight flats in the complex. 'Sometimes even my family complains that they hardly see me,' he laughs.

Patan is a small town in Gujarat, and in the early twentieth century, young Jains from there settled in Bombay. The Mandal, to help community members, and an elder, Seth Khoobchand Swaroopchand, gave ₹75,000 to start a housing project. One of his conditions was that the rent would be only ₹15, and nearly eighty years after the buildings came up, it continues to be the same; the price of each apartment in the open market can be anything upwards of ₹3 crore.

The original plan was to accommodate new migrants and their families who came to Bombay for work or business, till they found their bearings. Once their businesses started growing, they would vacate the flats and other families could move in. It was a good plan, and it did work in the early decades—residents used to live there for a few months or years and then move out.

But expectedly, the noble idea fell victim to the brutal realities of the Bombay housing market. By the 1970s, no one was showing any signs of leaving this prime property they were occupying for a laughably low rent. Even though they were financially successful, they stayed put.

The Mandal was in a fix—it did not want to start litigation, but it began talking to tenants to persuade them to move out. No one did. At the same time, they did not have any documentation that made them tenants or lessees; 'I was born in this house, and we have lived here since 1947, but I have no papers at all,' says Banker. That is the case with most of the 100-odd families who live in two of the buildings; the third transformed into a cooperative society a few years ago, after each flat's residents gave ₹30 lakh to the Mandal and became full-fledged owners of their apartments. Today a flat would go for ten times as much. Not surprisingly, the building is better maintained than the other two, which are under the control of the Mandal—cracks have appeared in the pillars, paint is peeling off the walls, but no one has yet taken a decision on the repair and rejuvenation that could cost upwards of ₹1 crore.

Many flats have been divided and subdivided internally so that no less than ten people from the same family—the original resident, his sons and their families—all live in the same 500-square-foot space. The younger generation does not want to move out, not the least because if they did, they fear they would lose rights after the parent dies.

The buildings are built around a small central atrium, and light falls directly on the floor on a large swastika painted in the centre. Inside, a marble plaque recounts the generous donation of Swaroopchand.

The community, consisting of around 3,400 families, is close-knit and meets at annual events. A 'vasti patra' directory has the names of all the members of the community; the Mandal has discreetly allowed people to 'sell' their properties (in a roundabout way—on paper it is handed back to the organization), but the condition is that it can only be transferred to other members of the community. Marriages have brought outsiders to the buildings, but Banker says everyone is relaxed about it—'even one Christian has come. They become part of the community, whoever they are.' No strictures are passed, no pressures put; the younger generation, feels Banker, is moving away from the traditions of the community, but it doesn't bother him. Both his daughters go to cosmopolitan schools and listen to the same music other youngsters listen to. Efforts are made to get youngsters together, to nudge them into finding grooms and brides within the community.

But the Mandal's rules don't allow homes to be transferred to daughters, so he feels at some stage after he passes away, the family might not be here. 'I think it should change, and I hope it changes.'

Instances of residents in possession of a property but with no documentation to show for it are not that unusual in Mumbai. Often, it leads to a legal fight, where the landlord wants to throw the residents out and reclaim the property. In the case of the Patan Jain Mandal, it is not hostile squatting, nor is the landlord trying to brutally throw them out—the residents moved in legitimately but then refused to move out. Nonetheless, despite the longevity of stay, the sword of Damocles—eviction—hangs over each and every resident of the two buildings.

These examples, of the terrace homes of Queen's Mansion and the tenacious residents of the Patan Mandal buildings, exemplify the extreme conditions of Mumbai, where to own a home is of course a far-fetched fantasy, but to even find a reasonably safe, secure and clean home to stay in is, for millions, unachievable in their lifetimes. People continue to find small spaces to burrow in and make habitable, unmindful of the legal status.

Mumbai abhors a vacuum. Empty space is wasted space, an opportunity lost to use it to its maximum potential. It needs to be immediately occupied and, if possible, monetized. Thus, a plot of land soon becomes a slum, a balcony, built originally to provide a sense of openness, is enclosed to make a room bigger, even the tiny space under a staircase becomes a small tailoring shop. The terrace of a building, thus, holds immense possibilities.

Behind this conundrum lies centuries of history of how Mumbai grew and developed, and the perpetual hunt for space in a city with a limited landmass but unlimited dreams. The circumstances of how the community on top of Queen's Mansion came to perch there and how the residents of the Patan Mandal buildings still live in their buildings all these decades later are seemingly different, but they both illustrate the same desire to somehow find a place and a roof over their heads in a city where even a toehold—whether to live or to hang on for dear life in a train—is enough, because that way you can continue to move.

'Bombay, like all other large cities, has a very acute housing problem. Not only is it customary for a whole family to live in one room, but this room frequently houses a number of other relations of the family. To meet the needs the Government are now undertaking the erection of a large number of tenement buildings to provide accommodation for 50,000 families. In view of the high price of land it has not been found practicable to provide for the poorer classes in other than blocks of tenement buildings,' wrote D.W. Davidge in his paper 'Development of Bombay', in 1924.

Just a few years before this, in his lecture on The Housing Question in Bombay to the Royal Society of Arts, London, which was published in 1910, G. Owen W. Dunn had said, 'The slender means of the working-classes necessitate their residing in as close proximity as possible to their work; their habits and customs lead them to congregate in communities of race, religion, and caste, and these people have not the most elementary ideas of sanitation.' Dunn had impressive credentials—he had been chief engineer of the Public Works Department and had held the position of not just the Commissioner of the Bombay Municipal Corporation but also the Bombay Improvement Trust, giving him an insight into the city's housing, infrastructure and sanitation. The Trust itself had been founded to decongest the city after vast swathes of neighbourhoods were hit by a plague in 1896, which was blamed on the cramped housing of the natives. The disease-ridden areas were seen as an example of the unhygienic native ways of living. More than the cultural aspects, what was apparent was that Bombay's biggest problem was congestion and overcrowding. The city's inherent geographical limitations, combined with a rapidly growing population and high property prices, meant that Bombay's residents had no option but to live in cramped conditions, a situation that is familiar even in the shiny, high-rise Mumbai of the early twenty-first century.

The islands that formed the Bombay archipelago could not have been this cramped in the seventeenth century. All visitors had reported that the swampy, disease-ridden space had scattered communities who were engaged in fishing, rice farming or toddy tapping. There were clusters of people living on the main island and in Mahim, which had once been important, but it was on Salsette that most of the trade took place.

The Portuguese, after acquiring Bombay from the sultan of Gujarat, rented it out to various influential families and to Jesuits, but the rulers based themselves mainly in Bassein, where their fort was a commercial and military headquarters, and in Mahim, a trading and customs outpost to collect duties from ships. Their mission was also to harvest souls on behalf of the Catholic Church, which they did, converting thousands of Indians to Christianity. The British recruited their early clerks and assistants. Not much is known about how the population lived, but it is unlikely that it was in very crowded conditions.

Things began to change when the East India Company acquired Bombay. When the second Company governor, Gerald Aungier, in the 1860s and '70s, welcomed settlers, mainly from Gujarat, to come and set up a base there, many responded—for a long time after that, the migrants were solely Gujaratis. (This is probably the genesis of the perpetual feeling among Gujaratis that they built the city.) Aungier and his successors had been based in Surat and knew the business prowess of the locals there, not just of the Banias, but also of the Khojas, the Memons, the Parsis and the Kutchis, all of whom displayed an adventurous spirit, especially when it came to business—*dhandho*—and making money.

These communities began moving to Bombay, and as usually happens, moved in clusters, creating enclaves—

or ghettos—where others of their own kind lived. British officials had residences in the Fort, and by the eighteenth century, Parsis had congregated there too. The Bhatias set themselves up in different locations, but a good number of them were in the north end of the Fort, as did the Bohras, near Bazaar Gate. One street there is still called Bora Bazaar, and a Bhatia mansion stands there even today. Just outside the Fort limits is Bhatia Baug, a charitable initiative by the community.

Houses around the mid-seventeenth century were of the most basic kind. The Portuguese had already been there for a century, and while the administration was in Bassein, many had settled in Bombay, Mazagaon, Parel and Mahim, which had now become part of the Company's domain.

In his book, *A New Account of East India and Persia, in Eight Letters,*[2] published in 1698, John Fryer, who arrived in Bombay in 1673 to take up his duties as a doctor for the Company, wrote about the houses he saw:

> At distance enough lies the Town, in which confusedly live the English, Portuguese, Topazes, Gentues, Moors, Coolie Christians, most Fishermen.
>
> It is a full Mile in length, the houses are low, and Thatched with Oleas of the Cocoe-tree, all but a few the Portugalls left and some few that the Company have built, the Custom House and Warehouses are tiled and plastered and instead of glass, use panes of Oister shells for their windows, (which, as they are cut in squares and polished, look gracefully enough). There is also a reasonably handsome *Buzzar.*

Beyond the Town, which was the Fort, lay villages and fields, and 'Massagoung (Mazagaon) a great fishing town, peculiarly noted for a fish called *Bumbello*,' he wrote. The island was not yet fully developed but more and more people were coming into this new settlement, with its promises of fortunes to be made.

By the eighteenth century, the population had increased and demarcations had become clear. The European quarter extended from Fort to the present-day Crawford Market on the east and Dhobi Talao—or Framjee Cawasjee tank, to give its official name—where Metro cinema stands, on the west. It is still called Dhobi Talao, even though the water body that existed there, which was used by washermen, was filled up long ago. Though not as grandly laid out as in the past, it still has open spaces, not the least because the ruling British wanted to keep attackers at bay and wanted to see them coming in advance.

That the infrastructure in the European quarter was much superior to that elsewhere is visible even today. The roads are broad, the footpaths wide, the maidans expansive and the architecture, whether Victorian or Art Deco, graceful. There has been very little new construction since the 1950s, whether in the old quarter, i.e., Fort and Frere Town, or in the post-1930s reclaimed land, where Marine Drive and modern apartment buildings were constructed in the 1930s–'50s period. Ballard Estate, which was reclaimed in the early part of the twentieth century by the Port Trust, has elegant Edwardian buildings, almost all of them commercial, and once again shows a high level of planning by the British.

The Fort area is congested, with narrow streets and haphazardly built residential and commercial structures. The central and southern parts are business districts, the north has some residential buildings, which appear to have remained the same for decades, perhaps since the early nineteenth century.

Fort at one time had its elegant parts too. Some houses in Fort were 'large, handsome and generally of three or four storeys high with wooden verandahs supported by wooden pillars projecting one above another. These pillars and fronts on the verandahs were beautifully carved,' wrote Bishop Heber in 1928.[3]

Almost a century earlier, in her book *Western India*,[4] travel writer Mrs Marianne Postans had described the itinerant merchants on the esplanade and the shops inside the Fort, which sold everything from ribbons to Chinese silks to other, mundane items of everyday use. A particular shop, 'or *Ducahn*', owned by Jangarjee Nusserwanjee, 'vends everything from purple velvet to raspberry jams'. The prized goods came from English and French ships that called on Bombay and found a ready market among the Europeans.

Outside these limits stood the 'native towns', which sprang up almost organically, and each of them today, approachable by separate entry points, retains some of the original characteristics. First, from the west, is Dhobi Talao, which connects to Girgaum and Thakurdwar, then Kalbadevi, followed by Bhuleshwar, which extends into the various specialist markets and finally, in the west, the present-day Muhammad Ali Road, which abuts Crawford Market, which leads to Bhendi Bazaar and Dongri, and is generally considered to be largely inhabited by Muslims. Each of these 'towns' has its own history, which is closely linked with the growth of the city and has contributed in many ways to making it the mosaic it is. Though much has changed, obviously, many significant markers of a hoary vintage still exist, in the form of various cultural, social, residential, commercial, educational and religious institutions and structures that still stand proudly.

Modernity, often in its ugliest manifestation, has begun to make inroads, mainly in the shape of tall buildings, most of them without any manifest character or style, but for the most part the native town is still a low-rise stretch, demonstrating once again that the Bombay of yore was constructed on a human scale, where the residents had a relationship with the street, and thus with the city. Even today, it is possible to see, in Kalbadevi and Bhuleshwar, structures built in the vernacular style, with cantilevered balconies and ornate, carved wooden brackets designed in a style that echoes the houses in the villages of Gujarat, where many of the residents come from.

The towns still give a good idea of how people lived and worked. The community enclaves were delineated, but they seamlessly merged with one another in a continuous flow, ensuring cosmopolitan intermingling. Whether it was the Muslim quarter, or the Maharashtrian wadi or indeed the Catholic 'village', all had open entrances and exits, and communities often had homes or commercial establishments in other areas. The idea of the 'gated' complex did not exist, barring very few instances.

The native towns were closely connected with the imperial administration. The Christians and the Maharashtrians, especially those who had taken to education, such as the Pathare Prabhus and the Brahmins, were the backbone of the civil administration, contributing clerks and secretaries to the courts and to various departments. The Gujaratis were into commercial activity, while many of those who lived in the town on the west—Muslims from different parts of India, especially the Konkan coast—were employed in marine activity. The residents of the other parts of Bombay, which had grown after the period of reclamation, which ended in the early nineteenth century—were employed as labour or in agriculture.

By the 1830s, the city's population had reached 2,36,000. Naturally, there was a need for housing. The native towns were dense and the Fort crowded. In between were large open tracts of land and beyond the native towns were orchards and villages. Land reclamation had started in 1780, beginning with a causeway that linked Bombay with Worli, followed by a long road connecting the east and the west, known later as Bellasis Road, which is still in use. Other islands like Mazagaon and Parel followed. This released a lot of land for construction.

Then in the nineteenth century came mass housing.

The rapid industrialization, which began with the setting up of the first textile mill in 1854 by the entrepreneur Cawasji Nanabhoy Dawar in Tardeo, meant that workers were needed. By 1870, there were thirteen mills, and as the century came to an end, seventy mills had come up. The numbers of workers grew exponentially, and they began living on whatever land they could find, in and around Parel, Currey Road and Byculla, where the mills were situated.

The mill owners decided to build housing for them, not out of benevolence but necessity and some government pressure. Private landowners too saw an opportunity and built chawls for the new migrants pouring into the city. Later, chawls were constructed by the government's Bombay Development Directorate, for mill workers and municipal employees.

These chawls were designed to be like hostels, where workers lived in single rooms, often five or six to a room, all of which were linked to a common corridor facing a central plot of ground, which was for the use of the community. Common toilets on each floor often led to tensions because of the sheer number of people wanting to use them at the same time, especially in the mornings.

Eventually, families moved in and the character of the chawls changed—now they were family homes, and several members lived and slept on the floor in the same room. Privacy was at a premium, especially for young couples. Because the corridors linked, everyone's lives were open for the others to see—what was being cooked, who was unwell, who drank too much in the evenings. Births, weddings and deaths were community affairs, and religious festivals were celebrated jointly with much gusto.

Those who lived in chawls and then left them often look back at this community living with nostalgia. Chawl life has been romanticized, and author P.L. Deshpande's play *Batatyachi Chawl* speaks fondly of the many oddballs who lived in a fictitious one.

Reality could, however, be difficult. As families grew, the space constraints began to tell. Living together was a strain—

newer generations craved their own apartments. Builders were attracted by the space and the locations of these chawls, which happened to be in either convenient south Mumbai or in the lucrative and rapidly developing central parts, close to the old mills, which were now prime real estate.

Agents approaching residents to sign over the rooms got an enthusiastic response—the money could be distributed among children and could help them buy a small but new flat in the distant suburbs.

All this development and growing prosperity brought more and more migrants from the hinterland.

Though there is no record of where the new migrants, especially the poor, lived, it is almost certain that they set up a home wherever they could. The word was not known then, but these would have been the earliest 'slums'.

Most urban historians agree that the word 'slum' originated among the poorer tenements in the East End of London in the 1820s and then became popular by the middle of the century. Till then the word to describe shanty towns was rookery; there is a record of Charles Dickens, in his powerful writings on the poorer parts of the city, using the term 'back-slum', referring to the back streets that had crowded housing amidst poverty and non-existent sanitation. The term came in widespread use after that.

There is no record of when the term was first used in India, but by the late nineteenth century, slums were visible in all parts of Bombay. In February 1915, *The Bombay Chronicle* reported a meeting of the Bombay Improvement Trust in which the officiating chairman Mr Hatch spoke of '1200 acres of slums' and how it would cost ₹1,500 lakhs to demolish all of them. He mentioned the 'Supreme advantages of the Birmingham Scheme of improvement over the Liverpool method of sweeping them away.'

Presumably this meant rehabilitation, but whatever the outcome, it did not stop the proliferation of such shanties, which kept growing, defeating all manner of well-meaning government schemes. The migrants and the poorer communities did not want to live in such primitive conditions—they simply had no choice. Over time, the communities were not limited to the poor—there is no dearth of graduates and post-graduates, and now white-collar workers too, living in slum-like conditions—it is critical to understand that these are people who are not 'poor' but just cannot afford a proper house in Mumbai. Nor do only recent migrants live in slums—many generations have continued to stay, and gradually, improved their living conditions by making pucca houses and adding embellishments and modern gadgets.

Estimates generally agree that half of Mumbai's population lives in slums—that, by a modest estimate, should put it at around six million people, a sobering number in a city with great pretensions of being a world-class metropolis. Not only do these six million not have proper homes, sanitation or even reliable water supply, but they have almost no hope of upgrading their lives and moving to a proper, constructed home—the simple law of the market won't allow it, and the state stopped considering housing as a public good a long time ago.

All kinds of formulae have been suggested to create 'affordable housing', a loaded word that is tossed around by politicians especially during the promise-heavy campaign time before elections, but nothing comes of it. Over the decades, builders have lobbied for all manner of concessions— the repeal of the Urban Land Ceiling Act in the 1970s, which put curbs on private ownership of land, more floor space index to create ever higher buildings, and various laws including the Slum Rehabilitation Act and the Transfer of Development Rights, which allowed them to build homes for the resident slum dwellers on a portion of the land and get the rest to construct expensive, marketable apartments. In each case assurances were given that the release of more land would end the 'slum menace' once and for all, but it made no difference. The slums continue to be a part of the urban fabric, right in the midst of our daily lives but invisible to us all.

Yet, despite this overwhelming presence on our physical landscape, in which entire clusters of slums are within our eyeline, and perhaps in the plot next door, not many people would have actually entered a slum. Most service-providers—maids, cooks, drivers—are likely to be from the slums, but it is a fair bet that their bosses have never been to their homes. The slum remains something out there, a dark, foreboding place, which could swallow any stranger who enters it.

Some vast slum colonies are less so—Dharavi is a good example. Often called the largest, or more modestly, second largest slum cluster in Asia, Dharavi, which started life as a small place at the mouth of Salsette just beyond the city's island limits, saw an explosion in growth in the early twentieth century.

The Kumbhar potters of the Matunga area were shifted there when the land was acquired by the colonial administration as part of the Bombay Improvement Trust in the 1920s, and there is still a neighbourhood called Kumbharwada within Dharavi. Gradually, the place expanded, and now estimates say it has a population of about a million people crammed into a little more than two square kilometres, with one of the highest densities in the country.

Over the years, Dharavi has gained much fame as a centre of great entrepreneurship—figures like one billion dollars as the annual turnover from there are glibly thrown around—and it has been studied and researched by scholars from around the world. Tour companies regularly take city slickers and tourists to see how the locals live in the narrow, fetid and filthy lanes, and builders covet the land, coming up with grandiose schemes to build free housing for residents and acquire the rest for building towers and office blocks for sale in the open market—its prime location within ten minutes' drive of the business hub known as Bandra Kurla Complex makes it extremely attractive, and the government keeps putting out calls for proposals, with lucrative incentives. A host of well-funded NGOs too operate there, pushing self-reliance and encouraging the locals to come up with their own community-based solutions for housing and keeping the builders out. It is a testing ground for all kinds of social experiments, but nothing ultimately changes, and the lives of those who have lived in Dharavi for generations go on as always, with virtually no improvement in civic infrastructure. There is more than an element of fetishization of the vast slum, with a lot of myth-making and even cultural exploitation. Despite all the attention it gets, however, it remains where it was; for families living there for decades and newcomers who find a job and room in its deep bowels, it remains home and a shelter in the big city, with its own rhythm and dynamics and a throbbing economy that keeps it going. There are small plots where vegetables are grown and rooms where workers toil away in oppressively hot conditions to tailor clothes that often land up in boutiques and stores all around the country; zardozi embroiderers with delicate fingers and sharp eyesight create patterns according to the instructions of well-known designers, which are then sold for price multiples of what the artisans make; fancy knock-offs of leather bags and shoes are produced by the score and even sold on the Dharavi main road to buyers; groups of women prepare papads for sale in shops, and idlis, pickles and even tea are sent out to restaurants. Young men and women form bands and B-boy dancing groups and make videos to upload on YouTube, nursery schools run in the mornings for local kids.

A bit of Dharavi falls on an important thoroughfare that links Sion with Bandra and thus connects the central suburbs with the west, and thousands of vehicles pass it every day. But the slum lies beyond what they see.

There are other slums that remain relatively away from the mainstream limelight—Ramabai Ambedkar Nagar, where several Dalits were killed in firing by the State Reserve Police in 1997, Malvani in Malad, built on a swamp, and Behrampada Chawl in Bandra East, which has a large Muslim population and was the scene of horrific riots during 1992 – 93.

The land on which Behrampada sits belongs to the collector of Mumbai. It was settled after 1947, when many Muslim families were moved from Mahim after the Partition violence. In those days there was a shamshan ghat for Hindus there, and an abattoir, which was eventually moved to Deonar. Gradually the slum grew. Now it spreads over seven acres.

Some Hindus live there, mostly in Makran gully, Lakdi gully and Koyla gully, but the population is overwhelmingly Muslim.

Behrampada is a few minutes away from the entrance to the eastern side of Bandra railway station, making it a prime locality for real estate development. A plot of land leads up to a few dilapidated buildings, low-income housing built by the Mumbai Metropolitan Region Development Authority, and a well-known construction company is supposed to have acquired it. One day, the buildings will disappear, and the garbage-strewn plot will be a playground for residents. Across the busy road, humming with traffic going to and from the station, stands a glass and chrome office building.

But it is the seven acres of Behrampada slum that will make the land mass a truly lucrative proposition. All that is required is to convince the thousands of people who live there to move out, i.e., leave their old homes in return for some financial compensation.

One of these is Bombil bai, more respectfully called Bombil aapa, who got the nickname because she sells only dry fish. She is a long-time resident of Behrampada.

I was taken to meet Bombil aapa by Zubeida, a volunteer in the Housing Rights Committee, which has an office nearby, who acted as a guide through the labyrinthian lanes. She is not a resident of Behrampada but knows it well; she leads the way, and I follow, quickly realizing that I would get lost within minutes of entering. The passage gets tighter and tighter, the dwellings become higher and soon, barely a sliver of sunlight seeps through. The feeling of being in an entirely different world, cut off from the rest, is heightened by the disappearance of street noise. Bombil aapa's home is deep inside Behrampada's belly.

On the way, we pass Perfect Tailors, Kohra Ironing shop, a foreign exchange shop, several goats, fish sellers, butchers displaying racks of mutton, and several groceries and kirana shops. Some of the structures here are five storeys tall, and the upper floors tend to lean inward, looking as if they will suddenly fall one day. The higher floors are accessed via an external ladder and are rented out; I wonder how the tenants of the last two storeys climb up and down several times a day.

Bombil aapa lives in Inga gully, named after one Inga, who used to have an abattoir there. Everyone knows her, she has been around for a long time; it turns out that many of the gully's homes are occupied by her relatives—a sister, an uncle, a niece.

She is lying down in a cramped position, wedged between a steel cupboard and a plastic barrel full of clothes. Her room looks to be less than 150 square feet. It is painted green. Pipes can be seen running down on one side. On the wall across are framed photographs of various Islamic and Sufi shrines. A tube light is on, though it is the middle of the afternoon—no light reaches here.

She gets up and waves away my apology for having disturbed her, saying she has just returned from her shop because the fish was sold out by 2 p.m. A chair is brought from somewhere outside for me; Zubeida and Bombil aapa are on the floor. The tiling on the floor is shiny and new—she got it done a year or two ago, she says.

I am from Solapur—you know Solapur? That is where Sushil Kumar Shinde comes from. His house is close to ours.

I came to Behrampada sixty years ago, when I got married as a young girl. My sister lived here. My marriage was arranged to a man from Bijapur. Both of us moved here.

In those days our kholi was *kutcha* and separated from the others by a gunny sack on one side and two wooden boards on the other two. It was very shaky and makeshift. Water used to regularly come into the house during the rains. There was no drainage, no running water, no electricity; every night we had to light up our homes with lamps.

We slowly got all of these, much of it because of the late Ahmed Zakaria, the MLA from here in 1980. He saw our condition and pushed first for electricity, then drainage and then eventually, running water. Today, I get running water inside my home. Sunil Dutt saab (the actor-turned-member of Parliament) was the other person who helped us a lot, by getting us pucca roads and much more.

By now, she is in full flow, enjoying reminiscing about the past.

Some twenty or thirty years ago, people started constructing a first floor, then a second and now most go up to the fourth floor.

I ask if the structures that have four or even five floors are safe.

Bombil aapa laughs and shows me the walls of her room—double brick, she says.

The upper storeys of her dwelling are for rent, though she says she has built them for her grandson. She rented out one of her other rooms, to a Hindu family—the man worked elsewhere, his wife and three children lived here—but when they left, she did not take another tenant.

Some non-Muslims do live in Behrampada, says Ghaus, her grandson, lovingly called Shah Rukh by his grandmother and aunts. He works in a shop selling fashionable clothes for young people; he left school after the ninth standard. His fiancée teaches in a school. '*Yateem hai bechari. Meine kitna bola Shah Rukh ko, padh le* (She's an orphan. I told Told Shah Rukh several times, study more),' says Bombil aapa.

Behrampada could be self-sustaining—it has almost everything within it, including meat shops and stables for cows. The slum economy in Mumbai is huge—goods and services are available for the population, from asbestos sheets for walls to masons to erect them, from doctors—qualified and otherwise—for medical services, to employment agents for the Middle East countries and fixers who arrange for crucial documentation. The documents are critical to establish longevity, which could help get housing. Often, the local branch of the Shiv Sena helps the residents get government identification papers and even intervenes to arrange admission to local schools; the Sena's strength is its local network of activists and volunteers, who are available to slum dwellers irrespective of religion—they will happily assist a Muslim as much as a Hindu. Bombil aapa, like her neighbours, has all the critical ID documents—a PAN card, passport, ration card, election card.

'Aapa, you don't have a TV,' I remark.

She immediately turns serious. 'I don't want a TV, I don't like TV. I have Makhdoom saab, Banda Nawaz (pointing to all the frames above her). Why do I want a TV? When I come home in the evening, my neighbours reduce the TV volume. I have no radio, no clock, no watch.'

But she keeps herself abreast of the news. 'They killed that Yakub Memon, innocent he was,' she says, referring to a recent report. 'Those who killed him will have to answer to God.'

I bring up the 1993 violence against Muslims—her memory is not so sharp, perhaps the unpleasant ones have been erased. 'Nothing happened here, really, it only happened outside, on the streets. Here it was peaceful.'

Which is not true, as Zubeida reminds her, prompting her to say, 'Yes, my nephew, Ali, was taken away and was given two life terms. His children have grown up. One nephew was killed in the firing.'

She was so angry and disturbed then, that another nephew offered to send her to Mecca; she came back feeling peaceful. 'Khuda looks after us, no?'

I ask if she will she continue to live in Behrampada.

'I will die in this flat; I will never sell it. But I know Behrampada is a gold mine. Many builders are looking at it with greed. If I get a flat, why not.'

For a slum dweller, especially a long-time resident, the social network and support system of the neighbours provides a certain level of comfort. By now, it is also well known that builders make a lot of tall promises when asking residents to sign agreements and move out but fail to meet their commitments. Apartments that looked attractive in the plans and brochures turn out to be small, shoddily built affairs, and there is no saying who their new neighbours will be. There is also no saying how long the construction of a new building will take—where will they go in the meantime?

Newcomers to Mumbai typically live in the distant suburbs and commute in harsh conditions every day. The city's slums have become expensive—the first floor of Bombil aapa's structure rents out for ₹6,000 a month, which, for a family man earning even ₹15,000, is untenable. Also, many shack owners are wary of letting out their properties, asking for all kinds of documents.

Sharing the room with five others is an option, though it gets very cramped. But for a migrant, it is important to save as much as possible and send it to the family in the village. And as the cost of living in the city is very high, roughing it out, however unpleasant, is the only option.

Some find novel solutions to this, like Suresh Yadav, who works with a security agency and is sent out as a watchman to residential buildings. After his duty is over in the mornings, he bathes in the bathroom provided by the building for employees, then, freshened up, sets out for his next job as a driver for a businessman, whose schedule works out very well for Yadav—all he has to do is drive his employer to his office and then, like clockwork, drive him back.

'He does not go anywhere during the day—I can sleep in the car, and if it is hot, I turn on the air conditioner.'

Once a week, Yadav visits his friends on Mira Road, on the extreme north of the suburban line, and stays over, paying out ₹100 per night. That way he saves on rent and the daily commute.

It's a precarious way to live, but the city drives a brutal bargain—if you want to go there to earn money, then you meet its terms.

The city is exclusionary to anyone from communities and groups of people who do not conform to mainstream, middle-class notions of normalcy. Minority communities, transpeople, single women, even meat-eaters—all have to confront these prejudices and obstacles to get a place to stay, to rent or to purchase.

Gauri Sawant, who is a celebrity of sorts, found this out the hard way. Gauri is a transperson identifying as she and refers to herself in the feminine gender. She has long been an activist and was the first signatory to the petition in the Supreme Court that resulted in the historic 2014 NALSA judgement, recognizing transgenders as the 'third gender'.

Three years later, she was the subject of a short ad film for Vicks, which showcased her real-life story of bringing up a little girl. It made her a star. 'Ola drivers who pick me up want to talk to me about the ad, in public places people come up to me and want to shake my hand,' she told me. From her fellow transgenders came some good-natured ribbing—'You have become too big, where do you have the time for us now?'

The ad film tells the story of a young girl on a bus journey who muses about her life, and her mother, who took her in when she was a child after her biological mother died, nurturing her and ensuring that she was admitted in a good school. It is slowly revealed that the mother is transgender—it is never mentioned overtly, but made fairly obvious. The last scene of the mother dropping her daughter off at boarding school and walking away is a lump-in-the-throat moment that won the hearts of thousands of viewers.

In real life, Gauri had literally snatched away a young child who would have fallen into the wrong hands after her mother, a prostitute, died over ten years ago. 'They were auctioning that poor prostitute's meagre goods and the child would have been auctioned too,' Gauri said. 'I just took the child and challenged anyone to fight me. Who will take on a *hijda*?' There was no sentimentality in her voice—she has seen life in its rawest and roughest form—but when she spoke about the child, her voice softened.

Despite her hardscrabble life, or perhaps because of it, Gauri had developed a thick skin and was ready to stand up to anybody. As someone who had run away from home as a young boy, faced public prejudice and police questioning and then been initiated into the complex rituals of becoming a full-fledged transperson, Gauri was not one to be cowed by criticism. 'After a few days, when no relative came to collect the child, I decided to keep her.'

Initially, she did have doubts, but 'one day the child, while sleeping next to me, put her arm around me. After that I knew I would never let her go.'

Gauri began raising the girl and took her to a school close to the slum where she lives. The school took her in, no questions asked. There were problems of course—other kids teased her. Gauri would sometimes send a couple of her fellow transgenders to drop the girl off at school, and one day she asked not to be accompanied. But these moments notwithstanding, a bond grew between Gauri and the child. Their story made it to the press and a few years after it was published, an ad agency came calling—they wanted her to be in a commercial for Vicks, the menthol chest rub much loved by Indians.

'I thought it was to be a small film—they said it would only be on YouTube. I said fine, but drew the line at using my daughter's face.' They agreed and shot it, and when it released, it was on television and soon became hugely popular, going viral on the internet.

The popularity took her by surprise, but it was welcome, because it helped her with her pet project, an old age home for transgenders where young, lost girls would also be looked after. 'I plan to call it *nani ka ghar*. A place for caring and nurturing.' Money came in from the most unexpected sources. She was made the brand ambassador of a microfinance company and for every loan made, she was given a small commission. Enthusiastic college kids banded together to raise funds for her. Reality shows approached her, but she firmly declined their offers as she knew such shows would invite ridicule. A nationally popular quiz show invited her to appear on the show.

But the street-smart Gauri, who left her home in her teens after her father stopped talking to her because of her effeminate gestures, was under no illusions. Every night, after meeting fundraisers, she would return to her fetid slum in Malad, built on marshy land, where transpersons occupy a small corner. 'The law changed, I am famous, but society hasn't. I still live in a slum. No one will want me as a tenant. When so-called respectable housing societies don't allow people from other religions or single women to rent apartments, who are we, mere hijdas?'

Nonetheless, she was able to stop working the streets, where transpersons beg for money. Nor did she have to dance at weddings and births, which many families consider auspicious and thus shower the dancers with money. And of course, no more sex work for her either, which every transperson has to do to survive; she now has the power and the money to move on. She still dresses in a sari—early on she was taught how to speak, move and even sit like a hijda. She demonstrated it to me, clapping and swaying her hips and switching to speaking coarsely, complete with insults and cuss words. All of them have a coded language, which outsiders don't understand, and it comes in handy in police stations when they are picked up.

Even those who are higher in the income and social chain don't have it easy, especially if they fall in one of these categories: single women (will have men visiting), Muslim, meat-eaters and, bizarrely, those working in the film business. A combination of these would of course put the hopeful tenant beyond the pale. Prejudice against Muslims is widespread all over the country, and Mumbai's middle-class housing societies are no different, but belonging to the film business is looked down upon because of the allegedly 'wild lifestyle' associated with it—drinking, parties, sex—and because incomes are uncertain and the tenant may not be able to pay regular rent.

Atika Chohan saw all this first-hand when she moved to Mumbai in 2013. She had come to work as a scriptwriter and was unmarried. Her first name raised questioning eyebrows, but the surname quickly assured landlords that she was most certainly a Hindu and an upper caste one.

She found a place and soon her boyfriend moved in. They lived together for two years and then got married—they were now respectable.

But some years later, when they separated and she wanted to move house, her broker was nervous about her single status.

'He told me to tell landlords that I was married. I refused. Then he suggested I get my mother to move in. He was pleading, so I asked my mother to come from Delhi, and that got me a place swiftly. She stayed with me for two months and then went back.'

This time nobody asked her questions because one of her films had just released, and her name was in it. But again, when she wanted to move, it was the same old story—single woman, films—and she faced rejection everywhere. Till she found a building in a good part of the suburbs, where all the residents were Muslims. 'They didn't care. Not many tenants come their way, so the landlord was happy. I got a great apartment at a convenient location. It's all good.'

Though some sections find it very difficult to find a place to stay, in general, apartment-hunting in the city has never been easy—prices are always that much more expensive than the average person can afford. Except in the aftermath of two exceptional events—the financial crash of the 1860s and the plague of 1896—the population of Bombay has never dipped, but has only kept rising, putting pressure on the scarce land in the city. Unlike other cities, Mumbai has no hinterland and can only expand towards the north, away from the busy south, or upwards.

With its sharp mercantile tendencies, no one was inclined to make free housing, and the government, whether colonial or Indian, didn't really care. After the formation of Maharashtra state in 1960, the new establishment looked at housing as a social good, and built colonies for various middle-class segments, but gradually, that policy was abandoned, and profiteering builders took over. Now, those very colonies, such as the one for the Middle-Income Group (MIG) with its sprawling campus, are being eyed by builders, and grandiose promises are being made to the current residents.

On its part, the government is on the lookout for any piece of vacant land that can be monetized and handed over to the builders—flat salt pan lands in the northern and eastern suburbs, held by families for over a century, marshy lands and even bus depots. Mumbai has become one big construction site, even if the population is now more or less stagnant and the apartments are unaffordable by the vast majority. In 2012, an international survey showed that it would take 308 years at current incomes for a middle-class professional to buy a 100-square-metre property in a prime area. In Hong Kong it would take ninety-six years and in Manhattan, a little over forty-eight. Even if this data is now outdated, since real estate prices are dynamic, Mumbai will no doubt remain in the top five or even top three category of the most expensive cities in the world. Nonetheless, luxury flats keep selling, no matter the economic conditions; the prices don't seem to deter buyers. Mumbai, the city that welcomed immigrants, is now a zone for those who can afford to live in her. The rest move further and further away, commuting inwards in the mornings, and then heading back to their homes to sleep.

3

A PANDEMIC HITS THE CITY

The Metro cinema junction at Dhobi Talao is always busy with traffic moving in several different directions. Five big arterial roads lead out of it, going towards Hutatma Chowk (Flora Fountain), the CSM terminus (better known as VT), Crawford Market, Marine Lines railway station and Dhobi Talao and Chira Bazaar, and beyond it to Thakurdwar. Hundreds of cars ply the roads, especially during peak hours; an underground path was built for pedestrians, but most prefer to use the roads, often slowing down the traffic as they try to cross the road without waiting for the green signal. In short, it's a typical Mumbai scene.

On one corner of this large crossroads stands a black marble statue of Dr Acacio Gabriel Viegas.

Dr Viegas is well connected to the neighbourhood. There is a Dr Viegas Road further down towards Chira Bazaar, and his father is buried in a church nearby. Dr Viegas is said to have been a resident of Cavel, a small, gated community of Catholics.

But Dr Viegas doesn't just belong to Cavel or Dhobi Talao. Though his name is long forgotten and doesn't spark much recognition or curiosity in the minds of citizens, his contribution to Mumbai is critical to understanding the city in the twentieth century. His pioneering work in public health, beginning from his role in discovering the beginnings of an epidemic, changed Mumbai for all time.

On 18 September 1896, Dr Viegas made a startling diagnosis when he went to see a patient in the Mandvi area, a crowded and poor neighbourhood. Observing the symptoms—weakness, drowsiness and an enlarged lymph node—he came to the alarming conclusion that she had the plague.

This was a disease that had not been heard of in Bombay, though there had been suspected cases in the Ahmedabad area—which was now in the Bombay Presidency—in the seventeenth and eighteenth centuries.

Dr Viegas swiftly submitted a report to the municipal corporation, and it emerged that such cases had occurred in Bombay in August, but had gone unrecognized, till his report on 23 September. After that the bubonic plague spread throughout the region, from Nasik to Surat to as far as Karachi.

Where did the plague originate? There were no answers. Speculation was rife, that it had come via a ship from Hong Kong, which perhaps had infected rodents. A wild rumour had it that some itinerant sadhus had brought it, though that was absurd. The colonial administration was quick to point fingers at the densely packed native areas and the filthy sewers, but while the overcrowding would have contributed to the rapid spreading of the disease, there had to be a source where it all began.

'The area of infection, which, extensive as it was at the close of the first year, was yet clearly limited, now practically covers the entire Presidency: Hubli, Dharwar, Satara, Surat, Nasik, Godhra, and many other large towns, in spite of every effort to save them while as yet they were only threatened, suffered from severe outbreaks.

'The reasons for this want of success may be found in our ignorance of the origin and modes of spread of the disease; in the failure of the people to comprehend its characteristics, and the value of the measures—in the proper enforcement of which their co-operation is essential; and in some measures, perhaps, to the limited scope of the measures themselves,' wrote Captain J. Condon, of the Indian Staff Corps, in his report, 'The Bombay Plague: Being a History of the Progress of Plague in the Bombay Presidency from September 1896 to June 1899', which had been commissioned by the government.[1]

As the infection spread and more cases began coming in, medical staff and others from the administration went from house to house to track down cases. Many residents resisted the entry into their homes by outsiders—in some cases it was because of the presence of women in the household and in many others, because of the castes of those who were working for the authorities. The residents simply did not want their homes to be polluted. In Poona, the conservative Hindus, especially of the higher castes, were appalled at what they described as tyrannical measures taken by the plague commissioner, Walter Charles Rand. Men stood guard in the houses when the teams entered, but they couldn't do much.

Their 'principal function was to shield Indian women from the unwelcome attention of the soldiers believed by many Indians to be possessed by "sheer animalism",' writes I.J. Catanach of the University of Canterbury, New Zealand, in a paper on the plague.[2]

So incensed were the people of Poona that their cause was taken up by Bal Gangadhar Tilak, the editor of the English weekly *Mahratta*, who wrote editorials denouncing Rand. 'Plague is more merciful to us than its human prototypes now reigning in the city.'[3]

Three brothers from the Chapekar family then plotted and killed Rand in Poona and were arrested. Tilak was charged with incitement to murder and sent to jail for eighteen months. When he was released, he had become a national hero.

Nothing as drastic happened in Bombay, but there was considerable resistance to the house-to-house searches. Rumours abounded, including one about how the sick were injected in hospitals and their hearts taken out and sent to the Queen of England. Quacks emerged too, offering to cure the sickness with medicines and mystic intervention to drive off spirits. A Dr P.S. Ganga, a specialist in consumption, advertised in *The Bombay Chronicle* in 1918, much after the epidemic had almost disappeared: 'Plague, 90 per cent Cure guaranteed by Mixed Treatment (Serum-Injections and Antiseptic Mixtures) if informed with 24 hours of the attack.' Daily prayers were offered in temples and churches to drive away the dreaded disease.

Local-language newspapers covered the plague in detail. Apart from giving details of daily infections and deaths, the papers were sharply critical of the authorities, including the municipal corporation. *The Champion* thundered about the 'incompetent Plague Committee, whose policy is detested by every citizen.' Would the municipal corporation have been so irresponsible in the discharge of its responsibilities had the epidemic broken out in the European quarter, asked the Gujarati paper *Akhbar-e-Saudagar*.

The *Indian Spectator*, while supporting the administration's efforts, also warned: 'Too much zeal ... It made one sick to hear of armed native police and European soldiers with revolvers in their hands rushing into zenanas and scattering the inmates before them.' The general tone of criticism was about the discriminatory treatment of the authorities towards the natives.

The numbers of the plague-infected kept growing—the bodies were piling up and the disease was spreading rapidly in the city and beyond. The administration concluded that the only solution was to evacuate people from their homes. Houses were marked with a red circle, with a date within, indicating that 'the pestilence had done its work and claimed its victim' wrote historian Sidney Low in his book *A Vision of India*, published in 1907.[4]

Low toured homes in the native areas, and while he noticed the shabby living conditions, he was less shaken than his compatriots: '… for poor filth, foulness, degradation, and outward misery, I am afraid that London has more painful sights to see than those which were brought before me in Bombay.' What disgusted him was the disparity in the quality of life: 'The Island city … has its palaces fit for a prince and its human kennels unfit for a dog.'

While the colonial gaze of the local authorities was unmistakable, they also had the monumental task of stopping the spread of the plague and quickly ending it. The administration was at its wits' end. With the death count increasing and tensions rising among the citizens, the government was forced to act.

Part of the plan was to move people out of their homes to faraway places outside town and wait till the plague died down, since it would take time to rid the old houses of infected rats. The populace would have to make their own arrangements, but the administration would provide sites and some infrastructure, as well as security. Police personnel would also guard the original homes, since people were worried that their homes would be robbed.

An SOS was also sent out to Waldemar Mordecai Haffkine, a Ukrainian bacteriologist who had come to India to promote his cholera vaccine.

He was given a research laboratory in Grant Medical College, and he set about working on a vaccine.

In Bombay alone, in the September 1896 to June 1897 period, 10,562 people died out of a total of 12,425 cases.

By June, the plague had subsided, but the administration continued its efforts to prevent another outbreak.

'Inspection of passengers by road and rail and sea; strict segregation of those arriving from infected places, prompt isolation and disinfection where, notwithstanding all precautions, cases had been imported—all these and many other measures were rigidly enforced to procure immunity and prevent infection from taking root,' wrote Condon in his report.

The efforts paid off, but only for a month. In July, the plague flared up again. 'All such hopes were, however, frustrated: all efforts unavailing. In the second year Plague struck the Presidency with twice the severity of the first year—established a wider area of infection—burst out in individual epidemics of greater severity—doubled the Plague death-roll,' Condon wrote.[5]

In the next year so, of the 17,907 cases, 16,562 people died in Bombay, a massive 92 per cent mortality rate. It was almost a given, therefore, that anyone who got the plague would not survive and would pass it on to those around them. There was a third period too, during which some parts of the vast Presidency were hit badly, but Bombay city escaped it.

By the end of 1897, Bombay, which extended up to Parel and with a population of a little over 8,00,000, saw its population decline by nearly half—driven by panic and fear, many had simply left the city, though many of them subsequently returned. There was a sudden shortage of labour, cooks, barbers, shop assistants and mill workers; worried that sanitation workers would also join the exodus and thus exacerbate the epidemic, the authorities declared all municipal employees as essential staff who could not leave or go on strike.

In January 1897, Haffkine had informed the government that he had developed an effective vaccine and suggested it be used. He had himself been vaccinated by a strong dose to prove its efficacy and had not just survived but would be immune to the plague. This was followed by administering the vaccine to '77 prominent Bombay citizens', which, the government hoped, would encourage people to get vaccinated. Scepticism still reigned among people, but the trials continued. The inmates of a correctional facility in Byculla, where a few cases and fatalities had occurred, were asked if they would volunteer—about half did. Of the 172 who refused, six died, but there was not a single death among the 147 who were inoculated. The news was widely disseminated, and hundreds came forward to be vaccinated.

The Presidency was huge, and the deaths continued, but wherever the inoculation drive was carried out, the mortality rate fell drastically. The vaccine was successful and eventually, the plague petered out. Haffkine was honoured with a knighthood by Queen Victoria in the 1897 list. He had already been given a fully equipped laboratory in Malabar Hill, and the Aga Khan, spiritual leader of the Khojas, made an offer of a donation and the offer of a large property in Mazagaon to expand the facility. Finally, the Government of India stepped in—'it had become an Imperial concern', Condon wrote, and under its orders, the governor's old house in Parel was declared the new headquarters for plague research. Haffkine Institute, as it is called now, still stands there and is a centre for communicable disease research and vaccine production.

The massive effort to tackle and end the plague epidemic was part of a larger plan on the part of Bombay's administrators to do something about the city's health. At the core of it was sanitary reform, an exercise to not just clean up the city but also to put in long-term measures to ensure proper sanitation. Till the early nineteenth century, the British were mainly concerned about the health of their own soldiers and civilian population, but gradually it dawned on them that general conditions had to be improved too.

British officials were critical of native habits, ranging from selling infected meat, overcrowding and generally living in filthy conditions. They were also convinced that Western habits and medicine were superior. As part of the reform process from the 1860s onwards, the municipal corporation set up a system of sweeping streets, cleaning up the sewers and arranging for potable water supply by creating the Vihar, Tulsi and Tansa lakes on the outskirts of Bombay. Gradually, helped by those Indians who saw value in the measures, the city's condition and health improved. 'Indian doctors were indeed the vital intermediaries,' writes Mridula Ramanna, author and academic, in her book.[6] 'They were familiar with the local natives, with cultural practices, and were in a better position to tackle the opposition and the reservations ...' Gradually, these changes took root.

There were two fallouts of the plague that had emptied the city and enervated the administration, which was now under pressure to take some long-term decisions to ensure that such a situation did not recur. Bombay's citizens wanted to see things change, and quickly.

First, in 1897, the government decided to pass the Epidemic Diseases Act, which would give the administration special powers to enable it to tackle any such outbreak of disease in the future. The second, which was to change the city in fundamental ways, was the setting up of the Bombay City Improvement Trust, popularly called the BIT, in 1898. The BIT's mandate was to remove unsanitary housing and develop the northern outskirt of the city to resolve the problem of overcrowding. It was creating schemes on part of the island to reduce overcrowding, which would create new housing.

It was an ambitious plan, to acquire agricultural land in the areas outside Parel, up to Sion and 'construct … sanitary dwellings for the poor and the police'. For this, the BIT could even reclaim land from the sea if required. The government would provide infrastructure, including roads, drainage and gardens, etc. The committee to manage the BIT consisted of senior officials from the government and the municipal corporation as well as representatives of the Port Trust, the Chamber of Commerce and the Millowners Association, whose president was Sir Sassoon J. David. Prominent citizens including Dinshaw Wacha were part of the committee too, as was Dr Viegas.

An earlier idea, initiated by Arthur Crawford, one-time municipal corporation commissioner, and called 'Development Plan for a New Bombay' had suggested something similar. Crawford had argued for all hazardous industries such as dyeing and tanneries to be shifted on the outskirts of the city, but he had been defeated by vested interests, including the big landowners and industrialists.

Crawford sent his brochure to Governor Sydenham Clarke, saying that he and two municipal officials had worked hard to create a plan for the systematic development of the city but had met with a lot of resistance:

> No sooner had Dr Hewlett and I drawn a line from the Prabadevi Temple in Mahim woods along the alignment of Elphinstone Foras Road to Parel—No sooner had we turned all dangerous trades out of the Island—except the common tanners, whom we located at Tannery Town (Dharavi) a very suitable position for the trade—No sooner had I proclaimed that no Factories of any kind should thence forth be built south of Elphinstone Road (the GIPR and the BB and CI Railway towns and workshops were already in course of construction at Anjir Baug: I bought the land for them)—No sooner, I say, had these essential steps been taken, than Kessowjee Naik brought his dyers back to their old quarters. I prosecuted them, but was defeated.
>
> Kessowjee Naik spent money like water, eminent physicians swore solemnly that dye-pits were beneficial to health, even the Press was nobbled by sums so large that their Editors could not resist the bait. This infamous success emboldened a powerful German firm to open a large steam Dyeing Factory close to Prabadevi Temple, whose refuse waters polluted the fair sands of Mahim Bay. Another German Firm (both were members of the Chamber of Commerce) followed suit with a huge Hide curing Factory.

It's a complaint familiar to the citizens of Mumbai even a century and a half later, but the new BIT was determined to forge ahead. With the civic arrangements of the city in the grip of vested interests such as landlords and industrialists, the BIT, which was formed as a parallel organization to the municipal corporation, was conceived as a noble project for the public good, to bring modern infrastructure to the citizens of Bombay.

It began well, with an ambitious plan to decongest areas and build east-west and north-south roads. The first four schemes were to be: a planned housing scheme in overcrowded Nagpada; a new road from south of Queen's Road to the Carnac Bridge, which ultimately became Princess Street; a road from the east of Chaupati (Chowpatty) ending at Elphinstone Bridge, which led to the docks; and creating roads between Chowpatty and Gowalia Tank, which would open up land for construction. All these roads are still in use, providing a critical link between the western and eastern parts of the city.

In the Nagpada project, over 2,000 residents already living there had to be shifted, and transit camps were built in Agripada. The intention was to reduce the density in Nagpada to 500 people per acre in three-storeyed chawls. By 1902 – 03, the committee proudly announced that most of the Nagpada project had been completed within three -and-a- half years, unlike similar schemes in London that had taken ten years to finish. Simultaneously, all other projects, including roads and reclamation—in Colaba—were nearing completion, and a report proudly announced that Princess Street was inaugurated by their Highnesses the Prince and Princess of Wales in November 1905.

But all these were in the developed part of Bombay, which was already urbanized. A far bigger plan was to take over villages beyond Parel, ostensibly to develop residential plots for housing for the poor. They would be moved out from their old, unsanitary living quarters and given an opportunity to live in cleaner surroundings.

In 1906, official sanction was given for other major schemes, two of which further increase the built-up parts of Bombay, by now witnessing another surge of population growth.

These were located in the belt beyond Parel to include Dadar, Matunga and Sion, thus covering a stretch about four kilometres long and mainly agricultural land. The colonial government saw this as an 'Improvement' exercise, a reflection of how it viewed native living as it existed. This was not without merit, since some of the living spaces in the city were almost inhuman, such as attics that were barely one foot high from floor to ceiling, and used only to sleep, the inhabitant accessing it by climbing a ladder. Some old chawls in areas like Currey Road, built by the administration mainly as hostels for textile workers, had this arrangement, though in most cases these were later additions by the residents. Owen Dunn, the chairman of the BIT for five years, in a lecture, described 'chals' (chawls), as 'unfit for human habitation'. 'The native chal landlord has, as a rule, ideas as to house property which are not altogether foreign to our own more advanced civilization,' he said, showing drawings of the floor plan.

Most of these chawls had been built in the wake of the textile factories boom and had been around for nearly fifty years. It took the plague for the administration to suddenly realize how overcrowded they were.

By 1909, the BIT was engaged in thirty-three schemes of development, including land reclamation in Colaba, including on the western side, where a seafront road and a seaside promenade were made, which was called Cuffe Parade, after a member of the Trust, T.W. Cuffe.

Big capital soon started influencing decisions and lobbied with the government to segregate housing and development according to income: the western shores would be for the rich, and Salsette island—from Bandra onwards—would be for the middle class. The idea of the Backbay Reclamation, which was on the west, was floated as the only viable solution to increase land availability. The reclamation of land at Colaba—where the Bombay, Baroda and Central India (BB&CI) Railway was laying a track for the convenience of the cotton trade—was an early effort in that direction.

The BIT's efforts were criticized by the media on many issues. Dunn was aware of the criticism and made light of it. He mentioned a piece of doggerel by a 'Local Rhymester' in the *Sind Observer*, apparently penned by a lawyer commenting on the lack of similar development in Karachi, then part of the Bombay Presidency.

We may not have a Ballard Pier and Passengers galore,
We may not Have a 'Taj Mahal' upon our sandy shore,
We may not have to live in an Apollo Bunder Flat,
But we haven't an Improvement Trust and thank the Lord for that!

For the residents on the lands to be newly developed—mainly farmers and labour in small industries such as tanning—

the BIT's efforts were nothing to cheer about. While new housing was to be created for others, their own land would be taken away. They protested, but their entreaties remained unheard.

The plan was to create layouts that would be comparable to those in the European quarter in South Bombay, where the post-1860 building boom had resulted in not just new construction but also the laying of new infrastructure. The wide roads and maidans were the envy of the rest of the citizenry, and though the native towns and chawls had grown in a haphazard manner, the government wanted to apply the latest urban planning principles to the new areas. A century later, it is difficult not to see that the efforts paid off.

The straight road from Dadar to Sion, then the very end of Bombay island, is much broader than roads elsewhere in Bombay, with generous footpaths to walk on. Each section between the two ends has a roundabout, which leads to the inner roads—the one at King's Circle, in Matunga, has a garden too. An ugly flyover built in the 1990s hides the beauty of the layout, but even so, it is possible to see how well designed it all was. The plan was to sell plots and create housing that would conform to new ideas—self-enclosed, multi-room apartments that would be hygienic and airy.

The government scheme also triggered private philanthropy in housing, especially among the Parsis of the city. Parsi charity and funding of institutions and projects for the public good had been seen on a large scale in Bombay in the nineteenth century—they gave their money for not just community causes but also for the general public. As far back as 1834, when big fortunes were being made, Jamsetjee Jeejeebhoy and Amichand Shah contributed jointly to set up the Panjrapole, a shelter in Bhuleshwar for stray animals, which eventually became mainly for Gir cows. Today, it looks after 350 pure-bred cows and sells their milk to the neighbourhood.

After the Fort walls came down in the 1860s, the big Parsi businessmen—and others, including Baghdadi Jews, Gujaratis, Kutchis and Maharashtrians—funded schools, hospitals and even crematoriums. But no one spent on housing on the scale that the Parsis did. As early as 1898, engineer Muncherji Murzban built two housing projects in Bombay—one near Gilder Lane at Agripada and another off Falkland Road—offering them to poor Parsis at extremely low rents. In 2016, the lowest rent for the smallest unit was ₹45—the highest was ₹932. The structures, made primarily of timber, are unique.

The residents, or 'inmates' as they were called, were to be 'poor Parsis who could not cope with the competition and crowding in Bombay,' says Simin Patel in an interview to me, a city historian who has written a thesis on the Parsis of colonial Bombay, 'The Making of British Bombay'.

In 1910, Jerbai Wadia, widow of the family patriarch Nowrosjee Wadia, built a few apartments for Parsi migrants from Gujarat who had come to Bombay to look for work. This was the beginning of her lifelong commitment to constructing more such gated complexes, which would be rented out to indigent Parsis in different parts of the world.

The 'baugs' that were made by her initiative and funds have provided homes to hundreds of community members.

Old-time residents of Cusrow Baug in Colaba recall their parents telling them about how very few people wanted to move to the colony when it was made in the 1930s. Today, the complex, with its gardens and other conveniences, situated in one of the southernmost parts of the city, is a coveted address for Parsis and there is a long queue of aspirants who have registered themselves with the Bombay Parsi Panchayat, which manages the place. It is possible to jump the queue by putting down a hefty, multi-million rupees 'deposit', which the others find very unfair.

But much before Cusrow Baug was built, the biggest and most ambitious housing project was conceived by a municipal engineer Muncherjee Joshi, who, quickly grasping the significance of the availability of an abundance of free land beyond Parel, immediately approached Parsi philanthropists to fund a housing complex. The municipal corporation had permitted him to build housing on the land.

The inner roads of the planned streets of the stretch that includes Dadar, Matunga, Wadala and Sion are green and with their own parks—the best one being Five Gardens in the middle of Dadar Parsi Colony. The colony was the first housing project in the new suburbs, and has maintained much of its pristine glory, thanks to an activist population of Parsis that wastes no time in fighting any intrusion into their idyllic world. In 2022, a plan to subdivide the colony into two wards became a big issue, and ultimately the municipal corporation had to relent and withdraw the proposal.

Entering the colony from the southern side, the visitor escapes the hustle and bustle of the main roads and thoroughfares of the city. The buildings have a maximum of three, sometimes four floors, though suddenly, the visitor comes across the imposing, multi-storeyed Delna Tower, with its pronounced friezes of scenes from Zoroastrian history on the façade. There is a school, an agiary and a community centre that is open to the general public for use too—this makes it an enclosed and inclusive area at the same time.

Somewhere in the centre of the colony lives Zarine Engineer, granddaughter of Muncherjee Joshi and a proud resident of the colony all her life. She has fond memories of her grandfather and calls him a pioneer and visionary.

'During the First World War, there were many Parsis in the Fort area, mainly middle class. Fort was becoming very congested, very tight. Muncherjee, a civil engineer with the Bombay Improvement Trust, wanted to do something for his fellow Parsis,' she tells me. 'Joshi went to his superior, E.G. Turner, who was the chairman of BIT and asked him for some land for Parsis. Turner offered him land in Dadar, which was marshy and wild. Those days monkeys and other animals used to freely roam about there.'

Joshi was greatly engaged with the idea of housing. In a speech to the Indian Institute of Architects in 1929 on 'The Housing Problem in Bombay', he said that half to three-fourths of the lower middle class—not middle class—families in the city were without a home. His painstaking calculations were based on the population of Bombay in March 1929, which was over 1.3 million, and by working out the number of buildings made and demolished, he arrived at his figures.

Joshi himself was of the middle class and decided that he would create housing for Parsis like him. Apart from being rough and wild, the land he was given was far away, especially for those who lived in the Fort area. But it was in abundance. He saw the possibilities of a large community enclave where Parsis could live in a modern way.

Bombay's communities already lived among their own, a tradition that began after the East India Company takeover in the seventeenth century. Though Fort had a somewhat mixed population, community clusters were the norm.

Joshi approached philanthropic Parsis as well as the Bombay Parsi Panchayat, the supreme community body with a hoary history going back to the eighteenth century, to seek funds for the construction of housing that could then be rented out.

He set about planning the project by first creating gardens. That legacy has remained—there are fourteen gardens there, and the roads are lined with trees of different species—mahogany, Ashoka, copper pod. It is the sheer variety of trees that gives the place its special character.

The first building came up in 1921 and in all, he made 113 buildings. With great foresight, he ensured that the land was leased to Parsis for 999 years. The flats were also early examples of 'apartments', with rooms clearly demarcated as living and sleeping spaces. Apartment living would soon become popular in the city.

Joshi's original plan included a proposal to build a wall around the colony, but that was shelved because the money ran out. A few years later, 'baugs' would spring up in different parts of Bombay—gated complexes where the community lives even today in a cocooned existence.

Dadar Parsi Colony became a model housing project, and the residents, in keeping with the original idea, refused to let any other community in. A few buildings were 'cosmopolitan'—a word regarded with some dread by many in Mumbai even now—and some families belonging to other communities did move there in the 1950s and even later, but on the whole, Dadar Parsi Colony has remained a Parsi universe.

In the early 2000s, three buildings were acquired by a Gujarati builder. As the residents looked on in horror, one of the buildings was demolished and flats were offered to the general public. In 2003, the Parsee Central Association Cooperative Housing Society, which was formed in 2001, sued. The city civil court agreed with the community and imposed a permanent injunction in December 2009 that these flats could only be sold to Parsis.

The Association now looks after twenty-three buildings and ensures that the essential character of the colony is not disturbed, writing petitions and approaching the civic corporation every time it comes across an infraction, but gradually, outside influences have been creeping in. It has not been able to stop the construction of buildings like Delna Tower—more are bound to come.

But so enamoured were others of this model of exclusivity, that they began clamouring for it. Right next to the Parsi Colony is a small estate for Catholics. On the opposite side of the wide, North Sound Road that connects Dadar to Sion, lies a Hindu colony, inspired by Parsi Colony.

While the colonies and houses differ in their designs, the central idea is the same—an enclave that only contains residents of a particular community, and, in the case of the Hindu colony, largely from the upper castes.

Further up lies Kapol Niwas, chiefly inhabited by members of the Kapol bania caste, and Matunga, often called, wrongly, Mini Madras, because of its large population of 'South Indians'—as those hailing from Tamil Nadu, the Andhra region, Karnataka and Kerala are collectively known. The temples, the spice shops, the flower stalls and the restaurants all give it a character redolent of a town in Tamil Nadu, though other communities are present there too. The so-called south Indian restaurants are run by those who came from Mangalore and Udupi, and there is a sizable presence of Gujaratis too.

Nonetheless, cosmopolitanism remained embedded in the city's ethos, with many micro communities, including some from other countries—Iran, Afghanistan and even Turkey—and migrants from every part of India living in the city. They were comfortable mixing with each other when it came to trading or commuting, but wanted to live among their own kind. They preferred to marry among their own religion, caste and even sub-caste and there were hundreds of community halls, temples, charity organizations, schools and neighbourhoods set up to service the members of particular communities. The more prosperous ones built hospitals, which were open to patients of every kind, but preference was given to those from their community.

These defensive walls were seen as important to protect a community's culture and traditions and provided a safety net to fellow community members. They were also predicated on the assumption of purity and uniqueness. For the Parsis—a minority group whose numbers are depleting—it was to ensure their unique way of life, which could get disturbed, even polluted, by the presence of 'outsiders'.

Most communities in Bombay have tried to resist the onslaught of practices such as inter-marriages, some more aggressively than others. A Parsi woman marrying a non-Parsi cannot get her children baptized in a fire temple and can also face barriers when trying to buy a house in a Parsi 'baug'. Other communities are not that strict, but many of them, especially those small in numbers, are bemoaning the tendency of the younger generation to inter-marry and their disinterest in the tradition and culture of their heritage.

The Dadar Parsi Colony and other similar precincts in the BIT's northwards expansion were a step forward in terms of town planning and the construction of living spaces, but the main city just followed the existing template of creating community enclaves. The mixed buildings and neighbourhoods that gave Bombay a true cosmopolitan flavour were yet to come.

4

BOMBAY TURNS WESTWARD

From the window of his sixth-floor apartment, Sevanti Parekh can see the distant horizon of the Arabian Sea. The window looks out on the entire Back Bay, which includes the arc of Marine Drive and beyond, extending towards the grand Raj Bhavan at the tip of Malabar Hill. Pollution often dims the views, but at night, the lights glitter on the curve of Marine Drive, justifying its popular name, Queen's Necklace, and on the tall buildings in the distance.

It is a view Sevantibhai, as he is locally known, has enjoyed for the last eighty years. At eighty-eight, he is probably one of the oldest continuous residents on Marine Drive.

His home is on the top floor of Bharatiya Bhavan, one of the buildings on the seafront.

He has lived there almost his entire life. He moved into his flat in 1939, when he was seven. The building, which was then called Jeevan Vihar, was built by his father. Three other partners in his firm did the same next door. (Three partners built on the plots next to Jeevan Vihar.)

The Marine Drive stretch, a little over three kilometres long, makes an arc that connects Nariman Point with Chowpatty and then on to Malabar Hill. On the western side is the sea, on the other, a row of buildings in the Art Deco style, followed by open grounds that are part of clubs, membership-only 'gymkhanas' for Parsis, Muslims, Hindus and Christians, who all played in the pentangular cricket tournaments in the 1920s representing their communities. The last gymkhana is for members of the police force. A few more buildings follow and then it tapers off. Marine Drive is a coveted part of Mumbai, built mainly in the 1940s and '50s, soon after a massive reclamation project that created land from the sea.

The promenade on the seaside is for walking, jogging, ambling and, for hundreds of young couples, canoodling. The spacious apartments lining Marine Drive may be out of reach, but the rest is a democratic, egalitarian and liberating public space. It is a busy thoroughfare, with traffic moving up and down all day and late into the night. Thousands of people converge here every day to 'eat the air'. Little children bring their tricycles, young exercise junkies run with gadgets strapped to their arms, middle-aged ladies walk briskly and retired gents sit and sort out all that is wrong with the world.

The couples sit, facing the sea, in self-absorbed isolation, communing only with themselves and the vast space in front of them—they don't care about the people behind them, and the crowds too leave them alone. In densely packed Mumbai, a bit of privacy is always welcome—what better place than Marine Drive, where it is possible to be alone in the middle of thousands?

Marine Drive is a place of abandon—the movies have often celebrated this by showing actors riding a motorcycle, their hair blowing in the wind, a song on their lips—whether for a drive or a leisurely walk or a purposeful run or just a few moments alone with a loved one before both part ways to go to their respective homes.

My own memory is as a child, when, along with my family, I used to walk on Sunday evenings from Churchgate to Marine Drive and down towards the end of the promenade where the Oberoi Hotel stands today. The business district of Nariman Point did not then exist. The seafront tapered off into a jagged strip of land where, every Sunday, crowds would gather to watch films projected on to a giant concrete screen. I found out much later that these were newsreels and not of any great entertainment value, with no songs or dances, but they provided an opportunity to congregate in a public place, breathe in the fresh sea air and simply gaze into the distance, with no tall concrete buildings in front to disturb the view.

For a little Bombay kid, this was the highlight of the week. I remember vividly how busy Marine Drive was on Sundays even then. At the time, the cars that came from Chowpatty did not continue into Nariman Point, an ugly creation of the 1970s with nothing but office buildings designed by architects and commissioned by developers with no regard for the Art Deco legacy or indeed any other style—they are not even fascinatingly brutalist, just indifferently put together concrete blocks laid haphazardly all over the place. None of that hideousness existed at the time. It was only the old buildings, the cars and the sea, Sevantibhai remembers.

Over the years Sevantibhai has come to realize how much he loves living here—the peaceful mornings, the glorious sunsets, the drama during the rains when huge waves crash on the wall that holds back the sea. He has resisted the temptation to move to a newer, swankier building. 'I used to go and see apartments in Malabar Hill, but none of them tempted me—there is no place like Marine Drive. My daughter and son-in-law live right here, and I am happy to see that they and my granddaughters too think the same.'

Parekh has seen Marine Drive grow from the very beginning. He remembers open plots where buildings now stand. 'After Seksaria Mansion, towards Chowpatty, there was nothing. Just one vast open ground. Our firm had bid for and won every plot, and these were sold piecemeal, one by one.'

After the construction of Jeevan Vihar was finished, Sevantibhai's father Jeevanbhai Parekh invited fellow traders and merchants to rent the apartments. The only condition was, they had to be vegetarians. 'We were strict Jains, and this was not negotiable.' This restricted the pool somewhat, but the bigger objection of the traders, most of whom lived in the native towns, was that this new neighbourhood was just too far. 'There is nothing here, no life at all, they said. Who will move all the way here?' The memory brings a smile to his face—how misplaced those fears were, since Marine Drive came to be a very convenient location.

The vegetarian condition was not universal—'The buildings on this side (the northern end) were all built by Gujarati and Marwari families, who were wealthy but very, very conservative and traditional.' On the other end (southwards), Sevantibhai says, all the buildings were 'cosmopolitan', i.e., open to every kind of tenant, community, religion and food habits. In the melting pot that Bombay was, 'cosmopolitan' was a loaded word, not just implying meat-eating, but also indicating an outlook and lifestyle that included drinking, dancing, partying and all things considered Western and therefore not Indian. The city wore its cosmopolitanism lightly, not surprising with its history of attracting people from all over India and the world, but that did not mean everyone had become Westernized. In time, Marine Drive and its environs would come to be associated most strongly with the cosmopolitan life, but early settlers were still rooted in their own traditions.

Many buildings, again on the south end, included guest houses, bed and breakfast places where mostly Europeans lived. Indeed, often landlords preferred Europeans—British and others—who would be temporary inhabitants and pay well.

The Bombay Club—it became Natraj Hotel later and then the Intercontinental—with its Burma teak panelling and modern furniture, became a popular haunt for Europeans, many of whom had flocked to Bombay in the 1930s to escape Nazi Germany.

When the tenants came, they were fussy and hard bargainers. 'Our building had slightly cheaper rents and even the one-time deposit of ₹30,000 was much less than the others, because we insisted on vegetarians. Yet, the tenants complained. One family took two flats on the second floor—the rent was ₹120 a month. Then they discovered the fourth floor had a better view, so they just moved in there. My father asked for a higher rent of ₹140, but they resisted, and finally it was settled at ₹130.' Many of them were also discomfited by the fact that the toilets were inside the apartments, even in the bedrooms. In Bombay, toilets were outside the main living structure of even the well-off, because they were considered impure. This innovation went against Indian culture and tradition.

Tenants had other demands too. 'I remember the buildings had boards announcing "To Let" prominently displayed. Tenants were hard to come by and were very fussy,' Dhun Lentin, a lifelong Marine Drive resident had once told me in an interview for a magazine. She was born in Soona Mahal and after her marriage to Bomi Lentin, a young lawyer who would once become a judge, had moved a few buildings up to Chateau Marine.

She married young Bomi Lentin, whose family lived five buildings down northwards in Chateau Marine. He went on to have a distinguished career in Bombay's judiciary but at the time was just a young lawyer. The building had been constructed by Bomi's father, and Dhun heard stories of how he was fed up with the constant demands of tenants who often used to rent only for a few months—mainly during the monsoons, to see the rains. 'Each new tenant used to have a list of demands, including the colour of the walls, all for those few months.' Lentin sold the building to the then Maharaja of Baroda whose family still owns it. The Lentins became tenants in the building they had constructed.

Across the Lentin flat lived a gawky young girl, Fatima, Bomi's childhood friend. 'She used to use this apartment's fire escape at the back to sneak back into her home,' says Dhun. Fatima morphed into a young woman who became hugely popular as Nargis, the star of the 1950s. The home belonged to her formidable mother, Jaddan Bai, a one-time singer, who held salons where hopefuls and eager producers congregated. Tenants had other demands too. 'I remember the buildings had boards announcing "To Let" prominently displayed. Tenants were hard to come by and were very fussy,' Dhun Lentin, a lifelong Marine Drive resident had once told me in an interview for a magazine. She was born in Soona Mahal and after her marriage to Bomi Lentin, a young lawyer who would once become a judge, had moved a few buildings up to Chateau Marine.

Manto wrote about these salons and the gossip that was freely exchanged. One particular target was the singing-star Suraiya, who was also a neighbour in Krishna Mahal, a few buildings down. In a column in a Pakistani Urdu daily he recounted Jaddan Bai saying that Suraiya's voice was bad, 'she could not hold a note, she had had no musical training, her teeth were bad and so on. I am sure had someone gone to Suraiya's home he would have witnessed the same kind of surgery performed on Nargis and Jaddan Bai.'[1]

In the 1940s, Marine Drive was still sparsely populated—those who lived there hurriedly moved out in 1942 after rumours spread that the Japanese would bomb the city, and the sea-facing locations would be the most vulnerable. 'People moved to their villages and towns in large numbers—we did too. When we returned, the whole of Marine Drive had "To Let" boards in the balconies,' Sevantibhai laughs. But by 1947, it was almost full up. The locals were joined by Sindhis fleeing from the newly formed Pakistan to India. Many from Karachi came to Bombay, where they already had business or family links and used to visit often. Those who could afford it moved to Churchgate, Colaba and Marine Drive, where the seafront reminded them of the home they had left behind. Marine Drive became a coveted address.

'It was just the most beautiful place to live in—no crowds, no traffic, just the sea.' The drive from his school, which was near the Victoria Terminus, took only a few minutes, the last bit covered in just a minute by his speeding car, which touched up to 80 miles an hour.

Though both people and cars have increased exponentially, the glamour of Marine Drive remains undimmed after all these years. Many of the buildings now look frayed, mostly because of neglect, and most need a paint job and structural work—in some poorly maintained buildings, slabs often fall off. Younger families may even find it fuddy-duddy, with hardly any children around and the buildings without the conveniences that the swanky new gated complexes provide—clubs, gyms, safe walking tracks and seclusion and security—here, the buildings have low walls and rely on a single watchman, rather than six layers of security. Eight decades, that too on the seafront, can take a toll, more so if there has been no investment in regular upkeep.

To the residents, these are surmountable problems. Where else would you get such large apartments—twelve-foot-high ceilings, large bedrooms, roomy kitchens? A lot of light, plentiful air circulation, a spectacular sunset every day, and in the monsoons, the stormy performance of the seas, as waves rise and crash on the promenade. All this, often for rents that are stuck at the rates of some sixty years ago. Not surprisingly, no one who lives here actually moves out and apartments rarely come up in the market—when families grow, it is not unusual for even adult children to stay put, fearing that leaving the flat could put their future claim at risk.

Over the years, Marine Drive has come to symbolize not just openness and expanse, but also freedom. Freedom not just from the suffocation of tiny apartments but also from convention and restriction. It is a place where nobody knows or cares about who the other is—you could live anywhere, do anything, but Marine Drive belongs to you as much as to that multi-millionaire stockbroker. The conveniently located train stations nearby mean homeward-bound commuters can take a short break here after work and soak in the openness before boarding impossibly crowded trains. They come here to stroll, to forget their troubles and be alone with their thoughts, to sit gazing at the horizon, waiting for the sun to set. Some adventurous ones venture down, stepping carefully on the tetrapod—large, four-pointed pyramids made of concrete and placed along the sea wall to break the waves and prevent erosions of the wall. Since they were placed there in the 1950s, they have become a fixture, a part of the Marine Drive experience, often a site for couples, photo enthusiasts and risk-taking youngsters, but also for a few who come here to defecate in the early light of dawn.

For old-timers, Marine Drive brings back memories of travelling by the 'C' route double-decker and trying to grab the front seat to see the road and feel the breeze on their faces. During the monsoon, it was an even bigger thrill. The C route turned to 123, when numericals were introduced, but the charm remained, till some dour, humourless bureaucrat took the double-deckers out of service and replaced them with single-decker buses.

The same mindset banned vendors who sold salted peanuts and roasted corn along the boulevard, a welcome snack at any time of the year. And every now and then, politicians wanting to impose 'Bharatiya Sanskriti' tried to banish the cosy couples sitting with their backs to the crowds, who come here to snatch a few moments of privacy in this maddening world. These efforts inevitably failed—Bombay doesn't take kindly to moral policing.

From the time of the reclamation and the construction of the many buildings on the promenade, Marine Drive emerged as a gathering place for its citizens—young and old, rich and indigent, men and women, all of whom came to enjoy the sea breeze and revel in the openness which sitting on the promenade and gazing at the horizon afforded them. There was a sense of liberation, literal and otherwise—they could enjoy, an escape from their small apartments further inland.

The buildings on Marine Drive on the other hand were large and were all in the most modern style—what came to be known as Art Deco. The entire promenade, of thirty-six modern buildings, were designed, built and financed by Indians. The buildings were designed in the modern style—what eventually came to be known as the Art Deco, reflecting a conscious decision by the architects to reject not just colonial Gothic grandeur but also the Indian vernacular. The creators of this new precinct saw the vast stretch of open land facing the sea as a blank slate on which they chose to write a new narrative; the typology of the buildings was the language of the modern that was sweeping the world at the time.

With this decision, the architects and the owners both decided they would shed the insularity that colonialism had wrought and become an international city, a link in a chain that included New York, London and Paris, and which later grew to include Hong Kong, Shanghai and Tokyo.

Bombay, which till then had faced the east, became a westward-looking city, a shift that changed the orientation of the city and its worldview. Marine Drive became a vector of modernity, allowing Bombay to reimagine itself in an entirely new way. It changed the way people in the city lived and thought. Apartment living was an entirely new idea in the city and demanded changes in behaviour and lifestyles. Toilets were en suite, a shocking idea for traditional Indians who kept such things at a distance, since it would otherwise mean cleaners of other castes entering the home.

In the new apartment buildings, as opposed to the old-style buildings and cottages, neighbours were invisible and distant. Doors were shut all the time, people kept to themselves, and privacy became important. In the 'cosmopolitan' buildings, your neighbour could be from any caste, community or even religion, a strange concept since people tended to live among their own. Bombay had always been home to people from different parts of the country and from across the world, who freely mixed with each other in offices and bazaars—now that mix was coming to living spaces too.

The genesis of what came to be known as Marine Drive was not auspicious. Before it could achieve fruition and the promenade was built, there was a huge scandal, thanks to exposés by a lawyer Rohinton Fali Nariman.

For over 250 years, all activity in Bombay was on the east, in keeping with the importance of the port. All commercial and social life grew around it. Areas such as Byculla, Mazagaon and Parel, where the governor lived, were important neighbourhoods where the rich had homes. The first governor, William Hornby, had moved into his mansion, called Sans Pareil, in 1771. In the mid-nineteenth century, Parel was where most of the cotton mills were established and mill workers too began living in the area.

The west was mainly water. Reclamation in the eighteenth and nineteenth centuries had created a landmass, but homes were few and far between. In the 1880s, the governor of Bombay moved his residence to Malabar Hill, which occupies a sylvan 225 acres on the very tip of the hill, so named because it was used as a lookout point for Malabar pirates. Some of the very rich followed, mainly Parsis, who built grand bungalows there. In the early part of the twentieth century, many potentates from princely states in Gujarat and central India built seaside homes along the west coast, up to Worli, the site of an old fishing village. Further north was Salsette, which in the early twentieth century was little more than paddy fields, palm trees and water-logged areas where farming communities, mainly Christians converted by the Portuguese, lived.

Where Marine Drive now stands was just the sea, starting from Chowpatty, all the way to the BB&CI (Western Railway) headquarters, and then till Colaba and Cuffe Parade, where large and elegant Victorian bungalows looked out on to the water. A widely circulated photograph on the internet shows Parsis praying in the sea right where the Churchgate station stands now.

The thought of filling up the sea and then reclaiming the south-western part of Bombay and then populating the west coast was long a goal of the British administration, which had already achieved its initial stated aim of joining all the islands into one landmass. The first reclamation of land to block the Worli creek and stop the flooding of Bombay's low-lying area in the 1780s was the beginning of the project to form a unified island. By then, officials were taken up with the idea of creating new land by filling up the sea, and almost continuously since then, some part of Bombay was being filled up. But all of this activity was in the east. In the 1860s, fired by the money the city was making because of increased cotton exports, a Back Bay reclamation company was formed, but after the American civil war ended in 1865, and there was no demand for Indian cotton, land prices fell dramatically and the ardour cooled.

The proposal got a new lease of life in the early twentieth century. The plague had prompted calls for decongesting the inner parts of the city where the natives lived. The Bombay Improvement Trust, set up by the government to handle the clean-up and creation of new housing, set about its task with vigour. But the elite of the city had more ambitious ideas—a syndicate of private capitalists set up a company to reclaim hundreds of acres between Back Bay and Colaba. This project was taken over by the government and handed over to the Bombay Development Directorate.

The original suggestions for the reclamation were very different from what it turned out to be. One such was to create well laid out housing for the middle class, but this idea was soon jettisoned.

'To provide for the pressing need for further accommodation in the business centre of the city, and immediately adjacent to the commercial enterprises in the Fort, a large scheme of reclamation is being carried out under the auspices of the Government. Some two square miles are being reclaimed from the sea in Back Bay,' wrote W.R. Davidge, a consultant town planner, in a proposal, The Development of Bombay, in 1924.[2]

'The town planning review area has been set aside for public buildings, legislative council, etc.; about a hundred acres will be devoted to office premises, the offices being grouped round shady quadrangles on the lines of Gray's Inn or the colleges at Oxford. A broad open space, lined with palm trees, under which there will be a "ride", will be laid out along the whole length of the reclamation terminating in an important public building at the extreme end of the vista, the northern end being directed on the famous clock tower built by Sir Gilbert Scott in 1878,' Davidge's proposal said.

Davidge's plan of 1924, 'which had envisaged broad avenues, laid out in a neo-classical pattern with Government buildings at each end of a central avenue, went nowhere,' wrote Sharada Dwivedi and Rahul Mehrotra in their book on Bombay's Art Deco.[3] Another plan, developed by George Wittet, consulting architect to the government, was also discarded, as was a third by the well-known architect Claude Batley, who had designed Cusrow Baug with apartment buildings around a central garden.

Instead, Marine Drive, the construction of which began in 1935, turned out to be a promenade with the seafront buildings getting a full view of the sea, while those built behind each block—four deep—had none. These were constructed by builders purely for profit, unlike the seafront buildings, which were owner-driven; not surprisingly, the construction is shoddy and the apartments smaller and unimaginatively designed. In addition, several flats don't get adequate light. An angry Batley called the final result 'a rather badly fitting set of false teeth to the city'. The buildings collectively look like many chests of drawers left open, but eighty years on, it is a much-loved part of Mumbai, and its prestigious standing has been reinforced by the granting of heritage status by the United Nations Educational, Scientific and Cultural Organization (UNESCO).

The Backbay Reclamation Project began in 1915 with the filling up of the sea from Chowpatty and was originally supposed to go all the way to Colaba. At the Chowpatty end stands a twenty-foot-high lamppost, commemorating the beginning of the reclamation, which was named Kennedy Sea Face, after Sir Michael Kennedy, who headed the Public Works Department.

The money ran out halfway through the project, and Marine Drive as we know it stops suddenly opposite the present National Centre for the Performing Arts. Across the bay are the gleaming towers of Cuffe Parade, built mostly in the 1970s, and on the left is the Colaba fishing village, which would have been wiped out had the proposed reclamation continued till Colaba. Today, politicians are forever eyeing it, coming up with new ideas on how to use the land, including the creation of public gardens, but the ultimate aim is always the same—to make available land on the seashore that can then be converted into luxury flats and office buildings.

The Bombay Development Directorate (BDD) was supposed to handle projects all over the city—reclamation was to be done in the Churchgate and Colaba areas, but the BDD was also to fill up the breach—a small stretch of water—at Warden Road and then construct chawls for workers in different parts of Bombay. One such are the BDD chawls in Worli, made for civic and other workers. This entire stretch is sought to be redeveloped by the state—a code word for building luxury flats—but the locals have been unimpressed with offers of bigger flats built separately for them.

Like all government initiatives, the BDD was propelled by good intentions and again, like many land-oriented projects, it fell victim to scandal, amid allegations of inefficiency and corruption. Vested interests—mainly merchants and big contractors—felt left out of the reclamation project because the selling of the plots was to be handled by the government and they had no finger in the pie. They failed in their attempts to stop it because the municipal corporation had been sidelined, and the scheme was approved in the Legislative Council, where big business actively supported it.

A campaign followed against BDD, specifically the Backbay Reclamation, which had the blessings of George Lloyd, governor of Bombay, pointing out all manner of failures, including the fact that it was very expensive. When a dredger broke down in the sea, the campaigners went to town, and the project was named Lloyd's Folly. By now newspapers and nationalists, led by the Congress, had gotten into the act. The campaign was led by a public-spirited lawyer, K.F. Nariman, and while there were suspicions that he was being goaded and propped up by the contractors' lobby, he managed to force the administration to appoint an inquiry into the reclamation project.

The municipal corporation, where the big contractors held significant sway and which was also smarting at having the project taken away from it by the government, condemned the Backbay Reclamation. The contention of the members was that the facts and figures presented by the government were misleading, and the scheme was destined for failure. 'A White Elephant,' said *The Bombay Chronicle* in 1926.

Eventually, though the scandal claimed George Lloyd, and the scope of the project itself was truncated, it did not stop the government from going ahead with it. Work continued apace, and stones and debris brought from far away continued to be poured into the sea, eventually creating over a thousand acres of land.

The public and the media appeared to have forgotten the scandal; *The Times of India*, displaying canny business sense, began publishing supplements on the progress of Marine Drive, complete with advertisements from suppliers and contractors. In 1940, noting that blocks of apartments had 'indeed arisen at a pace beyond anticipations', it said, approvingly, that while it was expected that 'even in favourable years' it would take ten to twelve years to finish the Churchgate reclamation, a large part of the available area had been done in two years.

'On the whole it seems the layout of the Churchgate Reclamation has achieved openness and freedom—most important essentials,' wrote the paper. Below the article, a half page advertisement of Shapoorji Pallonji, a civil contractor, claimed that works of over ₹50 lakh had been done on the buildings and 20,000 tonnes of ACC cement had been used. The hype was unmistakeable.[4]

At the time they were constructed, the style of buildings in the reclaimed area of Churchgate, Marine Drive and then parts of Colaba did not have a name—it was modern and en vogue. The projects were handled by Indian firms which had well-trained Indian architects. They were home-grown, but that did not stop them from absorbing international influences and tastes. This was a generation that was Western in its sensibilities, and this would eventually reflect in the essence of this new precinct that was coming up.

Marine Drive came up after the construction of the apartment blocks across the Oval Maidan, which had names such as Oval View, Palm Court, Queen's Court and Belvedere, though these were not strictly built on land reclaimed from the sea but after the old railway tracks leading from Churchgate to Colaba station—near present-day Badhwar Park—were uprooted and the land filled up.

Even before those, Regal cinema, the city's first Art Deco building, complete with soda fountain and underground parking, had opened in 1933 with *The Devil's Brother*, a film starring Laurel and Hardy. This was followed by other Art Deco cinemas—Metro with its streamlining, Eros with its ziggurat, and Liberty, built in 1949 and named to commemorate India's independence, with its long piano keyboard running down the side.

Financial institutions, such as banks and insurance companies, too chose the style, though their buildings were much more solid and imposing. The buildings loom over the street, without the cheerfulness of the residential ones, as if to impose confidence and trust but also awe. The architects tried to add a human touch wherever they could—the New India Assurance Building near Flora Fountain has two stone friezes of a man and a woman, toiling in the fields and in industry. They somewhat leaven the sternness of the structures, but they still look authoritarian.

Even as the buildings were being planned in the area around Churchgate station and Marine Drive, the Indian Institute of Architects, established in Bombay in 1929, held the 'Ideal Home Exhibition' in 1937, where thousands of visitors saw the latest styles of furniture, flooring and even refrigerators.

The architects, well informed about the latest movements across the world, chose what was loosely called the Moderne style that was spreading all over the world. The style included streamlining, ziggurats, curvilineal balconies, frozen fountains and sunbursts in the window grills and even nautical themes, which seemed particularly suitable for buildings situated on the Bombay seafront—Soona Mahal, which looks like a majestic ocean liner cutting through the seas, and Oceana, with porthole vignettes, are good examples.

The names of the buildings too were done in the new fonts that had become popular at the time—clean, geometric, sans serif letters, neatly but strikingly arranged.

To this, the architects added their Indian touches—the 'eyebrows' to protect the interiors from the rain, and balconies and windows to fully soak in the sunshine of the tropical city. The rooms were large and airy, and for the sea-facing apartments, full of light for most of the day. For the colours, the architects chose light pastel shades—powder blue, cotton candy pink, pistachio green, apart from an off-white, creamy shade that caught the evening sunlight perfectly, and these were the most popular.

The entrances to all such buildings are small and there is no lobby to speak of—just a few steps to the elevators. The available space seems to have been optimized to create large living spaces rather than grand lobbies that do little more than add vanity to the building. This is quite in contrast to the expansive entrances in modern towers, with glass frontages, chandeliers, couches and the latest security systems. Twelve-foot-high walls around these new gated properties prevent the general public from peering in and seeing the enviable lives of the residents. On the other hand, the Art Deco buildings have low, three-foot walls outside their compounds, which helps create a dialogue between the buildings and the passers-by. A lone watchman or two—not a security guard—stands at the entrance.

All kinds of phrases were used to describe the style—and the stylishness—of the buildings and the apartments. 'There are five upper floors consisting of four flats of the European type with the usual living and dining rooms, bedrooms with attached baths, kitchen and servants' rooms,' wrote *The Times of India* in its edition on 28 February 1940 about Soona Mahal, and waxed eloquent on the marble used on the staircases, the teakwood banister and the lighting.[5] The architects of the building were Suvarnapatki and Vora. It is the most recognized building of the Marine Drive stretch, with its distinctive high tower room on the terrace, a unique feature that looks like the bridge of a luxury liner, accentuating the building's nautical theme.

'The building was made by my grandfather F.C. Sidhwa, and he named it after his mother,' recalls Mehernosh Sidhwa, who only came to live there many years later. The staircases are today as they were eight decades ago, and his own is furnished with antique furniture, which he deals in. His flat is on the south side, where he can get a partial glimpse of the sea, but that is compensated for by an unbroken view of the east, taking in the high court and the university clock tower.

Eventually, this style spread to the rest of the city, especially to the newly created suburbs of Dadar, Hindu Colony, Matunga and Sion in the east and Shivaji Park, Mahim and Bandra in the west, where housing was being built for the middle classes. But it was in the Churchgate area and on Marine Drive where it flowered the earliest and the most creatively.

Not only were the owners, the architects and the contractors Indian, but the new owners also selected Indian products to beautify the interiors of their flats. For flooring, most architects turned to Bharat Tiles, an Indian company started in 1922 by Pherozesha Sidhwa, who was studying for a law degree and was inspired by the swadeshi movement.

'The idea was to produce such good products at almost half the price that there would be no market left for British goods in India,' says Sidhwa's daughter Dilnawaz Variava, who ran the company in the 2000s. The Indian connection was proudly declared—not just was the company named Bharat, but each tile used to have a map of India stamped at the back.

Till Bharat Tiles came along, the biggest supplier was Minton of England, whose clay tiles were used in the grand Gothic and Edwardian buildings of Bombay. Bharat, which regularly updated its designs, worked closely with architects, and soon its tiles were in great demand—the mass-produced designs were in terrazzo, made from chips of glass and other materials; for the more fastidious and those who were ready to spend more, the company produced specific designs based on intricate, geometric patterns. 'Someone from the company went abroad every two years and saw the latest trends and we then designed on those lines.'

The tiles were cheaper than imported ones, but still on the expensive side. A price list from 1929 – 30 shows that mass produced tiles were in the range of ₹50 per 100 square metres, while made-to-order ones could go up to ₹66. Flooring for a large flat could cost hundreds of rupees, not a small sum when incomes were low. For the wealthy owners, this was not a barrier, since they were determined to enhance their new acquisitions. The aspiration was to try out something new, the best available and as far as possible, Indian.

In 1942, the government requisitioned all the cement production in the country for the war effort. There was no more supply, and Bharat, like many other companies, had to shut down till the end of the war. When things returned to normal, trends had begun to change—terrazzo was more popular now, perhaps because personalized designs were more expensive. Gradually, newer styles came in.

It is still possible to see the stylish Art Deco flooring in many Bombay apartments, zealously protected by the residents. In one, the original wood panelling, the grills and the furniture are as they were then; it is like stepping into a museum of what a 1930s apartment looked like. 'We have resisted all temptation to remodel the flat and every family discussion ends with the same conclusion—don't change a thing,' says the lady of the house, who has lived there since her childhood. The tiles look as good as new.

The testimonials of users tell the story: 'The original Bharat Tiles have the same shine as they did over sixty years ago without any polish or other artificial means have to be used,' wrote one user in 2000. Another said his family home, built by his great-grandfather in the 1920s, still had the original tiles.[6]

Tiling was not a subject to be treated casually. Architects took it seriously, and the owners of the buildings—who were after all constructing for themselves and their families—were made to understand that. In 1935, Jal R. Kanga, a prominent engineer, in a lecture at the Indian Institute of Architects emphasized the importance of tiles and why it would be wrong to use shoddy tiles that may be cheaper but would wear out fast.

While price certainly had something to do with it, for many buyers, it was also a question of patronizing an Indian company, especially one that promised quality. The flats were to be homes for generations and were built in the latest style, and no one wanted to make do with the old.

By this time, when the new buildings began coming up in the late 1930s and early 1940s, there were enough companies and suppliers of goods and services that were fully homegrown, from the plumbing to the masonry, to the fittings and the furniture. The new precinct was to be the beginning of a new Bombay, so naturally everything about it, including the interiors, should be new too.

On the ground floor of the looming Industrial Assurance Building, with its stolid stone façade, is Kamdar, the landmark furniture store, decorators to the elite of Bombay and beyond. The tens of thousands of pedestrians—office-bound in the mornings and homebound in the evenings—scarcely have the time to stand and glance through its show windows, but if they did, they would see the latest styles of elegantly made furniture.

From 1941, Kamdar has stood at the same spot, and its vast showroom has reflected changing tastes and styles. Even in its early days, it became the interior decorator and furniture-maker to the residents of the most fashionable and stylish buildings of the era.

'My father, Bhagwandas Morarji Kamdar, who set up the company, was offered the space by Sir Chimanlal Setalwad, chairman of the Industrial Assurance company,' says Vikram, himself now in his seventies. 'We were first half the size, first we took one unit and then doubled it soon after. It was unaffordable, but my father had the vision to realize that we will require more space as we grew and got more business.'

Kamdar senior was an engineer with the government but quit his job in a burst of nationalist fervour to start his own business. He His loved woodwork and had made toys for

Montessori children. A request to make a table by a Bombay businessmen led him to explore furniture, and soon after, Kamdar was born.

His gamble of scaling up the business proved correct—buyers looking for furniture that was a la mode, well made and less expensive than the imported versions commissioned Kamdar's to create interiors for them. The company has never kept a catalogue of ready-made designs—every piece is bespoke, Vikram proudly says. Art Deco style furniture—sinkable chairs with gracefully curved armrests, smoothly finished bar cabinets, armoires and beds—they all rolled out of the Kamdar factory in large numbers. Vikram proudly says many of those pieces are still in service, eight decades letter—'You can't get that quality anymore—no nails, no screws, everything handmade.'

As business boomed, Kamdar's hired a young German, Ernst Messerschmidt, who had come to India to decorate the nursery at the palace of the Maharaja of Indore, whose wife was expecting a baby. The war in Europe interrupted and he could not return to Germany. Instead, he and many other Germans and Italians in India were interned in camps by the British authorities. Messerschmidt was in Deolali, where, incidentally, many German technicians from Bombay Talkies were also kept.

Like the others, Messerschmidt was released after the end of the war, and Kamdar senior, who had heard of him, invited him to join the company as a designer. It was a big leap of faith and imagination—a German in the employ of an Indian company that was also just finding its feet.

It was an inspired decision—the German, who liked India and whose family had perished in the war, created novel and utterly modern designs for interiors ranging from homes to offices to restaurants, which were proliferating all over South Bombay, especially just round the corner at Churchgate Street.

Vikram proudly pulls out a pile of papers with the designs, all done in water colours that hold fast all these decades later. 'This was done for a maharaja's dining room (a long table with twelve chairs on each side), this for a swank new restaurant (dining tables with orange chairs, a bar, a bandstand and low-hanging lights), a living room suite (everything from a bar, chairs, sofas and a drinks cabinet).'

The clients could visualize what their room would look like, and the result would be an exact match, down to the shade of the upholstery. Business took off.

The new apartment-style homes of Bombay, open and airy, with rooms clearly demarcated for their functionality, now had a personality of their own, with new flooring and furniture. They were like nothing that had been seen in the city or perhaps in India before. They could compare with the latest styles anywhere in the world. They were modern, and this, naturally, called for a modern lifestyle to go with them.

5

DINNER, DANCE, BUT NO DRINKS

In the early 1900s, perhaps 1902, a restaurant opened in Bombay, promising an entirely new experience to the city's upper classes. A. Vianelli, an Italian émigré, set up an eponymous fine dining place, which would serve Italian food to the many Europeans in the city as well as to wealthier Indians ready to try something new.

A photograph shows the exterior of the restaurant, with the name in tall letters, in the corner of a building at the end of Chowpatty, where the road currently diverges from Marine Drive towards Grant Road station. Marine Drive didn't exist, of course, so towards the south it was just the sea.

But the northern road led to Malabar Hill, home to the city's elite, both in terms of wealth and official power.

Not many details are available about the restaurant after that, till 1911, when a young Indian man, Bhimji Jairaj Makanji, newly returned from Japan where he had spent several years, bought out A. Vianelli. Bhimji Makanji's descendants have a photograph depicting both gentlemen standing outside the entrance to the restaurant, the young buyer looking stylish, with braces on his trousers and sporting a splendid handlebar moustache.

The setting up of a restaurant by Vianelli was unusual enough, but what made it a truly pioneering venture was its location. At the time, much of the city's population was in the eastern and central parts of Bombay. High-level British officials and some wealthy Indians lived on the western side, which was sparsely populated. Towards the south was the sea, and there were few houses on the coast towards the north. The old fishing villages in Worli and further down would hardly have been potential customers of Vianelli's. Investing in a restaurant may or may not have made immediate commercial sense, but it was a forerunner of many more to come—with the Backbay Reclamation just three decades or so away, the western coast was going to change forever, bringing with it not just new buildings and residents, but also a new cosmopolitan lifestyle and a new way of looking at the world and our own place in it. The transformation of Bombay was about to begin and alter it forever.

Bhimji may not have seen that far ahead, but he was somewhat of a maverick. He was the son of the fifth wife of Jairaj Makanji, a financier and tycoon who owned textile mills along with his partners the Khataus. At the time of his father's death, Bhimji was but a child and never received his share of the inheritance.

Bhimji grew up and began importing toys from Japan, and when he went there for business, he decided to stay there 'out of curiosity and love for the country and the language,' says his great-grand daughter Apnavi Makanji, a Geneva-based artist. Bhimji Jairaj authored a Japanese-to-Gujarati dictionary, possibly the first ever, and sent several postcards from Japan.

After his return, instead of joining the family firm, he decided to branch out on his own by investing in a restaurant. Somewhere along the way, Bhimji Jairaj changed his name from Makanji to Thakkar, apparently because the British kept calling him Mackenzie, which he disliked.

The Kutchi Bhatia community, small but influential and with a substantial number of wealthy businessmen, was appalled at Bhimji's decisions—both to change his name and to get into the restaurant business. 'They were very critical of him, but he did not care,' says Nalin Thakkar, his grandson. Nalin, also a restaurant man, spent his teenage years in Bombay and is now based in Geneva, where he has lived since the 1950s, when his father moved there.

At the time, in the early 1900s, the Kutchis were as conservative as most other Gujaratis, sticking closely to their culture and traditions. While they had to deal with the British, Parsis and various other communities in the course of doing business, social matters remained within community networks, many of them going back to Kutch.

Mostly a desert, Kutch is a harsh and difficult place to live in, and after the earthquake of the early nineteenth century, a large number of Kutchis—Memons, Khojas and Bhatias, among others—moved to Bombay, a newly emerging commercial centre that looked promising. Word of the opportunities, especially because it was on the sea, and of the burgeoning opium business were a big pull for the community, which knew all about trade across the seas.

The Kutchis had been conducting business with the Arabs and Africans for a long time and then with the Europeans who came to the western coast, mainly Gujarat, and Surat had emerged as a thriving trading centre. In Bombay, the Kutchis soon became successful traders. In the mid-nineteenth century, a few of them set up textile mills, carving a prominent place for themselves in a fast-growing city. The capital formation and wealth creation by the Kutchis made them among the very few Hindu business communities to get into industry, as the Parsis and Jews had done.

By the 1930s and '40s, the elites of the Kutchi communities rapidly became westernized. 'I had an aunt who went to Cambridge alone in the 1930s and eventually married a journalist from Madras,' says Javed Gaya, a lawyer and a Memon, whose family has lived in Bombay for over 200 years.

Among the Bhatias too, a younger generation smoothly transitioned to a more modern lifestyle. 'We were five sisters, and my parents were far more liberal than the others,' says Rohini Santos, who was born in the 1940s. The first had an arranged marriage, but the others chose husbands from different communities and religions. 'My mother had been a rebel and my father, poor man, had little choice.' Her brother, Deepak Khatau, himself married to a Singaporean Chinese, concurs: 'After the Second World War, the old traditional order crumbled, at least as far as the community elite was concerned.'[1]

On his part, Bhimji Thakkar had already demonstrated an adventurous spirit much earlier, no doubt imbibed from generations of Kutchis. His grandson, Nalin, who lives in Switzerland, remembers how the restaurant served non-vegetarian food and alcohol, quite contrary to his own traditional lifestyle at home, because his mother was still rooted in community values. 'She sat every evening in the restaurant, but never ate there. Advertisements in old Bombay newspapers mention the products that were available in Vianelli—"Red Wine for Invalids. Rich Port Wine made solely from PURE GRAPES at Baron Rothschild's famous cellars In Richon-le-zion" could be bought at ₹2 and 12 annas,' and, perhaps to go with it, the award-winning 'Hunter's Hames' (presumably another wine) could be picked up too, because it was ideal for 'picnics and yachting'. Foreign liquor was easily available in the 1920s, as were victuals from around the world, aimed at the European market.

After Bhimji died at an early age in the 1940s, his son Pratapsingh Bhimji Thakkar took over Vianelli's and ran the restaurant for around eighteen years. But then, in the 1950s, Bombay was hit badly by a new government policy that was to last for over two decades—prohibition. Liquor was banned, almost overnight, plunging many businessmen into bankruptcy and casting a pall of gloom over those who liked a drink or two.

Imposing prohibition had been a long-standing promise of the Congress party. It had been originally declared in 1939 by Dr M.D. Gilder, a minister in the state government and a big votary of temperance. Gilder was criticized by his fellow Parsis who had a big stake in the liquor business, and he was abused during a public meeting called to discuss it. The move collapsed when the Congress ministry resigned later that year in protest against Viceroy Lord Linlithgow's suo moto declaration of India as belligerent and therefore part of the Second World War without getting the views of Indians.

The city continued its merrymaking ways, and new restaurants were constantly opening up. Nalin's own Bombay days in the 1940s and 1950s were liberal: 'Restaurants, parties, dances,' he says with a twinkle in his eye. 'I was in my late teens and used to go to the top restaurants, where just mentioning my grandfather's name, I used to get favoured treatment—my uncle was a regular everywhere, especially the Ambassador Hotel, and his name opened doors.'[2]

In 1952, Morarji Desai took over as chief minister of Bombay state—he was an even bigger believer in the evils of drinking and enforced prohibition with greater vigour. The act had been passed by the government in 1949. 'Desai knew my father but of course that didn't mean he would make any exceptions,' Nalin remembers.

Pratapsingh, disgusted with this policy, sold off Vianelli, and a Kutchi food restaurant, Aram, took its place. The Thakkars moved to London initially and subsequently to Geneva where in 1957 he opened a new place, La Riviera. It was a tearoom serving Western snacks and sandwiches but Indian food for lunch and dinner. It became popular with

Indian diplomats stationed there and was a must-visit place for the Indian industrialists and millionaires who regularly went to the country to meet with their bankers—they all craved Indian food, mostly vegetarian, and a conversation in Gujarati, with the Thakkars, was definitely a bonus.

Once, Morarji Desai, who was on an official visit, came along to the restaurant—he knew Pratapsingh, who invited him to come back home. Young Nalin was introduced to the politician, upon which, he says, 'I said, I don't want to meet you; it was because of you we had to leave India.'

In 1968, Pratapsingh opened the Port Gitana Grill, a purely French restaurant with the exception of chicken or prawn curry and rice, which featured on the menu. It ran till 1974 when the state repossessed the building because of the building owner's debts. 'My grandfather Pratapsingh was again forced to shut down his business due to circumstances that had nothing to do with him,' says Apnavi.

The family stayed on in Switzerland, and Nalin took up a job in a popular restaurant chain. His daughter Apnavi is an artist, and keeps up her links with Bombay, where her family was a pioneer in a business we take for granted.

Restaurants or dining out were not really a big thing in Bombay when Vianelli opened. Though there were many places that served food, these were run for workers and single men from specific communities, including Muslims, Chinese and Maharashtrian. No respectable Indian family would go to them, and none would actually buy one to run. There is some speculation that an Irani café called Wellington was running from the 1890s in the Dhobi Talao area, but there is no evidence, though there was, till the 1940s, a cinema with that name across from the Metro theatre, which was built in 1938.

Many cafés were started in the early part of the twentieth century when Iranians left Persia for India for better opportunities. These served breakfast, lunch and dinner at very affordable prices, and their names reflected either their Iranian connections—Yazdani, Kayani, Sassanian and Bastani—or a nod to the British Raj—Coronation, Royal, Regal and Britannia. One, Café de la Paix in Girgaum, was so named because the landlord of the building had just returned from France and had liked the original Parisian café with that name.

The décor was similar in all of them—bentwood chairs imported from Europe, marble-topped tables, painted mirrors, a framed image of Zoroaster and a counter where the proprietor sat and collected payments. Most of them also had a bakery, which produced bread, pao and patties of various kinds. The restaurants served an important purpose as a neighbourhood resource for general goods and bread, besides being a place where groups of friends could congregate regularly over cheap cups of tea, discussing every subject under the sun. Lunch and dinner menus were rudimentary, usually meat dishes, one reason why Irani restaurants are not to be found in predominantly Hindu, and especially Gujarati-dominated neighbourhoods. Most were owned by those of the Zoroastrian faith, though there are Muslim Iranis too, and are thus often considered to be 'Parsi' restaurants, though that is not quite accurate.

A set of rules warning patrons not to discuss politics, waste time, ask for small change or comb their hair in the sink was prominently displayed, but was usually disregarded. The rudeness of the proprietor who has no time for small talk and the waiter who reels off the items available in one breath are also part of the Irani café's mythology.

A legend goes that these cafés were usually to be found at the corner of buildings because Hindus were superstitious about that section of a property, but that is not borne out by the fact that many Udupi restaurants occupy corner positions. Most of these Irani cafés were in the South Bombay area, where the population was most dense—Fort, Dhobi Talao, Girgaum and Grant Road—and where no dietary restrictions existed. By the 1930s, they emerged in the new suburbs of Dadar and Matunga and in far flung areas in Salsette, such as Bandra and Andheri. Lower real estate prices may have been one reason, but the market may have been attractive too.

As early as 1915, and possibly earlier, European-style restaurants and cafés were to be found mainly in the Fort area—Monginis, the Italian confectioner, was based in Churchgate Street and Cornaglia, 'Specialist in Wedding Cakes' and 'Importer of High Class Stores and Wines' had branches in Meadow's Street, the Esplanade and, additionally, in Poona. But these were still few and far between.

Bombay had a poor tradition of eating places and accommodation. Visitors to the city had to make their own arrangements. The natives either had relatives or made do in neighbourhoods where members of their communities could help. For Europeans, the 'letter of introduction' from someone back home usually did the trick, because local Europeans could be very helpful. Scholar Frank Conlon, in his seminal essay, 'Dining Out in Bombay',[3] quotes a popular proverb of the time, 'No hotel could succeed where the people were so hospitable.' But such letters were not available to all, and many had to try their luck in the tents on the Esplanade (makeshift lodges funded by the entrepreneurs), which were most uncomfortable in the cold weather.

'Accommodation, for visitors—both European and Indian—in Bombay remained problematic during the middle years of the nineteenth century. This changed in the mid-1860s, when a new hostelry opened to much fanfare—Watson's Hotel, with both a "restaurant with a billiard room attached" and a "dining saloon" for guests, soon became a popular haunt for local Europeans and visiting dignitaries,' wrote Conlon.

Watson's had 155 rooms, many of them looking out on the street to an expansive view of open space towards the east and south, where lay the sea, with ships in the harbour. There were no tall buildings in sight apart from St. Thomas Cathedral—everything, from the Gateway of India, the Taj Mahal Hotel and even Regal cinema and the buildings along Hornby Road, came up much later.

Much before Watson's, two other eating locations—one of them which has lasted till the twenty-first century and is still going strong—were opened, though again for Europeans. The Byculla Club was set up in 1833, somewhere near today's Bombay Central station, and a few years later, in 1846, the Royal Bombay Yacht Club came up at Colaba Pier, near the present-day Gateway of India, where it still boasts of a sturdy, colonial-era presence. These were gentlemen's clubs, modelled on their British counterparts, with all the familiar prejudices intact. Natives were naturally not allowed, and there are stories galore of Indians, even prominent ones, being turned away. More clubs were to come up, some even set up by Indians protesting against this discrimination, but the prejudices—in this instance against women and on the basis of class and pedigree—carried on.

In the 1880s, the Great Western Building facing the docks in Fort, which was an early residence of the late eighteenth century governor William Hornby, became a hotel by that name. It may be today one of the oldest surviving buildings in Bombay, and now has some residents and many offices and showrooms. Soon after, in 1903, the Taj Mahal hotel was opened, born out of Jamsetji Tata's desire to give the port city a hotel comparable to any in the world. The Tatas also acquired Green Mansions, which was next door and had mainly flats for Europeans, and converted it into a hotel. The managements were the same, but the ethos—the entertainment and the clientele—was vastly different, writes academic Rachel Lee, who has researched Bombay's hotels. 'Where the Taj was the epitome of aspirational manners and sophisticated socialising, Green's was impolite, loud and subversive', in the words of novelist Louis Bromfield in *Night in Bombay* (1940): 'The dinner went off pleasantly because the terrace at Green's Hotel made everything easy. You sat as you ate, overlooking the whole harbour with a fat, rich, hot moon overhead, and the food was good and around you, the people were fantastic and the spectacle entertaining—seafaring men who would have been embarrassed by the mid-Victorian imperial elegance of the Taj Mahal dining-room, English officers and civil servants and clerks who were there because Green's was Bohemian and as wild a place as they dared frequent in a community where everything, every move one made, sooner or later became known [...] And here and there a stray Russian tart or an "advanced" Parsee or Khoja woman dining alone with a man.'[4]

The Victorian elegance of the Taj pulled in a crowd from the rarefied upper echelons of Bombay, and this air of being a venue for and a part of the upper strata has remained its signature since. By the 1930s, it had become a popular venue for 'hot music', as jazz was called, with musicians from as far as the United States of America playing over dinner for the city's beau monde. It set the lead that would be followed by the rest of the city as restaurants cropped up in the early 1940s in the reclamation area.

But as dazzling as this impossibly glamourous venue was, the real excitement lay in the back streets, which held a magnet-like attraction for the seedier elements of not just Bombay, but visitors from across the seas. From behind the Taj right up to the Causeway, sailors roamed the streets at night in search of watering holes, 'tarts' and, presumably, fights. Police patrolling was a regular feature here, and smartly uniformed naval police used to walk, two men in perfect step, looking around for misdemeanours by naval ratings and to quickly whisk them to Bombay's naval base before they were arrested by the city's police. While there were sleazier precincts in the city, Colaba was convenient from the port and the naval base, and had restaurants and bars; plus, it had the promenade near the sea and, if only to look at, the majestic Taj Mahal hotel. Yet, in the dimly lit streets behind it, even many decades later, as you stepped out of the Crown and Anchor bar, you could almost sense that Mack the Knife was lurking around the corner.

The city around it changed, but Colaba—which had a fair proportion of families and legitimate commercial establishments—only consolidated its reputation as an exciting neighbourhood which offered more spicy possibilities that other, more respectable places, didn't.

In the 1960s and '70s came the hippies, rock music and opportunities for more youthful indiscretions and worse. Colaba, with its cheaply priced hotels such as Stiffles and hostels like the one run by the Salvation Army—both on Ormiston Road, now known as BEST Marg—was a popular neighbourhood with foreign travellers looking for the meaning of life in the mystic East and trying out various drugs in their quest to reach there. Drugs from Afghanistan and north India—initially ganja and charas and later the more dangerous heroin and brown sugar—were freely available in and around these joints. Dipti's Cold Drink House across the road was the hangout joint and among the hangers-on was one Charles Sobhraj, who became notorious as a serial murderer of hippies in southeast Asia. Further up Colaba was the seamy Blue Nile, a venue for bold striptease acts, which left nothing—nothing—to the imagination.

But this was all to come. The big revolution in Bombay's development of an entertainment and eating out culture had begun in the 1940s, after the creation of an entirely new section of the city—the Backbay Reclamation. Commercial activity was always in the south, and with the creation of more land, more institutions were built. People from all over the city had to come to 'town' to work. South Bombay became the most important and most prestigious part of the city, its residents the most envied and not a little lampooned as 'South Bombay types'.

In the beginning, it was just 'town', a generic description of the area that included Fort, Churchgate, Colaba, etc. For decades, those who lived in Salsette had referred to the southern part as 'Bombay' when they set out towards it. 'I am going to Bombay for the day' was a common phrase and perhaps is still in use among older citizens. The limits of the municipal corporation had been extended up to Andheri and Mulund in 1950, and 'Bombay' looked distant geographically and perhaps culturally.

'South Bombay' became the shorthand to denote a certain kind of resident and lifestyle, perhaps somewhat alien to the traditional Indian ethos, what used to be described as 'modern type'. This was not entirely accurate because the southern part of the island also included the older, native towns—'settled Bombay'—where families had lived for generations and were not necessarily in tune with the new habitats that had emerged after the reclamation.

But the 'South Bombay type' was soon to take the shape of a new tribe, with its own codes, personality and rituals. It is difficult to say if the rest of the city looked at them with envy or even aspiration—perhaps a combination of the two. But their own self-image, which formed gradually, was clear—they were the fortunate ones, lucky and privileged, maybe even deserving, who lived in the smartest and toniest part of the city, denizens of a universe that was a smaller bubble within the bubble that was Bombay.

It is almost trite to say that India was changing, but post-Independence India began to transform radically. With the great modernizer Nehru leading the way, the country was suffused with a determination to make India a great, proud nation. Nehru's modernity was laced with cosmopolitanism and a love for diversity, and that was reflected in this young, uninhibited city in myriad ways, not the least of them being in accepting all the world had to offer, whether in architecture and design or in attitudes and lifestyles. Bombay, as it had always done, embraced this ethos and now, physically looking westwards, let the breezes flow in from all over the world.

The reclamation, more than creating a residential enclave and institutional buildings, became a site for this new-found confidence. It opened the way to a lifestyle that was in sync with other parts of the world. In the 1940s, down Churchgate Street, starting from Marine Drive and moving towards the east, near St Thomas' Cathedral, a whole series of new restaurants opened up. Almost every building on the western side of Churchgate Street, till the railway station, had a restaurant, each offering a different type of cuisine; collectively, their food also reflected the cosmopolitanism of the times—Parisian (coffee shop), Berry's (fine dining), Kamling (Chinese), Purohit (vegetarian Indian), Bombelli's (Italian café and patisserie), and Gourdon's (French Italian). Later, Volga (with its jukebox), Gaylord, and beyond Flora Fountain, Bistro, came up too.

Hotels such as Ambassador, owned by a Greek, Jack Voyantis, with its society café, Ritz, which boasted The Little Hut (and the famous Italian chef Mario), and Astoria, whose Venice restaurant was known for its band, became the places for the city's Westernized elite to be seen in. These Europeans, who had come to India during the British Raj, stayed on after Independence and now welcomed Indian patrons.

Most of the restaurants and hotels offered nightly entertainment—a jazz band, a dance floor, an emcee who told jokes, and perhaps most popular of all, a 'cabaret', which meant a dancer, often costumed in ostrich feathers and sequinned two-piece outfits, who fluidly moved around the room to upbeat music and who, at the end, may or may not shed her clothes. Cabarets became popular in Bombay, Calcutta, Delhi and other urban centres that had already been exposed to Westernized lifestyles, and many of them became big draws.

Customers of these dining establishments would be dressed in their formal best, with the men in suits or dinner jackets and the women in gowns or sarees, hair cut in the latest style, glittering and a la mode. Dining out was serious business and could not be taken casually, especially when in an upscale restaurant. These restaurants introduced Bombay to a new cuisine—'conti'—short for continental but a pastiche of European and American dishes, some of which had disappeared in their home countries a long time ago.

Conti was an entry into a 'foreign' world, one that reflected a certain sophistication and cosmopolitan easiness. Besides, some of the dishes were easy for the Indian palate, which, while attuned to spiciness, also craved a novelty that did not demand too much adjustment. A Russian salad or a prawn cocktail, smothered in mayonnaise, was almost comfort food for Indians. There was a world of culinary adventure out there, waiting to be discovered—roast chicken, steaks with potatoes, grilled fish and so much more. Restaurants began serving 'exotic' dishes such as lobster thermidor and chicken a la kiev, dishes with a hoary legacy but not particularly au courant elsewhere. Clubs and hotels had been serving these in Bombay for a while, but those venues were only accessible to Europeans and wealthy Indians—restaurants brought them closer to a rising upper middle class and offered a new world full of possibilities. Along with the entertainment available in the evenings—and sometimes, in the mornings too.

The one crucial thing missing in this picture was alcohol. The strictly imposed policy of prohibition meant that no one could drink publicly. A few establishments discreetly offered their favourite customers a tipple, poured in teacups or mixed with dark beverages like Coca Cola, but many were wary of attracting the notice of the authorities, who would not hesitate to shut them down. The hotels had 'permit rooms', where foreigners and those lucky citizens who had a permit could legally consume liquor, but not everybody was so fortunate. Applying for a permit involved getting a medical certificate stating that the holder needed booze for health reasons, and there was a virtual epidemic of people who just couldn't survive without a few 'units' of alcohol, but the numbers were relatively small. Bootleggers were in great demand, as well as moonshiners and 'Aunties' who ran cheapo joints where illicit and possibly sinister and dangerous liquor was available, but consuming it required willpower and a cast-iron stomach.

This emergent lifestyle was glamorously portrayed in the Hindi films of the 1950s and '60s, especially in noirish crime films where the restaurant and the club were portrayed as little more than a front for shady activities, and the owner was often a respectable member of society who controlled the criminals. The dancers had names such as Rosie or Lillian, and they would move slinkily around the tables occupied by men and women in formal evening wear. A band was inevitably in attendance. The ambience was 'Western', and the subtext was clear—this was an alien, un-Indian way of life, with girls who were foreign and not surprisingly, connected to crime. This is how the rich live, the filmmakers were saying to the punters, but such images only enhanced, not diminished, the glamour and the appeal.

Marine Drive and its environs with its modern buildings, expensive-looking cars and wide, clean, tree-lined roads became a popular location for stories and songs. Cameras had become more portable, and shooting on the street was much easier than in the past. Only a decade ago, the images of South Bombay were unseen by a vast majority of filmgoers around the world. Now Bombay, the big city of big dreams, was being revealed like never before to wide-eyed audiences in dark theatres—the audience lapped it all up.

The neon-lit restaurants of Churchgate Street, in real life and as portrayed on the screen, thus became the site for many modernities, and while not everybody had access directly, they got a glimpse of what lay inside in a variety of other ways. During the day, it was college students especially who were the main customer base of these restaurants, for socializing, romancing and dancing to the latest Western music playing on the jukebox. The fare was cheap snacks, and the music was contemporary pop which the younger generation was dancing to. And these college students came from different parts of Bombay, even the country—the spirit of the place and the times soaked them too. By the late 1950s and '60s, the advent of pop music created a new market; if the formal, evening crowd had their jazz bands, the teenagers could listen to popstars—age, class, caste no bar.

South Bombay—that small part of the island on the western side—retained its hegemonic dominance through the 1970s and even after. Restaurants did open in other parts of the city, but South Bombay remained the entertainment district even if it was mainly for the elite and the new, burgeoning professional class.

The Jehangir Art Gallery, an exhibition space, had opened in 1952 and the public at large could see shows by the artists of the time, all of whom—collectively called India's modern masters—would go on to do great things. A bistro-like café, Samovar, opened up in an open corridor—on the one side was the gallery wall, and on the other a small garden, where cats freely came up to the patrons, appealing to be fed.

The founder of Samovar, Usha Khanna, had decided the café would serve home-style food—mainly Punjabi and north Indian—at reasonable prices, a promise she kept throughout the fifty years it ran. This encouraged skint students and indigent artists, struggling scriptwriters and hopeful novelists to congregate there, lending a bohemian air to the place. They lingered over pots of mint tea for hours, planning, thinking, arguing and then continuing their conversations on the steps of the Jehangir gallery, gazing at the magnificent Gothic structures like Elphinstone College, the David Sassoon library and the Rajabai Tower. Artists who were emerging as names to reckon with exhibited at the gallery and came to Samovar for a break, sitting there among the other patrons, chatting informally and freely. It was that kind of place—egalitarian, free-spirited and bohemian.

Across the road was Wayside Inn, altogether more formal, with its red-and-white chequered tablecloths, silver cutlery and uniformed waiters, a favourite with lawyers from the neighbouring courts who came in costume or in suits to have a lunch of steak and fries, followed by caramel custard. Both these places have gone, for a variety of reasons, but also because that world has gone.

Bigger changes were taking place in the background that would have far-reaching implications for the landscape and geography of the country, as well as for its social structure. In 1991, the Narasimha Rao government unleashed an economic liberalization programme that led to a boom in the financial markets and brought in investors and foreign companies eager to cash in on the growing middle class. Around the same time, the Maharashtra government loosened land regulations, which came as a huge bonanza for builders and developers. They cast their eyes on the old mills, many lying shuttered, and the state government opened up the land to them. New commercial and residential towers were built, swankier than everywhere else and with parking to boot. Buyers and tenants followed. This led to a boom in the floating population, one with money in their pockets, looking for places of leisure, and new restaurants and bars sprang up. It was the first blow to Nariman Point and South Bombay.

But more was to come, and the chief driver of this change was a government planning and development agency—the Mumbai Metropolitan Region Development Authority, MMRDA. In the late 1970s, the MMRDA came up with a plan to create a new business district within a city in an area of 370 hectares, which would be well planned, without encroachments and well connected to different parts of the city, with the airport within easy reach. Most of all, the plots would have the one thing that was rare in Bombay—clear titles. The city's past had meant that titles were always in dispute, but here, with no history weighing down upon it, this new landmass created out of a wasteland would be given unencumbered to buyers—no lengthy legal process, no wrangling with a host of claimants.

Enthusiastically the land was filled up and opened to bidders and buyers in 1980. Nobody came forward. The prices were attractive—₹3,000 a square metre—and MMRDA had promised to provide infrastructure, including good roads, but buyers were not convinced. For financial firms and banks, proximity to the markets and the Reserve Bank was crucial—South Bombay provided that, and it was close to restaurants and cultural centres as well. The Bandra Kurla Complex (BKC), as the new development was called, was simply too far.

The 1980s were pre-computerization and pre-economic liberalization days, and the world had not the slightest interest in India; a vast business district could not be sustained simply by relocating Indian businesses. A few intrepid investors got in early, but it was only after the economic reforms of 1991 that big players saw a future, not just in BKC but also in

India—suddenly, banks were interested in consolidating their operations in one place, and foreign investors were waking up to the 'India Story'. When MMRDA held its first auction in the early 1990s, land prices went up to ₹40,000 a square metre and still there was no dearth of buyers. They saw that the well-laid-out plans and the roads and other infrastructure were nothing like elsewhere in the city.

What made the BKC so different? 'One of the big pluses was that there was no elected politician here we had to deal with,' said U.P.S. Madan, who was the MMRDA commissioner when I met him. His top-floor office was itself the size of a modest apartment, and its glass windows offered views of all sides—glass and chrome buildings on one, unending marsh land on another, waiting to be filled up for more buildings that would spring up in the future.

'We had a clear mandate to create a new business centre, where international companies could come and set up base. That was achieved because we had a free hand.' The MMRDA reported directly to the state government, specifically to the chief minister, with no 'interference' from any other politician; this allowed it to bypass normal political oversight. Quick decisions were taken, and the results were visible; it was a model for the future, where an independent agency would control the growth and development of the city.

BKC as it turned out, was better planned than other, older business districts; it made Nariman Point look like a shabby, embarrassing cousin. The roads in BKC were broad, clean, and the footpaths were without street hawkers. Buildings had parking for their tenants, coffee shops at the ground level, food halls in the basement and multilayered security.

For those working in the centrally air-conditioned buildings, there was no need to step out in the heat at all. In time, plush and terribly expensive apartments too became available, all the better for senior executives to live in across their offices; a couple of expensive international schools were also at hand for their children.

For the rest, getting in and out of BKC was a tedious chore—there was no connectivity to the nearby railway stations, and every morning and evening, the access roads were choked with traffic. As always, the planners did not bother to think of the needs of the mass of white-collar workers who remained a low priority affair.

At the same time, prices of property in the nearby Bandra west area began shooting up. Bandra, which even in the 1970s and '80s was a calm, gentle place with families living there for generations, many of them in cottages and bungalows, drew the interest of buyers, renters, brokers and developers—they saw a great deal of potential in the small Bandra villages, with their tiled roofs and small garden patches, and a cleaner living environment; they saw yuppies moving in, new trendy restaurants opening up and eccentric old ladies as neighbours and landladies. Plus, the sea, which was within walking distance. It was, as bloggers love to describe it even thirty years later—quaint and quirky and most of all, cheap.

Builders, on the other hand, saw immense potential in tearing down old bungalows and erecting luxury apartments in their place—after all, the senior executives needed somewhere to live too, and what better place than Bandra, which most of all had the virtue of being twenty minutes away from their workplaces?

All of them were correct in their assessment. Bandra was all this and more—it had a history and culture going back centuries, and the close-knit communities were tied together by church, schools and graveyards. The families living there had deep relationships that had been passed down over generations. Everyone knew everyone in the parishes they went to, which their parents and grandparents had been part of.

This was the Catholic part of Bandra, but there were other areas too, more mixed but no less well networked, and then there was Pali Hill, tree-lined and cosy, where the film stars had moved in from the 1940s and '50s. Not every home was behind a wall of secrecy; film star kids played with everyone else's, and often went to the same schools. Spotting a big star like Dilip Kumar or Nargis did not excite comment, because they were seen often and because many of them were involved in community life. Like much of Bombay, Bandra was layered and yet intimate. Any outsider would love to become a part of this community.

At rapid speed, as the country opened up more and more, Bandra began changing. The construction boom in the 1990s saw bungalows being demolished and towers coming up. Prices and rents shot up. More and more people wanted a piece of Bandra—boutiques, cafés and coffee shops burgeoned. Ramshackle cottages were in greater demand than swanky flats. It was hipsterfication and gentrification at turbo speed, and the formerly quiet, almost sleepy suburb, became Brooklyn on the Mithi (the rancid river, not much more than a stream, which ran through BKC).

For anyone who has known Bandra in an earlier time, the suburb is a completely new planet and not a particularly habitable one either. It still has leafy roads, but many of the old bungalows and cottages are gone; instead, hipster coffee shops have sprung up, whose customers often crowd the narrow lanes; vehicles on the roads have increased exponentially, much more than the winding streets can handle; and property prices are at record levels. The gentrification is relentless. The temptation to sell and leave is strong, but not many old families want to give up their old connections and move to another place.

The East Indians who have been living there for centuries think of it as their own Bandra, never mind the aliens who have descended there. The aliens, meanwhile, are continually fascinated by the trumpet-playing musician or the old bakery selling fresh pao every morning. They invade the villages on the seafront on Sundays, photographing everything in sight for their social media pages.

The rise of BKC and Bandra has led almost directly to the decline of South Bombay in several different ways. In the 1990s, in the wake of new consumerism and a glamour-centric media that reported on the goings-on in society, 'Sobo', clearly an aspirational word coined to riff on Soho made its appearance in the papers. But the Sobo sobriquet came a bit late, at the same time, South Bombay was losing its earlier sheen. A combination of several factors—non-availability of affordable real estate and an ageing demographic—had resulted in a gradual decline in the residential population.

New suburbs were coming up in the north, and old-time residents in the once 'native' towns such as Girgaum and Kalbadevi began moving away, lured by the attractive prices being offered by developers for their small rooms—with that money they could buy a one- or two-bedroom flat in Andheri or Borivali. Large corporate houses, such as Hindustan Lever, upped from Churchgate and shifted to a larger property in Andheri, and banks leased whole buildings in BKC. The unkindest cut was that consulates of foreign missions too saw BKC as a lucrative proposition—'The space in town was much too small, and we need greater security too—BKC was ideal,' a diplomat once told me. The iconic Lincoln House in Breach Candy, a beautiful seaside Art Deco palace, which the US consulate had leased from the Maharaja of Wankaner, was shut down and the whole operation shifted to a new, heavily protected fortress in BKC. The long lines of hopeful visa seekers, who were seen every day outside the consulate in Breach Candy, moved there too.

Not surprisingly, entrepreneurs began looking at other precincts to set up restaurants and bars—Bandra became the new, cool place to live, work and party in. Bandra was where the new spending power was, and nobody was interested in the ageing demographic of town. South Bombay, especially the parts that were the social hub of the city, became forlorn and silent, and the jokes about 'requiring a visa to visit Bandra and the suburbs' began sounding tired and desperate. The grand hotels of South Bombay—the Taj Mahal and the Oberoi—began to notice a fall in clientele as new hotels sprang up in the suburbs; a business visitor landing at the airport could easily reach Bandra or Goregaon, where new offices had opened up, within minutes; the traffic to get to Nariman Point was a needless hardship.

Nariman Point too lost tenants, and while many who did not need too much space stayed on, the big companies had packed up. Rents crashed. Nariman Point was now facing competition not just from Bandra and BKC but also from

Parel, Andheri, Powai and Malad, suburbs in the far north that snooty South Bombay had never acknowledged. There was quality housing to be had at cheaper prices and often within fifteen minutes to the place of work; in the evenings, there was no dearth of hangout joints. It was these suburbs that were challenging the north-south axis (never south-north) of the past, just like the Backbay Reclamation had done in the 1940s and after. Bombay then had shifted focus from the east to the west—now it had moved from the south to the north. The north was dynamic, new and 'happening'; the south was dying, if not dead. The restaurants of Churchgate Street, where the city's elite went, were now empty on most nights. That lifestyle had also gone, though what it spawned had spread far and wide, except that it was now called globalized culture—American restaurant chains, high street fashion brands, and even a new body language.

Many large apartments were now almost empty, several with just one or two elderly people living there. The kids had decamped, either abroad or to the suburbs, which were dynamic and active. Rent control regulations mean that incumbent residents hang on to their apartments, which in turn discourages new buyers and renters. Landlords don't have any incentive to repair or maintain the buildings, which end up looking sad and forlorn. The market dealt the final blow. South Bombay, especially the reclamation area, still has charm, and the Gothic piles of the Fort stretch attract tourists and young, amateur historians, but the office crowd is depleting. Once again, Bombay has renewed itself and shed its old skin, even if this has meant abandoning a piece of history.

6

MILLS BECOME MALLS

Just off the bridge at the junction of Currey Road and Parel stations in Central Mumbai stands a magnificent, multiple-floor building, or tower as they are called. Pedestrians scurry from work to catch trains to go home. It is a convenient location, not too far from the business districts of both south Mumbai and the Bandra Kurla Complex, home to the big financial institutions and multinationals.

Currey Road station was originally built to ferry horses from the stables to Poona for the racing season. It also served as a landing point for those working in the textile industry, which was concentrated in the neighbourhood. In recent years, the profile of the commuter using it has changed—now it also sees young professionals who are employed in the many offices around here, in finance, hospitality and advertising.

'Introducing a lifestyle exclusively designed for a chosen few in the heart of Parel. Code Name Xclusive'—the he sign on the bus stop outside the building leaves no doubt about the project's credentials. One Avighna Park is pitched as a luxury address, and the promotional video, with a walk-through of the building, justifies that claim—a grand entrance with a waterfall, a small bistro, an indoor pool, a sports centre with facilities for soccer and basketball, a private theatre, a three-level podium garden and spectacular views from the apartments, day and night. All these can be acquired at a starting price of $1.5 million for a three-bedroom flat, going up to $3 million for a five-bedroom apartment. The surroundings provide a stark contrast to this modern structure—everything else around it is low-rise, a few with Mangalore tile roofing, which is the vernacular style of old Mumbai. But the neighbourhood doesn't really matter—for the resident, there will be enough to do indoors with little or no need to step out on the streets. The parking garage is within the building, and one can drive off straight to the office or the shopping mall close by or to the club in the evening. One could very well be living in any city, disconnected from the harsh realities around. This insulated living may appear sterile, but appeals to many, as the proliferation of gated buildings shows. These are islands where the multitudes cannot intrude.

Till a few years ago, the 6.5-acre plot where Avighna is built was home to around 650 tenants living in chawls that were over a century old. The plot itself is still called New

Islam Mills, which stood there for decades. A developer bought it out, built an unprepossessing structure for the previous tenants, which was mandatory under the rules, and began his main project of constructing a tower block of luxury flats for commercial sale. It soon ran into controversy, with allegations about several violations of the permitted plans—four additional floors—penthouses—were added illegally.

The civic authorities objected. This is par for the course in Mumbai, where builders and developers play fast and loose with the regulations, blatantly flouting them. Adding floors is the least of them—flats are often made smaller (or sometimes bigger) than what was decided, areas meant to be open are enclosed, promised amenities never materialize. Both the municipal government and the buyer are cheated—sometimes the official machinery halts further construction, or the matter goes to court, and then the builder either relents or pays the penalties, and the construction is 'regularized'. The stakes are huge; a fine may often be worth it. Eventually, the Avighna project got clearances and was completed. One more saga in the sordid world of Mumbai real estate came to an end. And one more bit of space associated with the city's past was erased.

Something similar is happening in another area close to the Avighna project, where mills existed and mill-workers lived. A little further towards the east from the Currey road station, across the Babasaheb Ambedkar Road, is Lalbaug, where history lives and breathes in every lane. It was on its corners that workers met and socialized, its maidans where meetings with fiery speakers went on till late at night and where families congregated to celebrate community festivals, the chawls lit up by paper lanterns during Diwali and other festivals.

The lanes are still there, but the fervour and energy of the past has gone. Many old families have moved out to the distant suburbs, to bigger flats that promise more room and more privacy. This shift comes at a price—the commute becomes longer, and with every passing year, the trains become more crowded and suffocating. But it is the loss of old friendships and networks that hurts the most.

The famous Lalbaugcha Raja, the fond name for the city's tallest Ganesh statue—it is about twenty feet tall—which began as a modest effort by some locals in 1936, now attracts millions of visitors during the eleven-day Ganpati festival. In 2018, it received donations of over ₹8 crore, including some in gold bricks and statues. The gifts are auctioned off and the funds raised go towards the charitable activities of the trust that manages the festival.

The festival gets bigger every year, but around it, one of the many old markers of another Bombay, the workers chawls are getting obliterated as the developers move in. A glittering new Mumbai has come up from the ruins of an older Bombay, with hardly anything to show of a past that made the city what it became. It was here, in Girangaon, the village of the mills, where one of the most enduring symbols of Bombay—the smoke-bellowing chimneys—stood, proud and tall; it was here that the machines throbbed, the sirens blared to signal the change of shift and thousands of workers lived and worked, often far away from their families, creating a self-contained world that the rest of Bombay knew little about.

It is here that the transition from a trading Bombay to a manufacturing centre occurred, and it is here that this metropolis once again shifted focus, from producing things to providing services. Where mills hummed stand either tony flats or vast offices or small, trendy boutiques and restaurants that draw a crowd that is completely unaware and unconcerned about that grimy but historical past.

This 'from mills to malls' shift came about in keeping with the city's ethos of being disinterested in the past and getting rid of it in a ruthless manner. Greed was the driving impulse, heritage be damned. Once the government cleared the way, the builders moved in, and the mills were brought down rapidly, the machinery thrown away as junk, and that most enduring symbol of Bombay—chimneys—demolished with abandon, uninhibited by any thoughts of history and legacy and propelled only by the lucrative monetization of the space that would become available. Now gated residential complexes, steel and chrome buildings of office blocks and shopping malls exist on the land where the machinery spun out textiles that brought so much prosperity for 130 years.

In the process, not only was a crucial part of the city's past wiped out, but significant demographic changes were accelerated. Old families were driven out, social networks built over generations were demolished and, lured by money and a pressing need for space, the residents were compelled to move to the distant suburbs.

Social observers say that most of those who have had to leave the city and settle far away are Marathi-speaking. There are no studies confirming that, but it does appear that areas like Parel and Girgaum, where new residents have moved in, have seen many Marathi speakers leave. For the most part, they have been bought out.

If this prognosis is accurate, it could have long-term social and political consequences. The political parties, who never tire of speaking loudly on behalf of this constituency, will be the most affected—they will lose a crucial base. The Shiv Sena, upholder of the interests of Marathi-manoos, is already fashioning itself to be a more broad-based party and is wooing other communities, which it had once wanted to throw out of Bombay. It wants to be seen as modern and is taking up causes like the environment and giving Mumbai a night life. It has trimmed its sails according to prevailing winds, hoping no one will notice that it too has been culpable in the takeover of the city by the builder community.

The big changes in the city happened from the 1990s onwards, when zoning laws were liberalized, first by the Congress and then by successive governments and gradually, the face of Parel was transformed.

Standing on the Currey Road bridge in Central Mumbai, Dilip Atyalkar looks at Avighna Park and then slowly at similar modern buildings further down. He remembers the chawl and what existed before the other structures came up. 'That's Jupiter Mills and the other one Mafatlal Mills.'

He remembers those mills well. In the early 1980s, Atyalkar had come from a small village in Kolhapur district looking for a job in a mill. He had relatives in Bombay, and they would find him employment. This had been the tradition over generations, which the mill owners too had come to accept. Those mills are long gone, and with them, the secure jobs. What survives, all around these towers, are chawls, one-room tenements built either by landlords or the British government in the 1920s in the aftermath of the plague when there was a sudden realization that the working class needed homes that had better ventilation and sanitation. It was a state-sponsored project, under the Bombay Development Directorate, and would have looked adequate at a time when housing for the natives was primitive and infrastructure was almost non-existent, but over the years, these chawls have become a byword for congested living.

At the time, however, textile mill workers were happy to get accommodation at subsidized prices, and so close to their places of work. Most of them were occupied by single men—their families were living in the villages—and soon, each small room—approximately 150 square feet—was occupied by many tenants, sometimes ten or more. They slept in round-the-clock shifts, corresponding with their working hours. The senior-most person in the room chose his spot, the others lay down where they could. They kept their belongings in their own trunks, which were neatly tucked away to ensure that space was not wasted.

'Many of the rooms were under the control of people from one village. That provided solidarity and comfort,' recalls Atyalkar, who used to stay in one of these rooms when he came to Bombay. 'You knew the person, his family, his antecedents. You got news from home, and you could send and receive things.'

One such cluster of BDD chawls is near Currey Road station, on N.M. Joshi Marg, or, as it is still popularly known, Delisle Road (named after a British official from the mid-nineteenth century, Lieutenant De Lisle). There are thirty-two buildings in all, each of three floors plus a ground floor, many of them with balconies that, in true Mumbai fashion, have been enclosed to expand living space. Though the buildings are still solid, many individual sections look dangerously close to collapsing and are propped up by girders.

For the most part the buildings look like prisons, with bars on the windows and common toilets at the ends of the corridors. Clearly, the colonial authorities wanted to 'upgrade' the habitats of the natives, but not by too much.

In its bid to redevelop this cluster, which includes recreational grounds and a community centre, the Maharashtra government has been planning to bring the chawls down and construct new accommodation. The state threw open bidding from interested developers, who had to compulsorily build alternative accommodation—in situ—for the tenants in return for surplus space on which they could erect fancy tower blocks for the richer buyers. The builders held many meetings with the tenants, showing them presentations of the homes and the lives they would get if only they would sign on the dotted line and move out so that the chawls could be brought down.

Billboards outside a chawl portray sketches of the future homes. Comfortable, roomy, airy, with all the gadgets and most of all, with enclosed toilets, but the canny residents have resisted moving out. They want bigger spaces but more than that, they want assurances that they will get what is promised. The Mumbai apartment buyer has been stung too often to take assurances at face value.

Kholi number 11 in building 16 in the BDD chawls is occupied by those from Shirole village in Kolhapur district.

Seven young men are sitting around on the floor. They look physically fit and sporty, in their T-shirts of a cricket team formed mainly of other young men from the chawls. One works in an office, another is an engineer on a construction site, a third a security guard and a fourth was looking for a job. 'There is an advocate among us who has just finished his law exam. He is not here today,' one of them says.

The room is neatly kept and sparse, with no extra furniture that could take up space. No bed, no table not even a chair or a stool. A small loft-like space had been created about eight feet above the ground, which could accommodate, they said, five sleepers. There is no ladder, but those who sleep in the loft climb up to it by placing one foot on two strategically placed switch panels that provide just enough of a toe hold, and then heave themselves up and into the loft. It is difficult to imagine even two people sleeping in that space, leave alone five—on Sunday night, the entire complement of fifteen people occupies the room. 'At one time up to forty people used to stay here,' says the engineer; it sounds like wild exaggeration but is probably close to the actual number. Rent is a negligible ₹200 a month.

The chawl is a home away from home, for bachelors and for married men, who come to the city to work. The grind of working in a dead-end and difficult mill job away from families was alleviated by the sense of community in the big city, which provided a support system.

Food for the textile workers came from *khanavals*, home kitchens run by the wives of mill workers, who cooked day and night to send dabbas—with chapati, vegetables, dal, rice and occasionally, mutton or chicken—to the workers.

The khanavals, which at one time were estimated to be around 650 in number, began folding up in the 1980s, as jobless workers migrated back to their villages and there was simply no demand.

Some have adjusted to the times. Shobha runs one in building 16, in a ground-floor room that was extended by a previous tenant. In the back room her daughter-in-law is making chapatis, her husband stirs the dal in the kitchen. Shobha herself is expertly managing two pots on the gas stove, giving instructions about some dabbas that are already packed and waiting to be picked up by the customers—they have to be returned washed.

Large 25-kg bags of rice and wheat are piled in one corner, a replacement LPG cylinder standing next to them.

It is the busy pre-dinner time, so Shobha is brisk with her answers. She makes thirty dabbas a day, twice a day, and charges ₹2,200 per customer per month. The enterprise is run by the family— 'You think I can afford staff? Things are very bad, raw material costs are going up.'

I ask how long she has been doing this. 'Oh, for decades, much before the textile strike.' (During 1982 – 83 strikes, which shut down every mill in the city. Tens of thousands of workers lost their jobs.) She is not particularly interested in the stranger who has come to her home, unannounced, at a very busy time.

Does she make enough for her family? Her husband, after the strike, had no job—her son works, but his income is not enough to support the family. They have been living in this place for two years, because the original tenant has gone to the village. He pays ₹100 a month, perhaps less, she is not sure; her family pays ₹13,000. She won't say how much she makes after costs, but the margins can't be that bad, given that there are no staff salaries, and she has quite a few mod cons—a flat-screen television, a washing machine, etc.

Demand for these rooms is slowing down, especially among young men who do not want to share accommodation with ten others. The moment they can afford it, or when they get married, they find another place, a flat, often in distant places, such as Dombivali or Nalla Sopara. Going back to the village is not an option. There is no work there, and no girl wants to marry a boy from a village.

At the exit of the building is placed a large idol of Ganesh, and a dhobi is ironing clothes in a tiny space in the corridor. Outside, we meet two young men. One of them, who works as a security guard, is wary of the grand plans to offer alternative houses.

'The builder has promised 450-square-foot flats to each resident, but the residents want 500 square feet. They have constructed a smart sample flat to show how two bedrooms will look. It is very tempting. But do people know that it will be expensive to maintain them?' Not surprisingly, progress has been slow, and the project has been stuck for years since there is no consensus among the locals about how to proceed.

Most of the residents of the BDD chawls and the many other buildings in the area are those who either worked in the mills or are families of former workers. They have seen the disappearance—destruction, really—of not just the mills and of livelihoods, but also of a community and a way of life. For anyone under the age of thirty-five, the great mill strike is little more than a family story, even a myth. For their parents, it is lived history that is, for the most part, bitter. The story begins with hope and determination and ends with disappointment and tragedy.

The shuttering of most mills finally broke Mumbai's connection with the industry that had built it. Driving the growth of the city in the nineteenth century—the time of grand Gothic structures that came to symbolize Bombay, the biggest jewel in the Crown—was a humble crop that grew far in the hinterland, and on which fortunes were made. If it were not for cotton, Bombay would have remained the backwater that it was for most of its existence.

Bombay had languished for most of the eighteenth century, a distant second to the imperial capital Calcutta, which was the centre of power. Bombay's administrators had to contend with hostility from the Surat council and indifference from everyone else. The reclamation project, which had started in 1780, was gradually creating a landmass that would then enable Bombay to become a cohesive whole and therefore better organized. Trade till then was waterborne, with ships plying up and down the west coast and, as they had done for centuries, to the Arabian Peninsula and as far as Africa.

One of the items that was traded was cotton. Indian muslins and calicoes were in great demand in Europe and 'practically till the end of the eighteenth century, no source of cotton other than Indian was known to the world,' wrote M.L. Dantwala in *A Hundred Years of Indian Cotton*, published by the East India Cotton Association in 1947.[1] The Association was celebrating its silver jubilee at the time and the foreword, by the Prime Minister Jawaharlal Nehru, said:

> The history of cotton and of textiles is not only the history of the growth of modern industry in India, but in a sense it might be considered the history of India during the past one hundred years. The British policy which dominated India during the period circled around cotton to a large extent.

The raw material was exported in substantial quantities to Britain during the eighteenth century, and the invention of machines like the jenny and the spinning frame around the same time had created new industries and therefore more demand for the raw material.

The British in India encouraged the growth of cotton, and while most of the early exports were from Calcutta—including to Britain—soon traders from the west coast too joined. Private opium trade in Bombay, in competition with Calcutta, was emerging, and the British rulers did their best to quash it. But there were no such problems with cotton—in fact, there was an urgency among the British to improve Indian produce.

Yet, India remained only a producer of the crop, and the value addition was done in the mills of Lancashire and then shipped back to be sold at a profit. The Industrial Revolution had not yet reached the shores of Hindustan, and it would be a while before fabric could be manufactured here.

On their part, the British wanted to improve the quality of Indian cotton because their own country was dependent on the Americans for the raw material. Machines for ginning had been brought to India by the late eighteenth century to remove pollutants from the crop.

In the first few decades of the nineteenth century, Bombay's new merchant princes, collectively called shetiyas, prospered by getting involved in the opium trade as exporters, shippers and financiers. Their wealth not only made them prominent citizens and community leaders, but also put them almost on par with the British establishment. In fact, so rich were they that one of them (and perhaps others) lent money to big British clients and came to be known as Readymoney, which the family gleefully adopted as its surname.

Some of these shetiyas were involved in the cotton trade too—the returns, despite the hardships of transporting cotton, were much too lucrative. Jamsetjee Jeejeebhoy was of course a prominent figure, as were several others, mainly Kutchis, who had been natural traders for generations. Kutch was an inhospitable place where little could grow, so the enterprising Kutchis became experts at trading, dealing with Arab and African traders.

Many of these wealthy Bombay merchants moved from trade to investment. In 1853, Cowasjee Nanabhai Davar inaugurated the first-ever textile mill in India, in Tardeo, Bombay. A mill had been set up in 1818 in Calcutta, but the venture had failed. Bombay Spinning and Weaving Company employed British engineers and operators and began production in 1856. Three years prior, on 16 April 1853, the first train journey was flagged off between Boribunder and Thane. The pieces that would form the city's and the country's industrial base were coming together.

Others shetiyas from different communities followed: Jews—the Sassoons were among the biggest mill owners—Parsis, Kutchi Bhatias and Muslims. These were all mercantile communities and would shape not just the industrial but also the public culture of Bombay. More mills were set up, and by 1865 the city had ten of them, humming to meet the demand of British mills and then, when exports collapsed after the end of the American civil war, for the domestic market and for other centres in Europe and the east. The city was now on its way to becoming a major commercial centre.

The mills needed labour and workers poured into the city, mainly from the hinterland. The Konkan region and present-day Marathwada were among the earliest sources, but soon enough they came from as far afield as the United Provinces (now UP), which had a long-standing tradition of weaving. Bombay's population and prosperity began growing. Apart from workers, a large number of others too were linked with the cotton business—farmers, middlemen, financiers, cargo handlers and cotton traders and speculators.

On the eastern side of Mumbai, on the Harbour line of the Central Railway, lies Cotton Green station. There is no cotton being grown there, and not much sign of natural greenery either; it is mostly an industrial wasteland. The vast warehouses are empty, and there are no residential complexes or factories. Very few people get off or on the train from there.

Right outside the station, abutting the port, is a low-rise, three-storey building, painted in light green. It looks incongruous—a long, sprawling structure in the middle of nowhere, standing alone and somewhat forlorn. This is the Cotton Exchange, of the Cotton Association, built in the 1920s. At one time, it was a humming place, with workers, clerks and wealthy merchants congregating there every day to conduct trade in that most precious of commodities, cotton.

Each floor has offices of cotton brokers on either side of long corridors. The shingle above the door identifies each occupant—these are the members of the Cotton Association of India, and are divided into sellers and buyers, with 'S' and 'B' clearly marked on each signboard. Almost all the names are of Gujaratis, who held a near monopoly of the trade. Some names stand out—Reliance Enterprises, China Cotton Exporters, Hindoostan Mills, Finlay Mills. At the entrance is also a statue of Sir Purushottam Das Tandon, KBE, CIE, D.Litt., industrialist and trader and a long-standing president of the Association in the early part of the twentieth century.

'The corridor used to be lined with samples of cotton, and there was a lot of activity at one time. Even till the late 1970s, this building was a very busy place,' says my guide, an employee of the Association. Now it is a silent, ghostly place, with a few open offices where clerks sit, surrounded by registers and files that speak of times past.

The trading hall that once buzzed with the cries of brokers lies empty, forgotten—it was once a venue for frenzied activity and where the price of cotton was set and large quantities of it were bought and sold. It is a vast and cavernous room, painted in salmon pink, with patchy walls badly in need of a touch up. A marble plaque on a wall informs one that the exchange building was inaugurated on 1 December 1925 by the governor Sir Leslie William Orme. The date is also mentioned in Hindi, Urdu, Gujarati, Japanese and Hebrew, testifying to the global business links of the cotton trade.

The headquarters of the Association must have been inaugurated with considerable fanfare as no less than the governor was present and the cotton trade was very influential in Bombay. In 1922, the East India Cotton Association was formed in the city, which was the pre-eminent centre of the trade. India by then had 271 mills and cotton production had grown tenfold in a hundred years. 'No doubt, during the nineteenth century India was ravaged by frequent famines and droughts and often failed to feed its own people. But we continued to grow more and more cotton to feed the textile industry,' writes Madhoo Pavaskar, one of the country's acknowledged experts on cotton.[2]

Till 1925, the trade operated out of Colaba, where cotton bales were brought from upcountry to the station specially made to handle the business. From there, the bales, packed securely, were shifted to the port, where ships lay in readiness to take them to far-off shores.

In the nineteenth century, the bales were kept in the open outside the Town Hall, on the Esplanade 'Greens', where the traders operated, till they found a more secure and permanent spot. Indian cotton was not the best, and often exporters were criticized for sending substandard stuff weighed down by adding water to the bales, but it still had a market, and during the 1860s, as American supplies were affected by the civil war, Indian produce was in great demand in Britain. The futures market was born in 1875, and the trade exploded—it was then moved to Colaba and finally, to its own building in Cotton Green.

But even this building became redundant by the 1930s. The Association, ambitious and expanding, began work on yet another building in Kalbadevi in 1936 and in 1938, a handsome Art Deco structure was inaugurated. This was then the tallest building in Bombay, and clearly a statement on the supremacy of the cotton trade in the city's economy.

But while the business prospered and made many people immensely rich, the benefits barely trickled down to the workers. It was a labour-intensive industry, and the back-breaking work and unhealthy working conditions took their toll on the workers. Strikes were frequent for the most basic of demands. The tycoons supported Gandhi and the Swadeshi movement but were negligent about their own employees.

The workers had become unionized in the early part of the twentieth century and frequently fought for better working conditions. They were also politically aware and ready, when the occasion arose, to show solidarity for important causes of the day. In 1908, when Bal Gangadhar Tilak, popularly known as 'Lokmanya', was sentenced to six years' imprisonment, workers, including from the textile mills, went on strike for six days. In 1928, the various unions representing workers came together to demand better working conditions, consultation before introducing new machinery and increased wages.

Changes were slow and for decades, the workers continued to work and live in the same conditions. They were well organized but no real, tangible benefits had come their way that improved their quality of life. Till the 1960s, communist unions held sway, which frightened the tycoons, who got even more worried with the rise of the left in West Bengal, the commercial rival of Maharashtra. Militant communists had not just begun to scare away capital but far left outfits were slowly spreading terror in Calcutta and in rural areas of the state.

A new political force began to grow in Maharashtra, aided and encouraged by the business sector—the Shiv Sena. The Sena, formed in 1966, had first targeted 'outsiders' such as migrants from the south of India for apparently stealing jobs, but they also clashed with the communists in Girangaon, the bastion of not just the textile industry but also of Maharashtrians. The party made tremendous gains and managed to take control of the Lalbaug–Parel–Dadar area, home to textile workers and the Marathi-speaking middle class.

By the mid-1960s, the afterglow of the creation of a separate Maharashtra state with Bombay as the capital had dissipated. The rosy promise of more jobs failed to materialize, not least because those who had fought for Maharashtra with such vigour had no particular economic plan to offer—charged emotions could only go so far. The youth, which had lent so much energy to the Samyukta Maharashtra agitation, was now adrift, jobless and with no prospects to speak of. The Sena, with its platform of jobs for 'sons of the soil', seemed attractive. The violent tactics of the Sena were almost cathartic.

By the late 1960s and '70s, the cotton business too had dwindled—futures trading had been banned by the government in 1966, and exports were no longer competitive. The halcyon days of King Cotton were gone—new synthetic fabrics were taking over, and much of the power loom business had shifted to towns like Bhiwandi on the outskirts of Bombay, where labour was cheaper and not organized. The mill owners were looking for ways to get out of the business. In 1972, the grand building at Kalbadevi was sold to a developer who created a jewellery mall. Manufacturing was dead—retail shopping was the way of the future.

'The mood for a long confrontation between the workers and textile mill managements was already building up for a long time. In November 1981 there was a one-day strike, which was followed by a strike in seven mills which went on for some time,' remembers Uday Bhat, now general secretary of the Lal Nishan Party, a left-oriented trade union that represents workers from different industries, formed after breaking away from the Communist Party of India in 1940.

Sitting in his modest office in Dadar in Central Mumbai, Uday fields phone calls and talks to the various union workers who walk in and out. The union office is in a shiny new building, constructed on the land where an older building had once existed and where the office was, but even in this new environment, the office retains its down to earth look and feel. On the wall are printed images of Marx, Lenin, Mao, Shivaji and Balasaheb Ambedkar, icons that tell their own story.

Uday, just out of college in 1981, knew all about labour unions—his father was a white-collar union leader, and the textile workers' strike was discussed in the house. The workers had a list of forty-two demands, including giving permanent status to *badli* (hired on a shift basis) workers who had been employed off and on for up to twenty years, with no regular salary or benefits. The mill owners did not want to give a pay hike because mills were labour-intensive and wage hikes ate into profits.

Various agitations had produced no results. The workers were losing faith in the Shiv Sena, which had taken the lead as the primary union in a wide coalition of other organizations.

'There was a big rally called at Kamgar Maidan and Bal Thackeray was to address it. You know Bal Thackeray, he always liked to make a big entrance. People were expectant, that he would come with news of a breakthrough,' says Uday. 'Thackeray came at 8 p.m. His first lines were, "I have just met Mr Antulay, chief minister. He has promised we will work out something. We should call off the strike".'

The moment he said that the workers began walking off, one by one. Within a few moments, the ground was empty. A large number of people landed up at the office of Datta Samant. Samant, a medical doctor, had practiced among quarry workers and had been appalled at their health problems, caused mainly because of lack of safety equipment and poor wages. He had organized them and won some concessions for them.

From there he had moved on to big industrial employers such as Associated Cement, Forbes and Godrej and Boyce. He made rousing speeches, often asking for, and occasionally getting, terms that no other union had ever managed to negotiate successfully. But he was also seen as a troublemaker, and violence inevitably followed wherever he tried to form a union. 'Datta Samant, Datta Samant … the name had come to be dreaded in industrial circles,' writes B.K. Karanjia in his biography of industrialist Naval Godrej, chairman of the eponymous group.[3] In 1978, Godrej was stabbed—as were his wife and daughter-in-law—by Shankar Sawardekar, a former employee of Godrej and Boyce who had been sacked from the company many years ago for violent activities and had been jailed. A member of Samant's union, Sawardekar was disgruntled and took to hanging around Naval Godrej's home, finally walking in one night and stabbing three members of the family.

That murder, by a member of Samant's union, did not dent the fiery leader's appeal among workers of other industries; certainly, the textile workers, by then disillusioned with their old unions and political leaders, were ready to go with him. It was a decision that would prove costly for them.

In 1982, two and a half lakh workers went on strike, led by the Maharashtra Girni Kamgar Union, which was headed by Dr Datta Samant. 'He was a hero to them, the man who would not just get them their just dues and better terms, but also give them dignity. The mill workers had been let down by one union after another—they were looking for a leader,' says Uday Bhat of the Lal Nishan Party.

Uday's father had joined hands with Datta Samant, so he saw the whole thing unfold.

'It began with a one-day strike on 1 December 1981, which was very successful. Buoyed by that success, the union called for a full strike on 18 January, and fifty-eight mills shut down. Nothing like this had been seen for a long time.'

The strike was total and appeared successful. Morale among textile workers was high, and support came from those who were employed in other industries not just as labour but also in white-collar jobs. Those tens of thousands of workers, unmindful of losing wages and hopeful of a better deal, were sticking it out. It was unprecedented.

Samant or one of the senior office bearers of the union would give daily press briefings during those days. I attended a few of them—he was a pugnacious man with sharp eyes and a determined look on his face. Always dressed in white, Samant addressed every question directly, mixing facts with rhetorical flourishes. The messaging was always the same—we are here for the long haul.

All kinds of methods were used to break the strike—goons were sent, union leaders were bashed up. George Fernandes, Bal Thackeray and Sharad Pawar, three prominent leaders from three different political strains, addressed a joint meeting at Shivaji Park, saying they would ensure that the strike was a failure. Rumours were spread that the mill owners wanted the strike. That the left wanted the strike to be called off. 'All this only strengthened the workers' resolve,' remembers Bhat.

A few months into the strike it began to weaken. Workers had gone to their villages. Those who remained were finding it very difficult to manage. Men had little work, so the women had begun working in people's homes. Others, more committed to the cause, continued their involvement, but the strain was beginning to tell.

Datta Iswalkar, of the Mumbai Girni Kamgar Union and one of the strike leaders, lived in the Parel area and felt the hardships acutely. 'It was very difficult. The children were small, it was difficult to explain why there was no money,' he told me many years later, showing me around the neighbourhood where he had spent most of his life. There was no money to feed the family—buying gifts or new clothes was simply out of the question. This was a common experience among workers—they had to look for alternative employment while their wives stepped out and worked as domestics in the neighbourhood homes.

After the strike, Iswalkar remained in the union. When the mill sale policy was announced, he was among the negotiators to ensure that retrenched workers of the mills being shuttered would get compensation and housing. Iswalkar said it was the politicians, cutting across parties, who let down the workers. 'The government saw it as a movement it had to crush, but even the other leaders, all professing sympathy for their workers, seemed to be acting on behalf of the mill owners.'

A year into the strike, there was no solution in sight, and the chief minister of Maharashtra had changed. A.R. Antulay had gone, felled by the judgement in the cement case which accused him of corruption in granting allotment of scarce cement supplies. Antulay's replacement Babasaheb Bhosale declared he would break the strike. He once told Datta Samant that he was under tremendous pressure from Indira Gandhi to ensure that the strike was a failure. There had been a major strike of public sector employees in Bangalore that had collapsed after two months.

Bhosale too did not last long. Vasantdada Patil, the new chief minister, banged on the table in his first press conference and said he would ensure the strike was ended in fifteen days. It didn't.

Samant had told the workers that the strike would be long drawn. The workers had said they would remain with him, but they could not have known that by the end, they would have nothing left, not the least because of poor strategic calculation by Samant.

'The astute leadership of a general strike on this scale required not only impeccable timing in initiating action but also in bringing it to an end,' wrote Rajnarayan Chandavarkar, a Cambridge University historian.[4] '... The prolongation of the strike beyond the capacity of the workers to bear appears to have been a catastrophic mistake. Perhaps, Datta Samant had given insufficient thought to a means of retreat ...'

Not just the mill owners, who dreaded Samant and were wary of handing him a success, but also the Congress—and other parties—were worried that if he got his way, he would become an all-powerful union leader in the country's commercial capital. Samant failed to read the signs—an old union comrade of his recalls him as 'obstinate and completely reluctant to listen to any other point of view'.

The strike lasted all of 1982, but by the new year, it began tapering off. Those who had gone home never came back. Some of those still in Bombay began drifting back to work. The mill owners had brought in outsiders, including goondas, to work and sleep inside the mills. Many workers got messages that this was a last chance for them to come back. They could not resist any longer.

The strike fizzled out, but was never called off, says Bhat. 'So technically it is still on.' But the industry was reduced to a pale shadow of its former glory. An estimated 1,50,000 workers lost their jobs. A long and glorious chapter in Bombay's history came to an end and soon, a new one would begin, which would create a new city with an entirely different culture and approach to its citizens. The mill workers who created the prosperity that built modern Bombay were cast by the wayside, with not even a token memorial to their name. Parel, where the mills once stood and the sirens blared to announce the shifts, became little more than a location for more shiny buildings that would mark the landscape of the future. A large new shopping mall was built where the glorious Phoenix Mill once stood; the only remaining memory of the mill marked by the chimney that was left standing. This was gentrification by a combination of powerful market forces and big money, helped along by policymakers.

7

GHETTOS, OLD AND NEW

'Dongri' is a darkish place, a warren of lanes and bylanes, where danger lurks. It is where Mumbai's criminals hold sway, plotting their nefarious activities, from murder to terrorism to smuggling. This is the Dongri of the city's imagination, further fuelled by news coverage and books such as *Dongri to Dubai : Six Decades of the Bombay Mafia*,[1] which tells stories of the city's biggest dons, many of them killed in bloody retribution or fugitives from the law.

It confirms all the stereotypes about Muslims—ghettoish, insular and backward, steeped in their own somewhat antediluvian religious practices, drifting towards hard-line Islam and from there, even to terrorism. Constant propaganda by militant Hindutva parties and organizations has only deepened those notions—housing societies disallow their members from renting out to Muslim tenants, and jobs, whether in the government or the private sector, are difficult to get.

This present-day perception completely ignores and erases the role of Muslims in the political, economic and social life of Bombay. Muslims—Kutchi Memons, Bohras, Chiliyas from Gujarat and Konkanis from the coastal areas among them—came to the city in the eighteenth century and soon established themselves as traders, merchant seamen and big businessmen. They also took full part in the nationalist struggle, joining Gandhi in his efforts to fight colonial rule. There was a sufficient body of influential Muslims, such as Umar Subhani and Syed Abdullah Brelvi, a well-known journalist, who positioned themselves against Jinnah and the Muslim League and supported Gandhi and the Congress.

The coastal shipping trade between Gujarat and Bombay and beyond, further south to the Konkan coast, was controlled almost totally by Muslim seafarers. Nakhuda Mohammad Ali Roghay and Haji Ismail Yusuf, whose family founded the first Indian-owned shipping firm, the Bombay Steamship Company, in the late nineteenth century, are among the pioneers of the trade. The Yusuf family is still among the biggest land and property owners of Bombay.

In 1888, a steamship, Vijali, sank off the coast of Gujarat during a storm as it approached Porbandar. Over 1,300 passengers, including many recently married couples, died. The incident is recorded in a popular song, '*Haji kasam tari*

Vijali' (Haji Kasam, your ship), commemorating the captain, a legendary navigator related to the Yusuf family, who too perished. His descendant, Ateeq Agboatwala—Agboat is a literal translation of steamship—is secretary of the Bombay Property Owners Association and administers the family's vast landholdings, which extend from land in the northern suburbs to buildings in south Mumbai. A lot of land has been encroached upon by slums or acquired by the government to create infrastructure or green areas; the family has been fighting long legal battles to get back some of the illegally occupied lands.

'The song is part of not just the family's but also the city's maritime lore,' he told me. Ateeq explains why Muslim families took to buying land and renting out flats and shops. 'Muslims did not invest in stocks or become informal money lending businessmen because earning interest and dividend is forbidden in Islam. Property was the only option left.'

Property also meant a steady income, much of which went into philanthropy and building mosques, rest-houses for travellers, hospitals and schools. 'But then, when the Rent Control Act was introduced, rents were frozen and have not been increased—the value of the income has progressively decreased,' Ateeq says.

This is echoed by Javed Gaya, a British-educated lawyer whose family too is among the older ones in the city, but he takes this even further. 'In the early years after the rent freeze, the income was sufficient, but Muslims really got hit in 1968, when the Enemy Property Act came into force.'

Many prominent Muslim families had sent one member to Pakistan in the 1940s when India was divided into two countries. Mohammed Ali Jinnah, himself a Bombay man, and a prominent lawyer, demanded and got a separate homeland for Muslims; in the city, however, the response to the new nation was less enthusiastic than in the northern provinces.

'There was a lot of reluctance to shift; apart from the displacement, many in the elite wanted to stay on in Bombay because of its easy-going cosmopolitanism—they felt Karachi would simply not be the same,' Gaya says. Many Muslim families had become extremely Westernized; 'My own family was among them—not just the men, the women too had gone to study in England. Two of my aunts went to Cambridge and one joined the British army. Ironically, she shifted to Pakistan and became a senior government official.' Jinnah was keen that professionals and investors move to Pakistan to help build the new nation.

'Those Muslims who did respond to Jinnah and the League and sent one son there did so more out of fear of the future,' says Gaya. 'The atmosphere was very tense in India—they wanted to hedge their bets, spread their risk, by opening a branch there. This was especially true of the bigger business families, who were not sure if they would be able to conduct business here.'

The Enemy Property Act of 1968, in the aftermath of a war between India and Pakistan in 1965, meant that all properties left behind in Bombay—and other places—by the departing families and relatives would now come into the hands of the government, which could dispose of them to the highest bidder. 'Overnight, people lost properties in prestigious areas—our family suffered too,' says Gaya. A famous case was that of Zulfiqar Ali Bhutto, whose family had owned the plot at Churchgate where Astoria Hotel now stands. Despite all efforts, it slipped out of their hands.

Till then, travel between the two countries was a routine affair; now it became difficult. Managing or disposing of the properties was not easy, nor was getting into protracted and expensive litigation.

The elite among the Muslims had moved away from Mohammed Ali Road and Dongri a long time ago. 'To the well-off, even the upper middle classes, Mohammed Ali Road seems backward; they look down upon it. Those Muslims who live in Colaba, Byculla, Bandra think this area is full of crime, bhais and what not. Frankly even I used to feel embarrassed and a bit ashamed,' says Nausheen, an activist lawyer who represents Muslim women in their divorce petitions. Her family has lived there for generations. She went to English-medium institutions, but as she saw more and more Muslim women, especially those from conservative families, struggling to fight for their rights, she chose to stay on. 'Now I feel the reverse—I think I must do something for the people, especially the women of my community. It is congested, but I feel safer in the home and area where we have lived for more than thirty years.'

The clichéd images leap out at the visitor in Dongri. On the face of it, it is no different from any other busy street in Mumbai—honking cars, women out shopping, men bustling about, vendors on the street selling their wares, everything from shoes to fruit to chicken. But the burqas and skullcaps are very much in evidence. The shopfronts have Urdu on them, though the Gujaratis or the Konkanis don't speak the language. Religious prayer books and framed images of the Ka'aba are on sale in roadside stalls. This would be a casting director's image of a 'Muslim' area.

Dongri, deriving its name from the Marathi word for stone, is in the very heart of the Mohammed Ali Road stretch, which runs for over three kilometres, from Crawford Market to Nagpada, after which Byculla begins. It was one of the several native quarters of the Raj and was long a melting pot of cultures—Chinese, Arabs, Turks, Afghans, Gujarati Muslims, Jains and Hindus all lived and worked there. Many of them were employed in the docks-linked business further to the east. Fitters in the Mazagaon Docks, labour with various contractors, ship repairers, sailors, vendors and even ship chandlers, they all found it convenient to live in the vicinity.

In time, Muslims from elsewhere—Konkan, Uttar Pradesh and Bihar—also moved there, and it became the city's Muslim quarter, with all the connotations it brings. Much of Mumbai sees it as a ghetto that is inherently backward in its social practices, best avoided unless there is specific work to be done there. The restaurants are a draw, especially during Ramzan, when food stalls appear on the streets and hundreds of people from different parts of the city throng there to taste 'Muslim' food. Chor Bazara, the thieves' market in Mutton Street, is a major attraction for collectors and others who want to buy furniture or old (likely fake) clocks and posters.

At one time, Mohammed Ali Road was an important north–south road, but in 2001, the government built a two-kilometre-long flyover that runs over the stretch—the distance from the reality on the ground and everything that goes on there is now complete, except for occasional glimpses of people's homes and the crowds below.

At Char Nal, on the biggest road in the neighbourhood, is a small police outpost, to keep a watch on the area. It is a busy and sultry Friday afternoon, and many men are rushing to the mosque for prayers, weaving through the traffic, handcart pullers, vendors selling everything from vegetables to footwear, burqa-clad women shopping and cars honking.

It is also a busy shopping area, selling household goods, meat and poultry, and clothes. But some establishments stand out—one sells copies of the Qur'an and shiny framed quotes from the Holy Book, another offers tours to Mecca, and a third is a specialty shop for ittar and surma, both still popular in these parts.

The Dada Nanji Kamarsi Surmawala store has what one would call 'an old-world charm'. From the signboard to the display of goods to the man behind the counter—they are all redolent of another era. Mohammed Anis Shaikh, in a kurta pyjama and wearing an embroidered white cap, who says he is around seventy, runs this shop, which was set up by his grandfather 'before I was born'. The entrance to the shop has a panel that announces in Gujarati that one can get 'budhe baba's surma, attar, spray, agarbattis and mehndi'. Inside, an optician's eye chart suggests that the establishment at one time also checked eyesight.

Shaikh appears happy to see customers in his shop, which is decidedly old fashioned compared to the flashy glass and chrome ittar stores close by. He offers to make an ittar to suit my personality and produces a handful of small bottles, each one with a somewhat overpowering scent—he rejects the rose and the jasmine, but after a bit of mix and match, applies a smidgeon of a rich, dense liquid to my wrist. '*Yeh aapko janchega*,' he says with a disarming smile. 'Very good for your general health and very manly,' he adds, his sales pitch perfected over decades. A tiny bottle of the perfume changes hands; I am convinced I'm being overcharged, even ripped off, and I suspect even he feels he has overdone it—a free gift of another bottle and a packet of mehndi is thrown in.

He admits he does not get too many customers—'The young men are not colouring their hair with mehndi or using surma like before. Ittar still sells, because Muslims don't use alcohol-based scents, but there is too much competition.'

A quick and refreshing cup of milky, sugary tea with a bun later (all for ₹20), I am ready for a tour with Ashar, a local boy who has now moved out of his old neighbourhood.

By any measure, Ashar would qualify as a dude. A graphic designer who runs a burger outlet in Breach Candy, Ashar says he felt stifled here and after marriage, chose to shift to the western suburbs. 'People just haven't moved on. I found my friends had no ambition and were content with their motorcycles and low-paying jobs. Their ultimate dream was to move to Dubai.' The 'ghetto mentality' meant they were not interested in exploring the world outside the borders. Ashar had other ideas.

'Every community of Muslims here lives in their own buildings,' says Ashar. He points them out, 'Shias only, Sunnis only.' Within those classifications, the divide is on pedigree and financial standing—belonging to the same sub-group is no guarantee of gaining entry into a housing complex, unless the applicant meets specific criteria—'older, richer families will not let in newcomers, however well off, unless they know them from before,' Ashar says.

All around are tiny enclaves exclusively for members of a specific community. Nearby is the enclosed Ismaili Khoja colony Karimabad, where non-Khojas cannot acquire apartments, across Mohammed Ali Road is Bhendi Bazaar, or Bohri Mohalla, which is overwhelmingly Bohra, though there is no restriction as such. There are lanes mainly occupied by those whose 'native place' is a particular village or district in Gujarat. These kinships have been forged over generations, and such networks are invaluable when it comes to offering support and assistance.

Less known are minuscule pockets of Jews, who have lived in the area for generations, though many have left for Israel.

Further down, we ask about a Yehudi masjid, wanting to go to the old synagogue, but are directed to a Jewish prayer room. It was originally set up in 1818 and now caters to the handful of Jews in the vicinity.

The prayer room is guarded by cops, who have become an ubiquitous presence outside Jewish synagogues since the 26/11 attacks. The policemen want to know who we are—it is difficult to explain that we are just walkers, interested in the gullies of the city. The word 'press' seems to work.

Inside, two men point towards a beautifully maintained room, with benches; 'At one time these used to be packed, now [there are] barely a few Jews left in the area,' says one. '[There are] many synagogues all over Mumbai, catering to hardly 4,000 Bene Israelis. Further to the south is a synagogue in a street called the Israeli Mohalla—the synagogue is locked, no one goes there anymore.'

Ashar then leads me towards Bhishti mohalla. It is not named after the water carriers; the word for them, who used to supply water in horse-skin bags to old structures, is *mashaq*. 'Very dangerous area, Bhishti mohalla.' It is a narrow, jagged side street, throbbing with handcarts, coolies, men hanging around and shops. A cookout is taking place on the main road—these are *bhatiyaras*, traditional cooks, who have set up their kitchens in small holes in the wall. They are caterers who take orders for parties and even small restaurants. At Al Rehman mutton shop, chunks of meat hang from cleavers.

Some of the buildings look new, constructed in a haphazard manner, looming over the street. There is no way such buildings could have got municipal permissions, yet, they are fully occupied by families, who have moved from within the area. 'This is graphic pollution,' says Ashar the graphic artist. 'Very misaligned.' A local had once told me, 'Muslims don't find flats easily elsewhere. Where else can they go when their families grow except within the mohalla?'

Right on cue, we hear shouts of 'chor chor' and a scared young boy with a plastic bag runs out of a building. Two young men run after him. The boy is cornered, because of the crowd. The men give him a couple of slaps, look into his bag, but seem to find nothing. During namaaz time on Fridays, thieves see an opportunity and enter homes while the menfolk are away, Ashar explains in a phlegmatic manner. He shrugs and turns away.

'All this is an education for me too—I have no idea about these parts,' says Shaikh, a young writer who has joined us. He grew up a few miles away from here and now lives in the western suburbs. 'Dongri is a strange place.'

This strange place was also, in the 1990s, the epicentre of Mumbai's worst-ever violence, when Hindus and Muslims clashed for days, weeks, and which ended in the deaths of 900 people, mostly Muslim. Thousands were displaced, their businesses and livelihoods destroyed. Many more thousands left Bombay, never to return.

Dongri became a battleground in the early 1990s when violence broke out in the aftermath of the demolition, by Hindutva fanatics, of the Babri Masjid, in faraway Ayodhya. The repercussions of that heinous act were felt all over the country, but nowhere as violently and barbarically as in Bombay, as it was then called. Hundreds of people died, thousands were displaced and in a matter of weeks, the city's sense of imagination of itself was destroyed.

Dongri was the epicentre of that danse macabre. 'It was a warzone,' remembers Abdullah Jam, a social worker and one-time journalist. Abdullah lives a mile or so away from Dongri but has walked these streets since childhood. His current occupation keeps him very engaged with the city, and this neighbourhood in particular—he draws maps for the Mumbai police. These maps help the police in many ways—to plan traffic and personnel movement during processions, to get a detailed layout of the area after a crime, to place policemen at strategic locations during a riot. Twenty-five years later, Abdullah remembers those days with great clarity.

The Babri Masjid was brought down by crowds armed with pickaxes and hammers on the morning of 6 December 1992. Even before the actual incident, for weeks and months, the Bharatiya Janata Party and the Shiv Sena had whipped up emotions by holding public gatherings declaring that the mosque would be destroyed. Muslim bodies held their own meetings where they demanded that the government not allow this to happen. The Prime Minister, Narasimha Rao, assured Parliament that the state would do everything to prevent this from happening.

'Many Muslims all over the country had hopes that this would not happen, but when the news came, they were shocked,' Abdullah remembers. 'The mood was so angry, I was worried about the worst.' Anger spilled out on to the streets of Bombay and hundreds of Muslims gathered at different places to protest. Tensions had simmered since the morning of the 6th, and a little after 12.30 p.m., when news came—on the BBC—that the mosque had come down, the crowds got restive. Reports of stone-throwing and even firing in parts of the city, spread—soon the anger exploded.

A little after 4 p.m., violence was reported in the Pydhonie and Bhendi Bazaar area and by the next morning, the city was 'aflame', in the words of the official report of the inquiry into the violence, which was headed by Justice Srikrishna.

The violence continued for the next five days, after which an uneasy calm settled on the city. The police came out in large numbers on the streets and particularly in the Mohammed Ali Road area, seen as a potential tinderbox by the government. On both sides of the road, the Muslim-majority areas were backed by neighbourhoods that had Hindu residents. The wide road around Char Null became the 'border' where brickbats rained from all sides.

Abdullah remembers, 'I had come out, spoke to some angry young men to stop the violence, spoke to their families too, but of course no one was in the mood to listen.' To some extent, it was understandable—this was war, and the 'other side' was not going to slow down either. Besides, many of the Muslims in Mohammed Ali Road and elsewhere were also battling another strong force that was endemically against them—the police.

Deep sectarian biases were embedded in the Mumbai police force; this was recorded in the Srikrishna report, but had been discussed for a long time before these riots.

To a Muslim, the men in uniform came across as implacably hostile at the best of times; there is always a visible police presence in Mohammed Ali Road as though it will explode at any time. During the riots, this aggressiveness was seen over and over again.

Farook Mapkar was one who experienced it first-hand.

Mapkar, a security guard in a small bank in Mazagaon, was working on 6 December when the first phase of the rioting broke out in the city. He decided to stay in the bank's premises rather than go home and stepped out only after five days, by which time the violence had somewhat abated.

The calm was deceptive, because in January it flared up again—this time it was to be bloodier and more vicious. On the morning of 10 January, Mapkar went to a mosque as always. 'It was quite normal in the city, no sign of any violence. I thought I would do my namaaz before going to work. The azaan sounded, and just around then, the police—it was the local cops and some central forces—began shooting inside.'

Nearly a hundred men were gathered there, and they began running helter-skelter in panic. The doors were shut hurriedly, but another round of firing came from an open window. 'I and a few others were injured,' Mapkar remembers.

A bullet hit him on his shoulder, but he did not feel a thing. 'I was sitting, looking after another man who had fallen. I felt a kind of sting, nothing more, and my shirt became damp and then wet; it was on my back, behind me, but I could see something red seeping down.'

The shooting, he says, was accompanied by abuses in a loud voice, but soon after, it ceased. 'I saw through the window, an officer—a Sikh, I could make out—order that the firing be stopped. We were all ordered to come out with our hands in the air.'

As they filed out, one of the injured men bent down to press his leg where a bullet had hit him. 'A Mumbai police officer reacted and shot him in his chest; the boy died instantly, right in front of us.'

The group was taken to a police station, where a bunch of men stood shouting slogans: 'I remember them saying, "*Jisko chahiye Pakistan, usko bhejo kabristan*".' Mapkar and others were made to sit, without food or water. 'One man kept asking for water, and died, because no one gave it to him.' By then, he was feeling restless, 'as if I had something in my body, churning around.'

Taken to KEM hospital to attend to their injuries, they were once again subject to mob fury. 'I told a policeman, please take me out of here, back to the police station, I will take my chances there.' In court the next morning, the police told the judge that they had arrested some of the men at another location, 'but it was not true—all of us, 183 in number, were taken either from the mosque or the immediate area around us.' A few were let off, but Mapkar was in custody till 27 January, when he was taken to a hospital where the bullet was finally taken out. He had been released on bail, pending the case being heard in the courts.

For Mapkar then began an endless round of courts, policemen who gave distorted statements and magistrates who disregarded witnesses, including one who was supposed to be a police witness but said that he had not seen any firing from the mosque, as the cops had claimed. This went on for years—he gave his testimony to the government-appointed Srikrishna Commission and was diligent in attending court, 'including on 26 July 2005, when Mumbai was flooded. Yet the police declared I was absconding.' Mapkar discovered new resources within himself, even cross-examining two policemen when his lawyer did not turn up. 'The magistrate was impressed, and he told my lawyer to learn from me.'

He was finally exonerated, but he did not give up. He wanted to see the policemen, especially the inspector who had shot the injured man in cold blood, caught and tried. His friends kept telling him to give it up and move on with his life, as thousands had done, as much of the wounded community too had done. His parents told everyone who asked, we don't know what he is up to, we don't ask.

The visits to the courts continued, the city moved on, the community had picked up the pieces and restored its life. 'Even the relatives of the others who died in the rioting or firing didn't want to pursue any case. Many of the victims were poor migrant workers from UP and Bihar—their families had no means to keep following up,' remembers Mapkar.

Not one policeman was held to account, forget being convicted. It just reinforced the widespread perception among Muslims that the police—as much of the government machinery—was fundamentally biased against them and they would not get justice.

'I saw the good side of the courts—I was let off and held completely innocent. But a few others in the legal system give the judiciary a bad name. It is not surprising that many people think that even the courts will not help them,' says Mapkar. The experience changed him. He now fights on behalf of others, 'anyone who needs help and doesn't know how to tackle the system, whatever their religion may be.'

Not all Muslims faced violence, but they felt its impact in some way or the other. The rioting mob and the police were limited to some areas only, where they were gathered in large numbers. Elsewhere, the growing feeling of a religious divide was more insidious.

'We had lived in our building for years—we had played with our neighbours' kids and my parents mixed socially with many of them. There was never any sense of being different. Then everything changed in December 1992.' For Sameera Khan, journalist and writer, seeing the Bombay she had grown up in change so suddenly and so drastically is a hurtful memory.

Atlas Apartments is one of the older, tall, multi-storeyed buildings in a corner of Nepean Sea Road, one of the city's toniest neighbourhoods, home to industrialists, senior executives, even film stars. Sameera Khan's father was in the multinational Hindustan Levers, well known around town and a former journalist himself.

For Sameera, the portents of what was to come became clear on 6 December itself. 'I was working in (the afternoon paper) *Mid-Day* and watched the demolition of Babri Masjid on the television set in the office. Someone said, "Muslims like you won't be affected." I suppose he meant people of my class.'

Then the riots began—they were taking place all over the city.

'The mood in the newsroom was horrendous. I used to wear salwar kameez and bindi. People started noticing this, that the colour of my salwar kameez was green. I started noticing that I was putting on a bindi, something I used to otherwise do casually.'

Next door to Atlas was a judges' colony, as was a branch of the Shiv Sena. 'One day, the secretary of the building called my mother, saying things like "how terrible things are". Watchmen started asking us, why do you go out for so long. Imagine a watchman asking a resident a question like this. For us, the atmosphere in the building was ruined.'

One day, Sameera came home and saw that the family's nameplate in the lobby had been taken off. 'All other names were there, but there was no 62A–Irfan Khan. I found it foolish. For one thing, it stood out. And it reflected the attitude of the building. Another day, there was a symbol made with chalk on our door—no one else had it.'

At a time when Muslim homes and businesses were being specifically targeted all over the city, this was a chilling signal. 'But I did not have words to articulate what I was feeling. We discussed this over the dinner table but didn't know what to say.'

In the office, the layout artists, who were mostly Muslims and lived in Muslim areas, were tense. 'There was an unsettled feeling. Bombay had turned against us.'

Khan's company was considerate and offered to shift them, but Sameera refused to move. 'I said nothing doing.'

Finally, when Sameera was getting documentation done to go for further studies abroad, Irfan Khan decided to move. 'We left discreetly, one bag at a time; someone asked us, where are you going, we said, to a relative's house, she is unwell. I packed chilli powder—when we eventually returned, my mother said she could not find the chilli powder. It had been in my bag all along,' she laughs.

It did not end there. One day Khan came back for something from his flat. A crowd had built up outside the building. The building's watchmen were hostile, telling him that they knew his licence plate number.

The building committee met to discuss what should be done about the Khans. There were some murmurs about asking them to leave. No voice except one spoke up against it—the actor Shashi Kapoor walked out of the meeting when the matter came up. The committee responded by telling him he should send away his manservant Jamal.

Eventually the Khans did move back, but something had broken. 'Through the eight years we lived there after, the name plate was never restored. I never forgot or forgave that,' she says.

The djinn of deep-seated prejudice that was hidden all these years gleefully burst out in the open, free of the demands of politesse and other social constraints. It was okay to now talk openly about 'those people' in veiled or even blatant terms. In elegant and cosmopolitan drawing rooms, guests were less inhibited about expressing their forthright views about 'the minorities' and their unreasonable demands.

Some hidden secrets emerged, for example, large, Hindu family-controlled companies that had never hired a Muslim in their entire existence; the unspoken restrictions on letting out apartments to Muslims were always there, now brokers and owners made it clear 'they' were not wanted.

The long, nation-wide rath yatra of the BJP leader L.K. Advani, the demolition of the mosque and the rioting had finally made communal biases legitimate. Bombay's cosmopolitan pretensions, always somewhat thin, were blown to bits.

On the ground, discrimination had always been felt by the city's Muslims—now it just acquired a nastier edge. There began a huge migration, both out of Bombay and within the city. An estimated 2,00,000 people had left the city in the immediate aftermath of the rioting; soon, Muslims who lived in Bombay began converging on community-dominated areas.

'Mohammed Ali Road became a magnet of sorts—people had always wanted to move out of here; now they were coming back. Property prices began moving up,' recalls Sarfaraz Arzoo, editor of the Urdu paper *Hindustan*, which had been launched by his father in 1940. Arzoo had covered the rioting as a reporter and was often stopped by the police. He shrugged it off as a professional hazard.

'The municipal corporation often says that the Mohammed Ali Road area and Dongri are full of illegal buildings—this is probably true, there are many legal discrepancies in them. But they came up in response to the demand after 1992 – 93, as Muslims came here in large numbers and needed accommodation.'

Others simply left the city and moved to the outskirts. One popular destination was Mumbra, just outside the city's municipal borders—forty-five kilometres from Fort—but serviced by the suburban train network, which made it very attractive. Till then a somewhat somnolent suburb soon after Thane, where Mumbai ends, Mumbra suddenly exploded with this influx and began growing—it hasn't stopped.

Mumbra was a somewhat obscure place for decades. The comfort zone for most Mumbai residents consists of where they live and where they work—if they don't need to go there, it doesn't exist. Mumbra sprang into the city's consciousness as more and more people—almost all of them Muslims—began moving there.

As soon as one gets off the train in Mumbra, the difference from any other part of Mumbai becomes starkly visible. The scene outside the station is a familiar one in any suburb, with the scrum of auto-rickshaws waiting for their fares, and a bustle on the roads and at shops, but the difference quickly becomes apparent—the population is predominantly and visibly Muslim—women in burqas and the men in 'Muslim' wear, loose pyjamas and shirts, beards and skullcaps.

I am here to see Shirin Dalvi, commentator and journalist who used to work for the newspaper *Hindustan* in Nagpada, Mumbai, but is a native of Mumbra. Dalvi is known to be a fearless voice, and she lost her job when one night a staffer added a photo of the notorious and controversial cartoon that had appeared in the satirical French magazine *Charlie Hebdo*. Conservative Muslims, who had never liked her, bayed for her blood, and after going underground for a few days, she had to resign.

She lives in a one-bedroom apartment on 'khadi machine road', named after the quarrying machines that have worked for years on the hills that loom over the suburb.

Also living with her are her daughter, son and daughter-in-law. The daughter is finishing a course in movie special effects, the son, in his twenties, is employed with his uncle who runs a travel agency, and the daughter-in-law, a commerce graduate, is planning to study further to become a teacher.

'When I was growing up in the 1970s, it was a very quiet, peaceful place—most of the land was used to grow rice, but all that began to disappear as the suburbs spread. In the late 1960s, many Muslims moved here after the riots in Bhiwandi (a small town fifteen kilometres away known for its power looms). In 1984, another bout of riots brought more families here.'

But it was only after the 1992–93 riots in Mumbai, which went on for two months with a break in between, that large numbers of migrants chose to move to Mumbra. 'People came in the thousands. Temporary camps were set up and soon, well-meaning philanthropists built one-room tenements that they sold for a mere ₹10,000; even this amount most refugees could not manage.

'Trucks and tempos used to leave for Bombay with food for those who had lost their homes, and they returned with families, most with little except the clothes on their backs. A few had lost family members. They came from all over, the Mohammed Ali Road area, Vikhroli, Bandra.'

Ironically, there was no violence in Mumbra itself. In neighbouring Thane, there were reports of rioting and killing, but Mumbra remained safe. 'There has never been any communal violence in Mumbra,' Shirin says, a note of pride in her voice.

The influx into Mumbra has continued, and the population has been growing steadily. The 2011 census showed it to be eleven lakhs, but it could be more. She shows me buildings that have come up, many of them without permission, to house the newcomers. Shirin says the system—in this case the local municipal corporation—has left Mumbra to its own devices and also discriminates against it. 'There are no power cuts in any of the suburbs around, but our power goes off routinely.'

One post-1993 refugee was Shaikh Alim, who was an eleven-year-old schoolboy when his family came to Mumbra after their home in Vikhroli was destroyed. He now runs Excellence Classes, a coaching centre for local students.

Excellence Classes is on the first floor of a rundown building but looks smart and swanky inside. The outer room serves as an office and reception, with the message 'May I help you' on the desk. On the wall are framed photos of the best students from Excellence, who scored the highest marks from the suburbs in state-level school and college exams. All the photos except one are of girls, most with their heads covered.

Shaikh, now in his late thirties, sits behind a desk in a small, air-conditioned room with a coffee dispensing machine in the corner. He is calm as he tells his story.

'We had lived in Hayali village in Vikhroli for about twenty years. My father worked in a transport company in Cotton Green. The "village" consisted of eighty-three one-room tenements, and just three of the families, including ours, were Muslims.'

In early December, when news of violence from different parts of Bombay spread, Alim's neighbours suggested that the family should move or send the children away. A shop close by had been burnt down but Hayali was untouched.

The Alim family moved to a relative's home but returned when it calmed down.

In January, the violence erupted again. This time, the family moved out immediately; they soon heard that their home had been ransacked and looted. 'I got to know that the looters were our neighbours, including older people who had played with us when we were children. That really hurt,' says Shaikh.

'One of our Muslim neighbours who moved to a house nearby told us her home was broken into and everything taken away and that she recognized all the vandals. At the same time, others hid in the home of another neighbour, a Hindu, who lied that there was no one in his house.' Some months later, when the Alims visited their home, they found that everything but the fans had been taken away. 'We took photographs of the empty room, but the photos were destroyed in the floods of 2005.'

The Alim family, having lost everything, went to their village in Azamgarh, but Shaikh's father, who had built up a small business, brought them back in March. On the day they landed, the city was bombed—thirteen coordinated blasts were heard in different parts of the city. As it came out later, this was an operation masterminded by a former Bombay underworld figure named Dawood Ibrahim, ostensibly to take revenge for the killing of Muslims. It left the city stunned; hundreds of people were detained by the police as a massive investigation was launched. Of the 129 people charged, 100 were found guilty, though many of them have still not been found.

The Shaikh family, which had found temporary accommodation, felt Bombay would never be safe; 'One day my father told us we were moving to Mumbra—we had never even heard of it. He showed us the house. It was around 605 square feet, and we got it for ₹2.10 lakh, which we could afford.'

Shaikh didn't take to Mumbra at all—he found it very different from his old home. His intellectual stimulation came from his school Anjuman-i-Islam, over an hour's train ride away in distant South Bombay. At the same time, his yearning for his old Vikhroli home was gone. For his older brothers, with stronger personal memories, Vikhroli was still where they had friends. 'They used to go there to get bread from the same shop we had bought it from for years. In our time it was called Shama Bakery, but they had changed the name to Maharashtra Bakery.'

'I like Mumbra, but the people here really don't want to develop themselves. The schools are of very poor quality, promoted by all kinds of shady operators. The other day I heard of a college that held a fancy-dress competition where one student came as Michael Jackson—why not think of yourselves as the Prime Minister, why a mere singer? Ambitions are low-grade, there is no sports worth the name,' Shaikh says.

Girls, he said, are doing far, far better than boys. 'I know this will create problems, is already creating problems. The boys have no ambition, they drop out and become auto drivers. Why would these smart girls marry these boys?'

The rising difference between them is flagged by many others. Zubair Azmi, a lawyer who runs Urdu Markaz, an organization to promote the language, in Madanpura, says he is often called to join counselling sessions to talk to couples where the difference in education levels causes serious rifts. 'The woman has often completed a post-graduate degree. But they are persuaded to marry boys who have barely completed school; how will it last?'

Increasingly, though, education has become a big priority among Muslims with young children. And they want them to study in an English-medium school.

I head to the Umar Rajjab municipal school, deep in the bylanes of Madanpura in the Nagpada area. Madanpura is the northern-most tip of the 'Muslim' area, which begins a few kilometres southwards at Crawford Market.

The school building is an unprepossessing structure, with classrooms on every floor. It was mainly an Urdu-medium school but saw its student population dwindle over the years because parents were reluctant to admit their kids. Inside, it has a rundown look, with peeling plaster and half-empty classrooms.

But on one side of the building, the corridors are freshly painted, and the classrooms are well lit, with new benches and blackboards. Each room is full, and teachers have charts, posters and much more to explain their subjects.

This is the newly started English-medium section, begun only in 2018, and already proving to be a great success with the local community. But so great is the demand that the people behind the initiative are finding it difficult to take in more students.

'Every parent now wants their child to join here—it's close by and the fee is negligible, almost free. But we have no capacity to absorb every child.' Rais Shaikh is the local municipal councillor who, with the help of a missionary school in the neighbourhood, set up this school. He convinced the municipal authorities to set aside some rooms for English-medium classes. It is he who is the face of the initiative and handles the parents, with a mixture of sympathy, warmth and firmness.

Outside the room where he sits every morning is a knot of people, and everyone is clutching sheets of paper, fidgeting, nervous, anxious. Many of the ladies are burqa-clad, some men are wearing skullcaps, visible markers of their identity, but in this group, they don't stand out.

Khan has a list before him that contains the names of children who have been admitted in the latest intake. He wants to help his constituents, but sometimes it just doesn't work out. Today he has to disappoint the father of a ten-year-old boy who had applied to join standard 4. 'Maulana saab, please see this list—we are allowed to take only forty children per class, and I already have a list of forty-four; I have to cut out four names.' The man, fully conversant with the ways of the system, says softly, 'Please adjust somehow. He will waste a year.'

Shaikh asks the boy to recite a poem, any poem, but in English. The boy freezes. Shaikh encourages him in a kind tone, but there is no response—he has been going to an English-medium school in the neighbourhood, but clearly hasn't become fluent in the language, not even enough to recite a few lines. His father stiffens more, and pleads with Shaikh, 'That is why I want him to come here, to get a real education.'

English-medium education has become big—the missionary schools, where the fee is modest, are very difficult to get into. New, fancier schools have sprung up, started by entrepreneurs, where big money is required, up to ₹25,000 per year, beyond the reach of most. An almost free English-medium school is a boon, except that it is full.

Muslims see education as the only route to upward mobility. 'Government jobs are almost totally closed to Muslims, but in recent years, the growing economy has opened up many possibilities,' Sarfaraz Arzoo told me. Retail is one such, where young Muslim boys and girls join outlets ranging from supermarkets to electronics stores. 'It brings structure to their lives—wearing a uniform, mixing with all kinds of customers, handling difficult situations.'

But not everyone is satisfied with such jobs. Some want white-collar jobs in banks and offices, others aim higher. Law and finance are in great demand, but in recent years, young Muslims have lined up to cram for the central services exams.

At the Haj House in Mumbai, which handles the regular traffic of Muslim pilgrims to Saudi Arabia, a year-long intensive coaching schedule prepares young Muslim aspirants to sit for the competitive exams. The coaching is subsidized by the government as part of its effort to bring more Muslims into the administrative services. Competition is intense and involves several stages, starting with preliminary exams, at which stage large numbers are weeded out, then are the main exams—involving nine different subjects—which reduce the number further for interviews and then the final selection. A million candidates start out and 800 or so are selected, very few of them Muslims.

Even to get into the coaching camp is a tough process. After regional tests around the country, interviews, then final exams and more interviews, barely forty make it. Barely one or two from the Haj House cohort finally get in; yet the number of hopefuls keeps going up. The prize makes all that work worth it—it could mean a prestigious government job for life, with power and status.

But will education and a career in the 'mainstream' remove the deeply rooted biases among others? Will Muslims be considered respectable? Muslims, educated or otherwise, find it very difficult to rent or buy an apartment—film stars, young couples, professionals—everyone has faced this situation at some time or another.

And when they cluster together, it becomes a ghetto. A ghetto that is considered beyond the pale, something different from the normal, perhaps even dirty and dangerous.

On a walk in Jogeshwari East, I go to visit Chota Pakistan. That is the name everyone around uses, including, it is said, the local policemen. Chota Pakistan is where Muslims live. There is another group of small 'pucca' houses close by, where Hindus live. It is not called Chota Hindustan. A street divides the two sides and is inevitably called the border.

Sitaram Shelar, an activist who has been working on housing and water issues with slum communities for the past twenty years, is showing me around. Both the Hindus and Muslims were among those who were moved to

Jogeshwari—dumped would be a better word—from various slum colonies in different parts of Bombay in the 1980s. Each family was given a small plot, and they all worked hard to make some money and build 'pucca' houses. Smaller clusters are still known as Colaba, Andheri, Bandra, referencing the areas they were brought from.

The families have moved up in life, and the community would qualify for being called neo-middle class; people with jobs, education and their own vehicles; most homes have refrigerators, flat-screen TV sets, even washing machines.

But there is a stark difference between the two sides of the border. The Hindu part is well laid out, with broader, paved roads and covered drains. It is clear that much more infrastructure investment has gone in there. There is a store selling 'designer clothes', another, paints for home interiors. 'The water pipes on the Muslim side are much narrower, which affects supply,' Sitaram points out. The drains are open and clearly not clean. Sitaram points to a Hanuman mandir, which was built with the help of Muslims.

While growing up, he himself was confused about the Muslims who lived around there, Sitaram says. He was a young boy when the riots broke out in 1992. 'I couldn't understand why people were taking the furniture of our neighbour and throwing it on a fire on the road. The neighbour had not done anything bad to us—we all used to go to his shop to get our hair cut.' It affected him greatly; his entire worldview changed. 'I could have joined in—instead I moved the other way.'

An activist from a local NGO, Janta Jagriti Manch, says things are gradually changing from even a few years ago.

'When there is an issue that concerns all the residents—housing, water connections, sanitation, etc.—everyone comes together, whoever they are, wherever they live.'

The Chota Pakistan tag is used less now, but has not yet died. It may even get a new lease of life, given the blatant anti-Muslims rhetoric in the country. Whatever the fact of their visible presence, their history in the city and their contributions, irrespective of the many high-profile people, including film stars, in the public eye—in cosmopolitan Mumbai, Muslims remain the Other.

For some years now, Muslims have been the target of prejudice and even legal assaults on their rights from the political establishment. Since 2014, when a new, Hindutva-oriented party, the BJP, came into power in Delhi and many other states, the marginalization of Muslims only got accelerated. There have been a number of cases where innocent Muslims have been lynched to death and new laws have been introduced that could potentially take away their citizenship. The social and institutional prejudices that remained under the surface have now got a sinister, official sanction.

Some have made adjustments with what they consider the inevitable.

In Radhabai chawl, which is now an almost overwhelmingly Muslim area, two men, both in their forties, are sitting on a doorstep. One of them, after chatting with us for a while, says, 'Who am I talking to?' I give him a card, mention I am a journalist. He is suddenly eager to talk.

'Those days it was very bad here. After the rioting stopped, the police took away many young men under TADA (Terrorist and Disruptive Activities [Prevention] Act).'

'Know anyone?' I ask him.

'There is one in front of you,' he replies.

His story comes out, in bits. 'I was taken to a local police station, then court, after which we were taken to TADA court. Then I was in [Yerawada] Central Jail in Pune. One of our number filed a petition in the Supreme Court and we were all freed. The well-known lawyer Majid Memon saab fought our case.

'Meet me at leisure and I will talk,' he says, toying with the card.

'Do you think,' he suddenly asks, 'I can get some compensation for being jailed? I have been declared not guilty. I will call you and tell you my full story.'

'What do you do now?' I ask.

He suddenly goes silent; his friend pipes up, 'He is now with the Shiv Sena. With Mr Waikar, who is a minister.'

8

SHIP-BREAKING AND SLUMS

Shanti Ravi knows the value of the land she is standing on. 'Look around you—this will one day become Smart City. Big big flats. Restaurants. Gardens. Cinemas,' she says, her hand moving in a wide arc to take in her surroundings. A smile is playing across her face.

Smart City is not the exact phrase that comes to mind when looking around. For the moment, the place is filthy and decrepit and full of 'informal housing', or, to be more accurate, slums. It is also completely illegal—on many official documents this colony of thousands of people does not even exist. The authorities have never come here to help with even basic amenities. It is, in fact, the very antithesis of smart.

And yet, on the ground here, at Koyla Bunder, the slums stand, as they have for over fifty years. Koyla Bunder is one of the many clusters in the area, which is known by its collective name Darukhana, or Gunpowder Place, named after the powder magazine kept there for British troops. Koyla Bunder itself literally translates as the dock where coal was unloaded. The other 'bunders'—an Arabic word meaning docks—are named after the goods that they serviced—Lakdi, Powder and Reti, the last for the sand that came in on Arab dhows—at a time when this area was humming with commercial and shipping activity.

Now, a fetid smell hangs in the air, a mixture of household garbage, industrial waste and machine oil. This is home to thousands of people in Mumbai, and if the slum dwellers weren't there, it would have been the perfect place to build plush apartments at prices that rival Manhattan's. The slums—no one knows the exact number, but a rough estimate says that around 50,000 people live here—are very near the water line, and a few are cheek by jowl of the edge of the small inlet where small ships and barges come in for repairs. The common toilets are in one corner, where, as in most slums, people queue up in the mornings, awaiting their chance to use them. By afternoon, there is an unbearable stink around them. It is an area unknown and unseen by the city and by the authorities who manage the metropolis. Further up on the Darukhana stretch is a dargah, a mausoleum of Sayyid Ali Mira Datar, said to be 300 years old. The lane leading to it is lined with shops selling flowers, sweets and 'chadars' to be placed on the grave. Many families bring their 'possessed' relatives here—probably those who are mentally ill—to get 'cured by a higher force'. Others are hopeful of getting rid of a curse, or possession by witches and demons. The dargah is steps away from a seashore, and many of the devotees have no hesitation in stepping into the putrid water, convinced it will wash off their ailments.

It is hard to believe, but this area was once a thriving dock. The landing stations had their own dock master and even a customs shed. In the 1980s, these were wound up. The ship-breaking, which provided employment to hundreds of Darukhana residents, halted around 2015.

Central Railway's Harbour Line, started in 1910, was intended to serve communities and commercial establishments along the city's eastern harbour. The names of the stations give an indication of their purpose—Dockyard Road, Cotton Green, Chuna Bhatti (Lime Kiln). Other stations are named after colonial administrators such as Sandhurst Road and Reay Road.

From Reay Road, with its sloping, tiled roofs, a decrepit van that should have been condemned years ago picks up passengers at ₹10 a seat for destinations such as Darukhana. The other way is to drive on P D'Mello Road, named after a well-known union leader, which runs parallel to the Harbour Line. P D'Mello Road is full of echoes of the past, when Bombay's trade was linked with towns all along the west coast—the streets are named after Calicut, Cochin, Goa, Surat and many more, evoking the city's seafaring past.

Once full of goods-laden trucks plying up and down, P D'Mello Road is now a link between south Mumbai and the eastern suburbs, but with the construction of a freeway that passes on top, traffic on this road has reduced significantly.

The road is populated by derelict warehouses, empty factories, scrapyards and barely surviving small businesses, the detritus of a past when Bombay was an industrial city and the port area was the hub of its international trade. Here also stands the sprawling headquarters of the Cotton Association of India, once frenetic with activity, now quiet and eerily empty, a ghost town and a melancholy reminder of the city's glorious past.

Bombay was built around the harbour, and also because of it. The East India Company, unhappy with its Surat base for many reasons, not the least because of the constant threat from inimical forces, both European and Indian, wanted to shift base and finally got legal occupation of Bombay in 1668.

The advantages of the island of Bombay were known to the English almost four decades before they actually got possession. Initially, it was more the isolation and the distance from various marauding Indian rulers that attracted them. But the deep harbour soon became the main attraction.

J. Gerson da Cunha, in his book *The Origin of Bombay*,[1] reveals an interesting detail—two frigates were being built in the harbour in the early seventeenth century, a clear indication that the Portuguese had begun using Bombay as a ship-building station. This news would have been conveyed to the Company's bosses, no doubt stoking further interest in this faraway place. In 1854, the Company directors approached Oliver Cromwell, Lord Protector, to enquire about the feasibility of leasing Bombay from the Portuguese, who had many other ports under their control.

When the Company finally got hold of the islands, they began to build infrastructure. Gerald Aungier, the second governor of Bombay, who can be called the founder of Bombay, invited people to come and set up their businesses in this new settlement, promising them complete freedom—economic, social, religious. He was an early town planner, setting up Bombay's judicial system, police force, land revenue system and customs—it was important to begin charging levies from ships moving in and out of the harbour. After all, this was where the Company would trade from. Before, Surat was the harbour where trade ships called and were berthed, and close by was Swally, which had shipbuilding and repair facilities. When the English moved in to take over Bombay, their first task therefore was to examine the feasibility of the harbour for trading and shipbuilding activities.

Correspondence began with the London headquarters and the Court of Directors gave clear instructions to start constructing a proper harbour with docks and to station an armed vessel there to protect the island and the trade. A proper dock, however, was not constructed till many decades later.

The Bombay administrators were in need of skilled labour of all kinds and in 1735, asked their Surat counterparts to send a carpenter to build a new 'grab', a kind of sailing ship popular on the Malabar coast. The man they sent was the master builder, Lowjee Nusserwanjee Wadia, who landed in Bombay sometime in March 1736. A Parsi, he was to settle down in Bombay; his descendants, the Wadias, are a prominent presence in the city. It is the shipbuilders who can be credited with giving the first boost to making Bombay an economic powerhouse. When, in 1813, the trading monopoly of the Company was lifted, Bombay had all the machinery and infrastructure to begin trading with the rest of the world. Indian merchants saw an opportunity to sail to places near and far to buy and sell goods and make their fortunes, and now, happily, they had ready access to ships.

The harbour also provided the perfect defence for Bombay from any attack that came from the sea. In 1686, the East India Marine became the Bombay Marine, and after much renaming, emerged as the Royal Indian Navy in 1932 and, after Independence, the Indian Navy.

By and by, the port expanded, and ships were built and berthed there. A major milestone in its development was the construction of the first dry dock in the 1870s. In 1873, the Bombay Port Trust (BPT) was set up as a proper corporation to administer the vast operations.

Ancillary ship-handling companies, scrap merchants, large warehouses, trucking companies and the natural corollary of this growth—labour—soon moved on to port-owned land. A few factories were also set up near Sewri, which the port had no particular need for. A special road and a railway line were built purely to cater to port activities and movement.

By the 1970s, however, the port could grow no more—harbour facilities were overbooked, and the city's population growth meant that the movement of trucks, etc., through residential areas was becoming untenable. A new port was built across the harbour in Nhava Sheva, and this was capable of handling ships with greater tonnage and modernized cargo ships.

The Bombay Port Trust had no immediate use for its land it owned around the port though it was getting restive about the growing slum population on some portions of it as well as the complex lease and tenancy arrangements that were now becoming very common. It had given out some parts of its vast holdings to factories, warehouses, commercial buildings and even residential structures on rents that were still pegged to decades-old agreements. Yet, business on these lands was booming where ship-breaking, for example, had become a profitable activity. It is this that brought in migrants from all over and they settled down in Darukhana, around the ship-breaking yards.

Shanti Ravi was born in Darukhana, as was her father, who worked in one such ship-breaking outfit. The family had prospered though they continued to live in slums on Port Trust lands. The slum structure expanded to several rooms on the ground floor and on the first floor, which has been rented out to The Believers, a Christian evangelical organization that meets for an assembly every Sunday. She makes the sign of the cross while mentioning this. The local Shiv Sena objected to the presence of a Christian missionary group, but Shanti Ravi has managed to stand up to them.

The original structure, perhaps a more modest one, was built by her grandfather when he came from Tamil Nadu in the 1960s. As her name suggests, she is from the 'lower' castes, but the family converted to Christianity somewhere along the way.

In her forty-two years, Shanti Ravi has seen the place transform, but in some ways, nothing has changed. Community toilets have been made, and each house has electricity, but the municipal corporation does not provide them running water, not even in common taps—everyone is left to their own devices, and to survive, they have to find ingenious and expensive methods.

A private enterprise—no one knows who set it up, no one knows who runs it—gets them that water, from no one knows—or admits—where. For a price. Both the water connection and the residents—or at least their homes—are illegal, even if the source is a legal one somewhere nearby. In 2019, after a lot of lobbying and representation, the Paani Haq Samiti, an NGO, got the municipal corporation to provide nine connections to residents. They now get piped water and pay the official rates for it, approximately ₹5 for 1,000 litres, while their neighbours shell out almost a hundred times more—about ₹40 for 100 litres. More official connections would have come but some politicians put a stop to it—supplying illegal water is big business, which benefits many players.

In its 2016 Development Report, which is prepared after every decade or so by the municipal corporation to plan for the future, the entire Darukhana slum did not show up in any official documents. The land belongs to the Mumbai Port Trust, and though the corporation has jurisdiction over the entire city, it went along with the Trust's claim that it was a vacant, unoccupied piece of land. The Port Trust was not in the business of building infrastructure for 'illegal' settlements that would then become even more entrenched. Showing it as unoccupied would have made it easier to get it vacated when the time for developing the property came. This lack of visibility meant that for decades, those who lived and worked on the land—mostly engaged in port-related activity—never got any civic amenities except electricity. They were in a state of limbo, ghost residents with no one to turn to. This changed in 2018, when an updated plan showed the place as a slum, but that is just the first step towards recognition. Much remains to be done.

Like many others, Shanti Ravi's husband works in a ship-repairing company as a painter, and her son, after failing in his exams, joined him. One daughter graduated from college and got married. She is back in the colony to look after her mother-in-law. The other is in the final year at St. Xavier's College, the most prestigious college in the city—it is something that makes Shanti Ravi immensely proud.

Her otherwise serious face breaks into a dazzling smile when she points out a ground where she says she got local youths to play soccer every evening. 'I got a coach to come to get these boys to play and get some exercise, instead of wasting their time.'

On cue, three young boys show up, their hair slicked back and their poses contrived to make them look cool. This attitude turns into sheepishness as Shanti Ravi asks them, pointedly, 'What were you doing before, eh?'

Getting the youth of her neighbourhood educated is one of her life's missions. She got many NGOs to open centres in Darukhana, but each one of them left, discouraged and frustrated. Shanti Ravi did not give up. She would take students to night school by herself, and then got a piece of land cleared where boys play football. She is the one who goes and argues with officials on any local matter. All this while running her household and making and selling idlis to earn some money. Her younger daughter teaches local children and brings volunteers from elsewhere to come and do the same.

As Shanti Ravi walks around, women come up to her with their issues about getting documentation done so they can put in a claim as legitimate residents deserving of alternative accommodation. There is nervousness about the future, but she assures them that she will take up their cause.

She stops outside a small home where the daughter of the house is washing clothes. 'Why isn't she going to college? She got good marks in her board exams.' The daughter remains silent as Shanti Ravi looks at the mother and admonishes her, 'Don't make her do all this, look after her education.' The mother mumbles an excuse.

Shanti Ravi knows that the Port Trust has its eye on reacquiring the land back from encroachers—the slums—and its tenants who are all paying old rents as part of its grand plans to develop the 'eastern seaboard', as it is being called. If all goes well, over 1,000 acres with a clear title will be available—in a city like Mumbai, that is a goldmine for developers. Darukhana is right on the edge of the water, and anything built there will be in great demand. The slum residents are occupying prime land, and to any developer and to the government, this is land not being monetized.

There is talk of entertainment centres, parks, a waterfront and marinas for the wealthy to park their yachts. It's an industrial wasteland, but in 2015 the then minister of shipping, Nitin Gadkari, saw a glittering future city in the area now being called Portlands, an echo of Docklands in London, which was transformed during Margaret Thatcher's time from a decrepit area into an ultra-luxury neighbourhood. With a gleam in his eye, Gadkari saw a London Eye-like attraction and a building taller than Dubai's Burj Khalifa, among other landmarks.

Nobody has yet mentioned luxury apartment blocks, but those will inevitably come. Over the years, smart politicians have realized that any suggestion that the real beneficiaries will be the city's rich will raise hackles all around. So, they couch their proposals as being 'for the people' but eventually, somehow, expensive properties are built.

An ultra-modern project here would be a real estate bonanza; the city's businessmen called it a 'win-win'; there would be hefty contracts of every kind and enough to go around for everyone. The Port Trust would get to monetize these lands and the city would get open spaces. Except that there are losers in this equation—those who have been staying on the lands. Shanti Ravi is determined to ensure that she and her fellow slum dwellers don't get a raw deal at the end of it.

The Mumbai Port Trust, as it is called now, is one of the biggest landowners in the city, with an estimated 1,800 acres, much of it contiguous and falling outside the purview of the local municipal corporation. The Port Trust is the supreme authority that not only owns and controls but also draws rent from the many tenants of its commercial and residential buildings. These range from godowns to fancy hotels like the Taj Mahal, from ramshackle old structures to spacious and airy apartments on Apollo Bunder—they are all built on land leased to them by the Port Trust.

The slum dwellers of Darukhana are not among the Port Trust's tenants. In fact, they are not anybody's tenants—they are on the far side of any legal status, hanging on to their tiny plots of land they or their forefathers occupied when they came to Bombay to look for work, as far back as the

1940s and '50s. At the time, nobody stopped them—there was an understanding that Bombay, and especially the port area, needed workers to work on marine-related businesses along the coastline. Ship repair was the main activity in and around Darukhana, and it was a labour-intensive job. The migrants were from as far as Tamil Nadu (then Madras State), and in the way these things evolve, each new visitor moved into that part of a slum where others from his own community had settled down; there is comfort in living among your own.

In time, the slum pockets grew exponentially, spreading over acres, precariously perched, physically and legally. The Port Trust did not care, because the workers were needed, and surplus land was not, though every now and then the civic authorities would march in and demolish the houses. Yet the workers stuck on, eking out a living and by and by, making their structures better.

The approach road to Koyla Bunder is dangerously bumpy and runs alongside an open pit full of sludge. Trash—mounds of it—covers the edge of the street and beyond it is the accumulated waste of industrial activity, most of it emanating from the ship-breaking yards nearby. Everything that could possibly be of any use has already been taken away from the vessels; what is left behind is the fuel that flowed from their stripped engines. Over the months, the years, the liquid from scores of ships has accumulated and turned into a viscous organism that floats menacingly on the surface of the pit.

On the eastern side is the sea, lapping the slums on the edge of it, and on the south along the coast are the Mumbai docks and further up, the Naval Dockyard, where the famous ship builders of Surat, the Wadias, came in the eighteenth century.

Till up to the 1980s, the Mumbai harbour was very busy, and ships lined up in the sea waiting for a berth, which had a waiting period. The main preoccupation of the top management of the Port Trust was to prioritize the entry and exit of the ships into the port, ensuring that critical items were unloaded first. India was a net grain importer, and it was vital to keep the supply chain running.

As a consequence, there was no time to focus on other issues, such as real estate. The Port Trust's attitude was one of benign neglect. Many of the godowns, factories and other buildings had been leased out in the 1920s, most of them for sixty years, and these leases had lapsed. The lease holders stayed on, however, and every now and then, when the estate office turned its attention to these expired leases and demanded that the properties be vacated, the tenants, especially the big companies, went to court.

Slums too began to proliferate, mainly in the Reay Road area. Cheap labour, needed for the ship maintenance business and for other assorted activities around the landing docks, moved to the informal settlements that came up here.

No authority provided any utilities or facilities—this was not the municipal corporation's territory. Periodically, especially when elections were approaching, a politician turned up and promised them all kinds of help, but there was no fundamental change in their lives. Possession, it is said, is nine-tenths of the law, but that would work to their advantage in any other part of the city. Here, they had no standing under any law—they were just there, unseen and unwelcome.

By the 1990s and in the 2000s, as marine trade in Bombay shifted and ships had moved to the newer, more efficient facility in Nhava Sheva, the Port Trust woke up to its land holdings. On the day I went to visit Darukhana for the second time, Shanti Ravi told me of a crackdown a few days before. A few huts, probably new ones, had been broken down, but the old ones looked safe, for the time being at least.

She is sanguine that her own neighbourhood will be secure. The local member of Parliament (MP) had come and assured the residents that they would be accommodated elsewhere when this land was taken over for 'development'. Grand plans were already being made, and once these plans were finalized, everyone from Darukhana would be given alternative accommodation, though he did not say where that would be—if past experience was any guide, it would be in the remote eastern suburbs, where they would be out of sight.

The problem is the land available is not contiguous—the ambitious plan to develop the area would require empty, unencumbered land, and not just the slum dwellers, but factories, warehouses, small businesses and clearing agents, who have functioned there for decades, would have to be forced out. In 2015, the Port Trust began that job in earnest.

In May of that year, officials of the Port Trust, accompanied by the police for security, walked into the Nazir Building in Ballard Estate and threw out the belongings, including furniture and computers, of the occupants. The Port Trust claimed that the lease had run out long ago and they wanted the premises back.

Factually and legally, it was right. But it was a far more complicated issue. Nazir Building had been leased out to a Jimmy Nazir in the 1930s for fifty years. Sometime in 1986, the lessee 'sold' the lease to a third party. The Port Trust did not recognize the transfer; instead, it sued both of them. The tenants, many of whom were holding on to subleases of doubtful legal status, were left in limbo; on the orders of the court, they began depositing the rent with the court and the 'buyer' of the lease kept collecting it, says Pervez Cooper, who had an office in the building since the 1980s. 'But she did not hand it over to the Trust.' This went on for three decades, till one day the Port Trust decided to take possession of the building—'We got one hour's notice'—and the tenants' belongings were simply moved on to the road. Decades-old businesses were simply wiped out.

Pervez laughs bitterly at the grand visions of the government. 'Burj Khalifa? By all means build those, but why at the cost of our livelihood and our lives?'

There are thousands of tenants like this, hanging in mid-air as original lessees who have sold out, migrated or died are not around, and the Port Trust does not recognize the new ones.

Cooper, like many others, tried to convince the Port Trust to take into account the changed circumstances—recognizing the transferred leases would have benefited tens of thousands of people. 'For years, the Port Trust wouldn't take any action against all those people who had illegally transferred their leases. It wouldn't even acknowledge something was wrong. Tenants who went to ask who they should pay the rent to were shooed away. Life just went on—we even hoped for proper, permanent tenancies.'

There was a legal complication too—the Port Trust is using the Public Premises (Eviction of Unauthorised Occupants) Act of 1971, a law that was originally devised to prevent government servants from taking over housing given to them as part of their jobs. 'That law does not apply to us—it is completely unfair,' says Cooper.

The Trust's website lists nearly 800 leaseholders and 2,005 'tenants', but the number of residents in these properties runs into lakhs. Rooms from as small as 200 square feet to small garages to large apartments and huge offices, warehouses and even iconic buildings like the Taj Mahal Hotel—are all 'owned' by the Port Trust, but leased out. Some bitter tenants claim that influential lessees managed to keep getting extensions of fifteen months at a time. 'This couldn't have happened without some greasing of palms,' says a tenant who did not want to be named.

'My grandfather had taken an entire floor in Madhav Bhavan, a building near Darukhana, in 1942,' says Shridhar Shenoy, who runs a small restaurant near Chhatrapati Shivaji Terminus. In those days of informal arrangements, various relatives came to Bombay from their villages, moved into the rooms, leaving a small portion for the Shenoys, where Shridhar, his wife and two daughters live. The upper floors too were occupied by tenants.

In the 1950s, the building's lease passed on to another buyer, but the Port Trust did not react then. Taxes and rent began mounting, and every now and then the Port Trust and the Bombay Municipal Corporation made demands on the tenants; till recently they collectively somehow managed to pay the lakhs of rupees in arrears. But doing that is no longer easy. The Port Trust does not recognize the new lessee, but at the same time has not been able to track down the original one (who, it turns out, died a long time ago). The tenants are caught in the middle. 'It is an unfair situation—we have to pay and there is no guarantee that if there is any resolution we will get to keep the place, even as tenants,' says Shenoy. 'We could be thrown out at any time,' adds his worried wife, Preeti.

While these problems are not new, the Port Trust has gone into overdrive to get hold of its properties, never mind if there are people living and working in them. This thrust is clearly linked to Gadkari's grandiose plans to overhaul the area, turning an old, rundown section of Mumbai into a glittering smart city by the sea.

'It's our land and naturally we want it back,' said Sanjay Bhatia, the chairman of the Port Trust. An affable IAS officer, who was brought in from the Navi Mumbai development agency, CIDCO, Bhatia understands the dilemma of the tenants but uses the legal argument: 'They don't pay market rents, and we lose money and rights. With the new development plans, we cannot afford to waste our own properties.'

As far as the slums are concerned, the situation has somewhat changed—at first the Trust did not acknowledge them, then, when the politicians got into the act, it promised them alternative accommodation, and finally suggested they would get housing somewhere close by instead of far away.

Then there is the problem of commercial tenants. The big warehouses and factories that hummed once are now lying shut. But the smaller establishments that sprung up around shipping activities—ship chandlers, cargo agents, but mainly scrap merchants—still function. Where will they go?

'We have been fighting our case for a long time, but it looks like we will be thrown out any day now,' says a pessimistic Zoeb Sahiwalla, a former president of the Darukhana Iron and Scrap Merchants Association. The Association has around 1,000 members, a few of them running agencies that are almost a century old.

'Many original tenants, now long gone, leased their premises out and there are further subleases. BPT says it will deal only with original tenants, but it is impossible to trace them. There are nearly 4,000 scrap dealers around and around two lakh workers will be affected if we are thrown out. Originally, the scrap dealers came here because the Port Trust wanted us—now they want to chuck us out.'

Sahiwalla says the Port Trust shows double standards in its approach to occupants—it goes after legitimate ones who pay rent but is wary about throwing out slum dwellers, who are illegal occupants, because there will be an uproar.

At the heart of it is land, the most valuable resource in Mumbai. It is not often that an enormous land parcel comes into the Mumbai land market. In the 1990s, over 600 acres became available in Central Mumbai after the great mill strike of 1982 devastated the textile industry. All manner of noble declarations were made that the mill land would be utilized for building not just apartment blocks and offices but also public amenities and 'affordable' housing for the thousands of mill workers who were thrown out of their jobs. The way it turned out was exactly the opposite—there are no parks or public amenities in the area but a lot of malls and high-rises; the workers were left high and dry.

In 2014, Nitin Gadkari set up a committee under a former Port Trust chairperson Rani Jadhav to outline the future of the Portlands; promises were made that the report would be ready in three months. It was never made public, and activists unearthed it and put it online. Some of its observations did not go down well with the government. The report recommends that 30 per cent of the land must be used for creating open spaces, public amenities and transport infrastructure, which would be anathema.

Apli Mumbai produced its own report—'A Citizens' Plan to Re-imagine Mumbai' where, again, there were renderings of beautiful promenades, day and night eateries, luxury yachts and nature parks, plus a 'Sanskriti corridor', which would be created around an old British-built fort in Sewri that otherwise lies neglected. Redevelopment, tourism hub, marinas—all the buzz words and phrases are present, but the intractable—and human—problem of how to deal with long-resident tenants still looms.

At a seminar organized by Apli Mumbai at the Indian Merchants' Chamber, Sanjay Bhatia acknowledged that all the stakeholders would have to be taken on board. These include not just those who are in occupation of Port Trust land, including slums and 'unauthorized occupants' but also the Trust's employees and pensioners, numbering a mammoth 35,000 people. 'There are many aspirations, ranging from public utilities such as gardens, to a waterfront, restaurants, public transportation hubs, hotels, Burj Khalifa, an international cruise terminal, water sports, etc.' There is another impediment, however—as things stand, the land use policy only allows for port-related activities; 'some changes will have to take place,' he said.

What these changes will be is what worries citizens' groups. Darryl D'Monte, the late journalist and environmental activist, who wrote extensively on how the city's mill lands were appropriated for constructing luxury towers and malls, says a bigger pattern is emerging to completely alter the city. 'The politicians are blinded by the notion of "development", but what they are planning isn't *vikas* (development) it is *vinash* (destruction).' Therein lies the nub, the heart of the problem of what Bombay was and what the policymakers along with businessmen and builders want to make Mumbai—a city that not just looks and feels different but also creates an entirely different ethos, one in which the more vulnerable are either hidden from sight or simply vanish into the darkness, unless they provide specific and useful services to the rich.

Central to the entire issue is the question of what to do with those who occupy Port Trust land. While slum dwellers may get alternative housing at distant places, and institutions such as oil companies and large corporations have the clout to get the best possible deal, it is the tenants who are going to get hit the hardest.

Milind Deora, the former MP in whose constituency most of this land falls, says he had almost worked out a solution to this long pending issue. 'The Mumbai Port Trust is one of the three in India which holds so much property. When I was the minister of State for shipping, I had proposed that the Port Trust regularize tenants with some kind of one-time payment and a reasonable rent. We are talking of lakhs of people here. But our government got voted out and the proposal was forgotten. Now they are talking of eviction and huge rent increases.'

It's going to be a long and tediously slow process, but the direction has been set—the ugly old must give way to the shimmering new, whatever the human cost.

Shanti Ravi, however, will not give up without a fight. It is a losing battle, and she probably knows that, but she—for herself and for her fellow slum dwellers—will ensure that they get a fair deal. After decades of being useful to the port's activities and leading a difficult existence with no support from any government agency, they are going to make sure that they get what is their due—a decent home to live in.

9

THE RED LIGHT FADES

'The term Kamathipura is commonly used to denote the prostitutes' quarter, and the same may be said for Grant Road and Shuklaji Street, both of which names connote a good deal more than geography.'

What Samuel T. Sheppard wrote in his book *Bombay Place-Names and Street-Names* in 1917 is still valid. The book is a compendium of the origins of various streets and bylanes of the city at that time. The city stopped at Parel, so most names are of the European quarter and the native towns. Clearly, Kamathipura existed at the time, and was already a thriving place with an unsavoury reputation.

Sheppard tells us that it was where the Kamatis, labourers from the Nizam's dominion in the Deccan, had arrived in the late eighteenth century and settled down: 'It contains no building of interest and is occupied, for the most part, by the lowest classes of the population.'[1] The lowest classes were migrant labourers, but also prostitutes, as sex workers were known.

A century later, the names Kamathipura and Shuklaji Street still evoke the same response, though they have been transformed beyond recognition. Someone with a sly look will still sidle up to an outsider entering Kamathipura, but the energy and buzz has gone. The visitor is more likely to come across housewives shopping for vegetables than anyone from the sex trade. Many of the old brothels have been converted to small-scale industrial units, engaged in everything from jewellery-making to embroidering saris or even assembling engine parts. As dusk settles, a few women looking for customers can be seen venturing out, but they are probably the last of the very few left here—the sex trade as it was in this sprawling precinct, which included notorious streets like Falkland Road, Foras Road and Pila House (a corruption of Pleasure House), seems to have vanished into thin air. Kamathipura has been 'gentrified', not by coffee shops but by the most dreaded marauding beast of them all—real estate prices.

'It is completely wrong to say that Kamathipura is the home of prostitutes. Those days are gone. This is a middle-class area, we are middle-class, respectable people,' said Rajendra Satla, the general secretary of the Kamathipura Landlords' Welfare Association, when I met him in the area.

Satla, who owns scores of properties here, has been trying to 'redevelop' the precinct, turning the low-rise, ramshackle tenements into brand new towers for middle-class buyers. 'Look at the location, close to everything.' There are around 500 landlords who own over 8,000 properties, he says.

More than the commercial and profit-making prospects of such an enterprise, this is also an attempt—if only a long simmering hope—to make the area 'respectable'. There are no ATMs or coffee shops here, that would be too much to expect, but like everyone else in the city, the residents and landlords of Kamathipura have aspirations of upward social mobility. The economic or the social profile of the place is no longer what it was. As a venue of entertainment and recreation for the working classes of the city, it has outlived its utility; Mumbai is now changing, and has no need for such sleazy places; besides, land is expensive. Kamathipura is well located and builders have their eye on it. The denizens of the area too hope they will be included in any development plans.

I am here to see a presentation on the redevelopment plans for Kamathipura to the local public. A minister has been invited to get the government's blessings and to add some credibility to the initiative—the public here is sceptical of such ambitious plans, which surface every now and then, make headlines and then sink into oblivion—no one has faith in the landlords, the builders or the government.

In March 2016, a *Hindustan Times* report declared, 'Kamathipura all set for a facelift, to become a plush township'. Years later, nothing had changed. The press had reported that there was excitement among landlords, the thousands of tenants, and most of all developers, who saw mouth-watering prospects in the thirty-nine acres of land that would become available.

The same scheme has been resurrected and will now be presented to the new minister.

The small hall in the 10th lane is filling up with local residents. I am here on the invitation of Amin Patel, a much-liked and respected state-level legislator, who represents the area. 'Come along, and see how the city is changing,' he had told me.

Though redevelopment is not new in the city, I was intrigued by the prospect of an entire neighbourhood being transformed, where the old one disappeared and an entirely new-looking landscape came up in its place. In Kamathipura's case, it would not merely be a physical change—towers where low-rise structures once stood—but a profound social one. The very name had for long signified something unsavoury and sleazy. Could this century-old perception be changed by altering its landscape? And what did the locals think about it?

I entered Kamathipura from the Bellasis Road side, at the corner where Alexandra Cinema once stood. The small theatre, one of the oldest in Mumbai, was a big draw for Kamathipura's residents and showed old semi-porn and English films, the titles translated in the most inventive fashion. Alexandra's titles always raised a big laugh in the city; they would now be called memes: *Blow Hot Blow Cold* became *Kabhi Naram, Kabhi Garam*, and a Laurel and Hardy film was called *Ullu ke Paththe*. The cinema fell on bad times, then in 2017, it quietly turned into a mosque and Islamic centre run by a trust; the front has been shuttered to discourage anyone peeping in.

Within a minute of my entering Kamathipura, a young man comes up to me and begins mumbling something—the undertone is difficult to catch in a crowded street, but 'chokri' catches my ear. The best course is to keep moving; after a few steps, he drops back. Clearly, I am not worth investing time in.

This ritual continues for a little while more as others too approach and then withdraw. It is still daylight, but a few women, looking hopeful, are already out on the streets. The majority of the people bustling about, however, are shoppers, vendors and others going about their business. Many of the women are in burqas, quite a few in saris worn in the Gujarati style. A few are with children; there are any number of schools in the area, including a few schools run by missionaries and very sought after by parents in the neighbourhood. An English-medium school is a ticket to a good future. Parents everywhere have the same aspirations, and many children have gone on to study further and leave the area.

The streets to the venue of the meeting have posters and buntings announcing the event. Directions to the venue are swiftly provided—no one gives me a second glance.

The hall itself is a smallish affair, with a capacity of about 250 people. A few chairs are taken, mainly by middle-aged folks—these are not the kinds in white-collar jobs. The first two rows are reserved for the VIPs who will come—the minister and his entourage and some local movers and shakers. Someone is fiddling with the sound system.

People keep trickling in, and I can hear hushed whispers about the latest whereabouts of the minister. Indians have vast reservoirs of patience and don't get restless while waiting, especially for a Very Important Person. We are ten minutes behind the scheduled timing of the meeting, so no one looks particularly bothered. The smarter ones know they must come later. The humidity is getting oppressive by now.

By and by the hall fills up, the women on one side, the men on the other. In the third row, two men have occupied the chairs on my right. After a while I turn to them and ask, 'So what do you think the minister is going to say today?' They take stock of me, for perhaps ten seconds, and one of them replies: 'We have been hearing all this for years. He will come, promise quick action, declare he and his government are different, get some applause, and leave.' The rest is left unsaid, but I can hear it: 'And things will remain the same.'

A volunteer approaches me with an enquiring look. 'I am a guest of Shri Patel,' I say. He immediately requests me to shift to the front row—clearly, I am a VIP by association on this occasion.

Shortly after, the minister arrives. Jitendra Awhad is a well-known face, an aggressive spokesman of the Nationalist Congress Party on television and is now handling the housing portfolio. He has a casual swagger, but like many other politicians, has the ability to connect with the general public, an invaluable skill in a local representative. He sits down next to me, and we are introduced. The word 'press' seems to please him. 'I am planning a book on Mumbai's slums,' he tells me.

The speeches begin, and Sailesh Mahimtura of the eponymous architectural firm steps forward to make a presentation of what could be in store for the precinct if all things go well.

Mahimtura's slides begin with a brief history of the place and then a photograph offers an aerial view of Kamathipura and its environs at night. The lit-up streets appear well laid out among low-lying structures, many of them triangular, hugging the street corners, with majestic towers in the far background, their lights twinkling, as if to say, we are the future. It's the vista of any modern metropolis anywhere in the world.

Soon we get to see the harsh reality in the daytime—buildings looking as if they will fall down any minute, the corroded insides and the façades with patchwork and wooden doorframes that should have been discarded years ago. This is the life of thousands of people, which they have no choice but to stoically accept.

So, when the slides move from these grim images to what is on offer, it is a sense of relief. In English, the new slides list these coming attractions: mini cricket ground, clubs with gyms, theme park, jogging track, amphitheatre, stilt parking, good quality elevators, and buildings with good quality fittings, tiles, plumbing and switches and wiring, crucial in old buildings where a jumble of wires can often cause electrical fires. It all seems so unreal and distant—and, having seen all this before, the locals can testify that it is unreal and distant.

A jumble of figures and calculations follow, all in very fine print, where a key operative point is at the very end—the developer will make a profit of over ₹2,000 crores, or roughly $300 million. All this provided the whole project is given for development to one group, which will then raze all the buildings and work on the open land.

Then comes the part where dreams are woven, with a texture so fine that it has the ability to mesmerize. The 'Concept Design' part of the presentation begins with a top shot of the entire area, probably taken from Google Maps. It offers a remote and detached overview, which shows neither grime nor the messy reality of the ground. The next slide, in soothing green, replaces that with a bird's-eye view of buildings laid out in a spacious and well-planned way, surrounded by gardens, parks, playgrounds and tree-lined streets. And next to this densely packed cluster of buildings, presumably tall ones to fit in all the residents, a vast, open space, also in green, with the legend 'Sale Area' printed on it. It's all there, transparent, for anyone to see that almost half of Kamathipura will be sold to buyers in the open market. The old-time residents will get 500-square-foot apartments, highly subsidized, the landlords will be paid off, and the profits will come from the open sale.

Going by the plans and the layouts, the living spaces designed for the residents are something most may never even have dreamed of, much less experienced—two bedrooms of about 90 square feet each, two ensuite toilets, a kitchen with a counter and a sink, a living room with a dining room attached—it's the kind of flat any young couple starting out would love, if they could afford it. The three-dimensional model, created on a computer, is even more dazzling—beds, cupboards, large flat-screen televisions; it is an unimaginable luxury for those currently living in Kamathipura, where many people live in a cramped 180 square feet area.

The buildings, especially on the upper floors, will have generous views of the city, and at the street level—as per the architects' vision—will be broad pavements to walk dogs, shops selling Prada and Louis Vuitton, and hatted white women in shorts, cycling. At this point, the presentation ends, and the stardust in the air settles down.

It is now time for the minister to go up and address the crowds; Awhad is a man of the people; he says he himself came from a humble background and knows this area well. Kamathipura is world famous, he said, though not always for the right reasons—this redevelopment will remove the notoriety of the past.

'Earlier governments made promises, but nothing happened. But we are different—within a week you will hear from my officials (pointing to two senior bureaucrats who have come along with him) and they will work out the details. Soon the work will begin,' he assures everyone. There is mild applause when he finishes, the locals presumably jaded by promises over the years. The landlords seem somewhat more enthused—'With the government's encouragement and backing now, things can finally start moving forward,' one of them tells me and his colleagues. 'Kamathipura can look forward to a complete makeover.'

The landlords and builders are relying on a scheme of the Maharashtra government introduced in 2014 for 'cluster redevelopment', which allows for an entire precinct to be completely razed and then rebuilt, with all the locals rehabilitated in buildings in situ; this releases a lot of vacant land that can be commercially exploited for an open market sale. The builder—usually just the one—can then make enough profit to compensate for the funds spent on the free housing. Naturally, to maximize profits, builders will build shoddy structures for the residents and shiny new ones for sale. Care will also be taken to ensure that the ugly structures are not in the eyeline of the other buildings, so a buyer who has spent top rupee for a glorious vista from his balcony doesn't have to see his neighbours, who have lived on the same land for generations.

On paper, the policy sounded like a win-win, as politicians are wont to say; it was, the government explained, a fine example of 'public-private partnership', where everyone cooperated and got something out of it. But it was not so easy—builders had to get the approval of 70 per cent of the landlords and residents to move out and then demolish all the old, low-rise buildings. In the meantime, the residents would have to be given alternative accommodation or rent to stay elsewhere. In a widespread area with hundreds of landlords and thousands of tenants, this was an impossible task—landlords got greedy and old residents remained suspicious of builders, not without reason, and a few proposals that were made never took off. Till one day, a new proposal was made, and it looked promising. The market perked up with interest.

Bhendi Bazaar is a typical example of an old 'native town', one of the many neighbourhoods that came up outside the European quarter and which eventually became ghettoized by different communities. The one furthest east and closest to the port became populated by Muslims of different denominations and from different regions—Gujarat, Konkan, the hinterland of what is now Maharashtra and even as far afield as the northern provinces. It is the Gujaratis who dominated the area—Khojas, Bohras, Memons and many others, all of whom swiftly carved out streets and lanes for their own communities. Since both the harbour to the east and the bazaars to the south were close by, all those who worked or traded with them found this area very convenient.

Others, such as Iranians, Turks, Armenians and even the Chinese, also lived and mingled there in the bazaars. The origins of the name Bhendi Bazaar are ambiguous—some say the area had many okra plants (known as bhindi in Hindi) while others claim it stands for 'behind the bazaar' where it is located. Either way, it is a catchy name that has come to stand for many things, chiefly the Chor Bazaar (Thieves' Market), where fake antiques, reconstructed furniture and car parts are sold in small kiosks; and the food stalls that spring up during Ramzan, pulling customers from all over the city. The area is also dominated by the Bohra community, known among locals as the Mohalla, which immediately brands it as a closed, conservative and backward ghetto. The narrow lanes, the old buildings, many of them looking as if they will collapse at any moment (and some of them do) and tiny, dark rooms that often leak from above are characteristic of the place. But very few people move out because their businesses are within walking distance.

The high priest of the Bohra community, the Syedna, holds great sway over its members worldwide and has a substantial following in the Mohalla. Concerned with the living conditions of his fellow Bohris, he created a new body, the

Saifee Burhani Upliftment Trust (SBUT), under which new towers would be built and every resident, including the few non-Bohris who lived there, would be given a free apartment. Till the towers were fully constructed, the tenants would be given temporary one-room apartments to live in, which were not just new, but also airy, full of light, and had amenities such as a proper kitchen, toilets and even washing machines. The area SBUT wanted to redevelop was over sixteen acres, over which 250 structures were spread; if all the residents were shifted to skyscrapers, it would leave enough free space for four more sixty-storey plus towers for sale in the free market. The sketches showed attractive, tree-lined boulevards and dazzling shopfronts selling the finest brands like Bose and Cantabil. For an area without even a coffee shop or pizza chain outlet, it sounded very attractive, if somewhat ambitious. It was to be a ₹40 billion project, free to the locals, the money to be recovered from the sale of the other apartments. The Trust's ultimate ambition was to 'uplift' the 3,200 families who lived in tiny apartments in the Bhendi Bazaar precinct. The cluster scheme presented a good opportunity, and consultants and architects were brought in to design it.

The key reason why the scheme took off in Bhendi Bazaar and not elsewhere was the clout of the Syedna—as the supreme authority, there were not many who would disobey him. While a few held out—they were dissatisfied with the documentary assurances given—and many landlords upped their demands for compensation, many families did move out, and some were so taken by their temporary flats that they did not want to move back. The state government gave the project its full support, with files moving quickly and approvals coming fast. Even with all these advantages, the scale of the project was overwhelming—it inevitably slowed down, hampered by not just the logistics but also the changing market conditions sometime after 2016, when the expenditure mounted. The real estate market crashed, with buyers showing no interest in new buildings anywhere in the city. By 2019, one forty-one-storey tower had been built for the old residents, and 600 or so families moved in of the 3,200 families who were to be eventually rehoused.

Urban planning experts pointed out that it would raise density in the area dramatically, and this would put pressure on the infrastructure, but the new owners did not seem to mind that. For most, it was an upgrade of their lives—the flats were tiled, and were sunny and airy with running water and a great view; there was greenery on the roof of the podium, fast elevators, parking, and best of all, it hadn't cost the old residents a penny.

The Bhendi Bazaar project inspired the Kamathipura landlords—'It will be a model for us,' Satla said. He is convinced that the old Kamathipura is on its way out and a completely new one is imminent, and everyone will benefit. Whether the new landlords of Kamathipura will be as benevolent to their tenants is highly debatable; property owners and builders tend to be a calculating lot and their relationship with their old tenants is vastly different from that of the Syedna with his followers.

In any case, upgrading Kamathipura is a remote prospect. Raising the funds, getting builders interested, rallying the support of thousands of tenants and landlords and then attracting investors and buyers, to say nothing of obtaining government permission is a long-term exercise, and for years, the efforts of the locals have not paid off. They keep trying, of course, but nothing has moved.

On its own steam, however, Kamathipura has completely transmuted, even if the look is the same as before. It is no longer the centre of the city's sex trade but a thriving commercial area where small units hum all day and night long. Women can still be found, but most of the 'cages', where garishly made-up women stood under coloured lights at night, trying to look provocative in just a blouse and a petticoat, are long gone. The stark image of women standing next to grilled windows, beckoning customers, does not define Kamathipura anymore.

These cages at one time were notorious the world over—various documentaries were made, shot deep inside Kamathipura's lanes. Mary Ellen Mark's photo essay on 'Falkland Road', also in the same vicinity, showed the sad world of the red-light areas of Grant Road. 'Madam, cage girls are the lowest—they only charge ₹2.' (Seven rupees equalled one dollar) reads one of the captions, and it was true, at least in the 1970s. These women were past their best, but still had some capacity to earn. The madam, or 'gharwali' as she was called locally, usually a retired prostitute, was the owner-protector of the girls under her wing, responsible for their well-being but mostly for their earnings, which they had to hand over to her. She dealt with the outside world, mainly the police.

The women, many of them from Nepal, had been brought there by force and sometimes by commercial incentives given to their families, their resistance overcome by brute force and violence. They were then made to work in the harshest of conditions, making money not just for themselves but for their pimps, their brothel madams—often former prostitutes—and to send back home. Escape was impossible—they were not called cages for nothing.

Friends from India and abroad who came to Bombay in the 1980s and onwards often asked to be taken there. The fascination lay in its infamy—the place was a draw, a forbidden zone that no 'respectable' Bombay person visited. The two bus routes—66 and 69—passing through there towards South Bombay brought many school children headed home in the afternoon—they were told to avert their eyes.

But the visitor to the city had no such compulsions. He wanted to go there, and go there at night, when the place was humming. A few wanted to try out what was on offer.

During my many forays there, I gradually began to realize that the 'sex economy' was not limited to the workers, madams or pimps.

The landlord gained from letting out the poorly designed rooms that served as the brothel—they were narrow, constricted rooms, with beds on either side, sealed off by a curtain, with just enough room to squeeze in, finish the job and push off. The idea was to have quick turnover. A visiting friend, fired up about tasting all of Bombay's flavours, mustered up the courage to go forth but returned without success, appalled by the narrow corridor, the curtained-off bed and the quick negotiation, both of the commercial part and the actual deed. He came out crestfallen, depressed by the cold, impersonal nature of the transaction and affected by the living conditions.

The brothels were poorly ventilated, badly lit and unsanitary to dangerous levels. The girls' quarters were at the low-rise mezzanine level, accessible by stairs, where customers were not allowed. All of it was a mood downer, guaranteed to put off all erotic thoughts, a far cry from the delicate descriptions of sex in the Kama Sutra. But for the property owner, who could not get any better clients, it was a money earner.

Then there were the restaurants, the bars and even the paanwallahs, selling cigarettes and sometimes drugs—on one such visit, one of them bridled at being asked directions. Nobody wanted to be seen as associated with this disreputable trade, even if they benefited from it.

Above all were the policemen—an operation like this could not function without the patronage of local politicians and the law-and-order machinery. The state turned a blind eye to this sore and ugly spot in the middle of the city, but in return demanded a cut in it to keep the wheels lubricated and the machinery turning.

Selling sex was not illegal—soliciting and acting as a middleman was. The actual law, with the ironic name of SITA (Suppression of Immoral Traffic Act) was rarely applied, but it existed and was occasionally used and misused, if only to show that the state would not countenance such illicit and immoral activity.

It was not always like this. In the early days of Kamathipura, the British Raj viewed it somewhat more indulgently. Bombay was a prominent port city, on the route to and from the west, with ships from both Hong Kong on the one side and Europe on the other stopping over, many of them carrying British sailors. The docks were close by, and the Raj administration realized these sailors needed an outlet for rest and relaxation, and the lanes and bylanes of Kamathipura were the perfect place. Kamathipura was also near the bazaars, which were to the north, and the textile mill area, which was to its south-west.

By and by, European women, most of them from the continent, and others from Britain and even the Middle East, began settling down in Kamathipura. The opening of the Suez Canal had made travel to Bombay easier, and among the travellers were women too. A small enclave emerged, which is still identified as 'Safed Galli', White Lane, where the white-skinned women took up residence. Many of them were Jews. There is an Arab Galli too, and a Chini Galli, but it is not known if these were specifically where women from the Arab world or from the Far East lived. The readymade market in the vicinity made Kamathipura a good place to set up shop, as were the cheap rents.

The administration usually deported the British women but ignored the rest of the white ones. Legalized prostitution had been banned in the UK in the late 1880s, but the attitude in the colonies was different. Occasionally in Bombay there was a wave of outrage, and some efforts were made to stop public solicitation, but within the confines of the Kamathipura-Falkland Road axis, the business kept growing.

Kamathipura was not the only place of 'vice' in the city. Prostitutes were present in large numbers in the larger Girgaum-Thakurdwar area, and along the Muslim quarter, now known as Mohammed Ali Road, opium dens and dancing girls were a big draw. S.M. Edwardes, a former police commissioner and indefatigable chronicler of the city, wrote a regular column in *The Times of India* under the title, 'By-ways of Bombay', which described a 'Kasumba den', where 'Bombay and Gujarat Mohammedans, men from Hindustan and one or two Dawoodi Bohras', who were regular customers, paid a price for a glass of weak opium water, and a bit more for the less diluted version; after his quota, the drinker called for a 'kharbanjan', mainly sweets and sago-grain, otherwise known as 'khir'. This removed the bitter aftertaste. After which a more poetic and merry opium-drinker would recite flowery shayari to the others.[2]

For the real thing of course the well-heeled could go to the house of Nur Jehan, the singing queen, who would chant the 'subtle melodies of Hindustan and even English roundelays for the delectation of the English guests; We had remarked her delicate hands, the great dark eyes, the dainty profile, the little ivory feet and above all the gentle profile and the courteous bearing.' This was all in the 1910–1912 period, as the city prospered, and in the post-plague period, as the numbers of migrants grew.

For the more respectable citizens, there were other entertainment centres—theatre houses and gradually, cinemas. The Europeans and the Indian gentry went to Capitol, Edward and Alfred, the rest to less grand venues in the Grant Road belt, located close to the native towns, the working-class neighbourhoods and the red-light areas.

Kamathipura continued to grow and thrive, unconcerned with the debates around it. Women were being brought in from the neighbouring regions of Bombay and from further south, in the Deccan. And the issue continued to exercise the minds of legislators, the police and citizens.

In 1930, the Bombay Council discussed the Prostitution Bill during which the government declared that many brothels would be abolished, a claim that the other members scoffed at for its improbability. Miss Ida Dickinson, listed several advantages of shutting down brothels, including, 'the end of the glaring advertisement of vice which is a potent factor in the lowering of all standards of decency, and the reduction of the incidence of venereal diseases.' She got an ovation for her address.

Two years later, the Bombay Vigilance Association felt compelled to tell the press that its campaign had been misunderstood. The Association, formed in 1926, stood for 'public decency, the maintenance of a high standard of morals for both men and women, and the edutain of public opinion against the toleration of a vice area in the city,' reported *The Bombay Chronicle*, under the headline 'Bombay Vigilance Association Justifies Itself, Is Opposed to Segregated Areas and Aims at Complete Extermination of Brothels'.

The Association regularly issued leaflets to educate the public and lobbied with the authorities, but its efforts do not seem to have changed anything. All the pieties and vigilance did not work, and the business only grew. It had a demand and moreover too many livelihoods were dependent on it. Nor were the police able to clamp down on trafficking, despite regular raids and arrests.

'Living on Married Girl's Earnings' was the headline of a small news item in *The Times of India* in 1932, which reported how a mill worker was arrested for having 'enticed' a seventeen-year-old girl, married her and forced her to do sex work in a rented room in the '14th lane in Kamathipura. He then lived off her earnings. He was charged with both offences, 'procuring a minor girl' and forcing her to be a prostitute. Minors being brought into the area was and remained an endemic problem.

But this also meant that Kamathipura and the areas around it became increasingly isolated, with municipal services barely reaching there. Sanitation, hygiene and even ventilation were missing, the workers suffered from severe health conditions and criminal activity increased. Street crime was rare—no one wanted customers to be scared away—but trafficking was increasing, with a whole supply chain bringing women from other parts of India and even outside.

The 'safed' women gradually began decreasing in number, and by the 1940s, had almost disappeared. In time, the traffickers discovered another source, Nepal. Travel between the two countries was visa-free, and many Nepali men were already employed in Bombay, mainly as security guards, or more accurately, 'watchmen'. Taking advantage of the open and relatively unsecured borders, and with the help of corruption and coercion, an entire supply chain sprang up.

Off and on, horrific stories of cruelty and violence would surface, but Kamathipura was a blind spot of sorts, and the traffic, barring occasional efforts to bust it, went unchecked. The criminal gangs involved in it were too resourceful and too powerful. A cop familiar with the area once told me that he had been surprised at the efficiency of the operation. 'It's a business. At the source, there are networks which scour for women, pay the middlemen and occasionally the families, bring the women down to Bombay mainly by road all the way and then sell them off. Then they break down her resistance, by violence if necessary, and get her started. They have made an investment and they intend to recover it. Police interventions once in a while do not matter.'

This business generated big money. The initial 'investment' of paying off the middleman (and often, middle-woman) in Nepal was just the beginning—there were transportation and other costs, mainly of greasing various palms along the way, all of which added up. They also took the huge risks involved in the process and had to deliver the girl to the eventual buyer. The profits had to be good to make it worthwhile undertaking the venture.

By the 1970s, Nepali women were visible all over the red-light area, though other regions were affected too. Rates for one session went as low as ₹2, climbing up to ₹10, but this was for publicly available fare. According to legend, for higher paying customers, much more exclusive and expensive deals were available. On one occasion during recent research, an old-time pimp, obviously fallen on bad days, recalled how the street had been agog in the 1990s when a woman would allegedly be sent to a VVIP for '₹1 lakh for the whole night'.

Kantibhai—as he called himself—seated on a cot at the end of his lane in the heart of Kamathipura, said, '*Sab badal gaya hai. Woh din bhi kya din the* (Everything has changed. Those were indeed the days),' with a sigh of nostalgia. When I met him in 2018, Kantibhai looked as if he was in his late seventies but, as he informed me, was only sixty-four or sixty-five. He now tends to a local temple, which began life as a few painted tiles on a wall but has now morphed into a small, cemented canopy with an idol, a few framed photos and a collection box, in which passers-by put coins and notes. 'All the money goes to feed cows, and if we have good collections, I give it to an NGO here that teaches local children,' he says, pre-empting my curiosity and possible scepticism. Kantibhai has lived in Kamathipura his entire life.

'*Bachpan mein mujhe dar lagta tha, par ahiste ahiste, main hoshiyar ho gaya* (When I was young, I used to be afraid, but then I slowly learnt, became street smart).' He went to school for a few years and then apprenticed with a local pimp. 'Everything available—*aadmi, aurat, chokra, chokri, hijda, jawan, buddhhi bhi* (men, women, boys, girls, eunuchs, young men, even old women).' Each taste was catered for and here, he gets into gossipy mode, recounting stories of the perversions of some well-known names in the entertainment business. It's clearly all hearsay, much of the gossip known beyond these borders.

Kantibhai is not without moral standards. He finds homosexuality repulsive and immoral. '*Chokra* (boy) …' he shakes his head, '*Chi-chi. Paap hai* (It's a sin).' His boss, and later he, never offered male prostitutes, though he had no compunctions about pimping women.

Kantibhai went out on his own when his boss fell ill and became a success. The girls used to like him, he says, because he played fair and did not get them unsavoury customers. But, '*Gharwali ko bhi khush rakhna tha* (The madams too had to be kept happy),' so targets had to be met.

He quit the business a long time ago, became a 'social worker', an omnibus term that covers everything from a busybody to a ground-level operator for politicians to genuine social work with an NGO. He has regrets and some complaints, but not about his chosen profession—'Things were different—the women were mainly Nepali, and they were easy to manage. Now a lot of Bangladeshi women have come, some brought by their own menfolk. Very aggressive. *Haath uthate hain logon par* (They hit people).'

The place has changed drastically too—'*Abhi ladkilog ka dhandha nahin idhar* (There are no longer any girls here).' Small businesses, iron workshops, and, most worryingly, he says, real estate sharks have moved in, lured by the possibility of huge profits when redevelopment finally comes. For the businessmen, cheaply priced small rooms work well to set up, say, a jewellery assembling unit or a zari-making workshop. The madams have been bought out, the women have gone home or shifted, mainly to the distant suburbs, near the entry points to the city where truck drivers take a break. And of course, technology has altered how business is done—there are scores, if not hundreds, of solicitation offers on the internet, in easy-to-understand codes—'escort', 'for intimate friendship', 'to show good time' and the hardy perennial, 'massage at home'. WhatsApp plays a crucial role in communication and coordination. The streetwalker is long gone, in its place we have the tech-savvy, young, professional woman.

In Kamathipura, changes were coming as far back as the 1980s, when many voluntary organizations were moving into the area, mainly to spread the message of a deadly virus that would decimate scores of sex workers and damage the entire 'business'. AIDS was rapidly spreading throughout the world, and unprotected sex was one of the biggest causes.

Prostitutes began dying in significant numbers—customers refused to wear condoms, and the sex workers could not insist on it, not with their gharwalis dismissing their concerns. The idea that the virus could cause death was not yet widely known at the time. Nor was the disease limited to the red-light areas. Many from the higher economic strata were affected too, but the sex-worker was the most vulnerable because of multiple sexual encounters, often on the same night.

Doctors, the civic authorities and NGOs began awareness campaigns, only to be met with scepticism and hostility. Alarming statistics and warnings about the dangers of unprotected sex made no difference. Ignorance and the commercial imperative made it impossible to get through to both the sex workers and their managers. Plus, there was a stigma attached to the disease.

The relentless march of the disease finally made everyone realize that this was a deadly affair, which, among other things, would also be bad for business. NGOs were distributing free condoms, and that began to finally pay off. The sex workers themselves formed organizations that would talk to the community and make them understand the grave dangers confronting them.

In 2001, several years after AIDS had already hit not just the red-light area but also the wider community, UNAIDS released a report, titled 'India: HIV and AIDS-related Discrimination, Stigmatization and Denial',[3] which found not just ignorance but deep prejudice against any AIDS patient. Families, friends, employers, all simply distanced themselves from anyone with the virus; the most shocking part was how doctors and medical staff dealt with it.

The report quoted a surgeon as saying a young doctor had recommended that a patient desperately needing surgery (for an unrelated ailment) should be discharged because he had tested positive. A woman, who was not told her bridegroom had been diagnosed with HIV, and had herself become HIV positive, said her in-laws did not want her in their home and her sister and family too were hostile. By then, a treatment for AIDS had been discovered and was in use, and many of those who were HIV-positive were leading normal lives. But the word still caused dread and fear.

In the 1990s, the vice business in Kamathipura was going strong, but subterranean changes were taking place. AIDS, growing worldwide awareness, campaigns by NGOs and, less noticed, changing land economics in Bombay collectively impacted Kamathipura and its environs. The closure of the mills and the fall in the numbers of textile mill workers had reduced the potential customer base.

To the women of Kamathipura, this change was slow in coming. Their lives continued as before. An Emmy award-winning CBC documentary, *Selling the Innocents*, made in 1997, took viewers inside the brothels, with their narrow corridors and curtained rabbit warrens where the women practiced their trade. The film spoke about how women were often raped if they resisted joining the business and were told they had to pay off the cost incurred in procuring them—this could go on for up to ten years. The most unnerving part of this trade was the selling of children, who were brought to Bombay to be 'married', often to much older men.

Ruchira Gupta, who produced the film, said it took her some time to gain the confidence of the locals, especially the influential madams, before they would allow her in. 'A local politician Vinod Gupta was very helpful, and the madams too, once they realized we were supportive, helped us,' she remembers. In the film Gupta says the situation could change for the better if the government supported NGOs who were trying to rescue the girls. Clearly, that support was not forthcoming.

Gupta then launched her own NGO, Apne Aap, making it her mission to fight sex-trafficking and provide education, job skills, and legal help to women not just in Mumbai but also in the smaller centres from where the women were brought.

Kamathipura has come a long way since then. The sex trade looks tired and jaded, and brothels have given way to workshops. By day, it looks like any other neighbourhood, bustling with shoppers and workers. At night, it is a pale shadow of its old self. This is not a place one can romanticize about; the old was wretched and foul, but closely linked with the city—there is no use pretending it did not exist. The new has not yet come. When it does, it can only be hoped that it is not yet another soulless projection of the Shanghai fantasies of policymakers and architects or completely ignores its history. Way before the brothels came, this is where the builders of Bombay came and lived and worked to give shape to the buildings we consider our legacy. The sex workers were forcibly brought here, but they too remain a part of this legacy. The future Mumbai can never forget that.

10

THE GLITTERING CITY

On a hot summer's afternoon, a chilled drink is always welcome, and this is the first thing offered to us as we get down from the car. The server, in a dark suit, smilingly emerges from under a canopy, the entrance to an under-construction building, looking out of place around workers in hard hats and stained clothes. If he is uncomfortable, he doesn't show it.

He offers us two champagne flutes filled with cold, sparkling apple juice. A valet quickly materializes to drive the car off to park it. Two young executives are waiting to escort us into an air-conditioned lobby, where we are once again offered coconut water and cold towels by a liveried waiter.

A model of the building under construction, encased in glass, stands in one corner. A young woman stands behind the reception.

We are led to the seating area and settle down on a plush sofa—there is a bookshelf behind us, and on the facing wall hangs a gilded photo frame, empty except for the words 'A Masterpiece by PABLO PICASSO—Unveiling soon' on it. The lobby will eventually display the only Picasso painting in India, said an executive. 'Which one?' I ask. The response: 'I don't really know, only management does, but apparently it has been bought. It will hang in the lobby.'

While we sip our drinks, the executives start their sales talk. The building under construction is only for a chosen few; just thirty-odd apartments, on a plot that is a bit less than an acre. Some buyers are buying duplexes, two flats on consecutive floors joined internally by a staircase; for some reason, it is always pronounced in real estate circles as 'duplets'. The 'floor plate' of each apartment is 4,000 square feet.

'This area is very exclusive, very rarefied. There has not been a new apartment block here for sale in the last nearly twenty years, though the famous home of a tycoon came up a few metres ahead; but that multi-storeyed building was for his own family,' the executive drones on, experienced with his practiced sales patter. Only a chosen few will live here, and we could be among them—we are here because our names came up in a database of those who were fit enough to be invited to see the property. 'We don't want anybody and everybody who can afford these apartments; it is important to be selective. They should be familiar with living in South

Bombay; not someone from Malad or some such distant suburb,' he says.

Onwards to see the actual apartments. Though the building is not fully ready, one show-flat has been made to demonstrate what a good, well-appointed apartment could look like.

We don safety helmets and go up in the construction cage. The building was constructed in record time, with a new technology involving lots of steel, upping the cost of construction. This being a neighbourhood with rich and influential citizens, care was taken not to disturb them—no construction on Sundays, half a day on Saturdays. In the rest of the city, these strict rules are rarely followed.

That didn't prevent some neighbours from selling their apartments and moving out. The noise and the dust had disturbed many in the neighbourhood; and most critically, the view of the sea would be blocked by this huge tower.

Couldn't the same one day happen to the residents of this new building, I wanted to know. 'Not really,' comes the reply. No one will get permission to build a tower near it. The builder—who happens to be a prominent politician—gave some land to the municipal corporation elsewhere, as compensation. The implication of this is a bit mystifying, but whatever it is, for the future residents of this building, the view of the setting sun and the sea in the distance will always be available.

On the twenty-seventh floor we encase our footwear in plastic booties to ensure that our shoes do not scratch the expensive marble flooring. Two golden elevators will bring residents and guests to a floor. 'This landing outside the elevator is for your exclusive use. You can put plants, paintings, etc. It is included in your square footage.' What this means is that the buyer will have to pay for common areas, which are not built up, adding to the overall price.

We then walk into the pages of a glossy design magazine, where everything looks expensive and perfectly placed; this is not a lived-in space, but carefully curated to impress a potential buyer who can now imagine and dream of what living here could be like. A shining piano stands on one side, a seating arrangement is on the other, all facing a spectacular view of the city. In the distance is the sea, shimmering in the mid-day sun. Not the slightest sound filters inside—the expensive and imported double glazing on the windows ensures that. Below, the dinky cars and tiny figures—the little people—can be seen moving. 'It is far away from the rest of the city,' says an executive. In crowded Mumbai, to be away from the rest of the rabble, literally far above it, is much desired. With tall buildings coming up all over the city, it is a dream within reach for more people, but at a price.

One door leads to a terrace, where the lucky resident can have a sundowner while looking at the glittering city, the puny structures all around, the cars crawling up Pedder Road. Up here, the city looks like a CGI creation, useful to establish location and context, but otherwise of limited interest—just a view that will confer bragging rights.

Each room opens up to a vista—Haji Ali mosque and the Bandra-Worli Sea Link on one side, the dock areas in the far east, which too will one day be filled with skyscrapers, and within shouting distance, the glamourous and overwhelming neighbour Antilia, tall and imposing and the big man of the neighbourhood; it blocks a large part of the view of the sea, but then Antilia, owned by one of the richest men in the world, is itself a national monument, and builders can easily sell 'Antilia-view' flats.

Whoever designed the show-flat did not spare any expense and undoubtedly had in mind a potential resident who would want something not loud and garish but subdued—understated elegance is what he must have been aiming for. There are greys and beiges in the living spaces, which reflect studied informality but spell evening conversations about art investment and high finance. The American living model, as imagined from here, is also in evidence—an island kitchen, where friends can sit and have a drink while the host rustles up a simple meal in the fitted kitchen on a lazy Sunday afternoon.

But formal occasions are also kept in mind. The dining area has a table set for eight, down to the wine glasses—I was keen to see the wine selection but refrained from asking. There is a cheerful kids' room, a master bedroom with automated curtains and a television set that glides down into a frame at night, 'because you don't want to see a TV set first thing in the morning especially when the view is so glorious.' A few books—best sellers and on management techniques—are placed strategically, as part of the decor. They've thought of everything.

The bathroom too has a TV set for viewing while bathing in the tub. While sitting on the commode, one can distract oneself by looking down on other buildings and the traffic—'Don't worry, no one can see from the outside. No building is tall and besides, the glass is dark from the outside.'

The resident will have a choice of two kitchens—one for cordon bleu cuisine, with the fashionable island and the best new mod-cons, and a more casual set-up where the family can assemble for a coffee and eggs on the weekends. 'There is a sliding door that keeps the servants away from these intimate family moments.'

As another gloved waiter brings coffee and biscuits, the big question pops up—how much for all this? The senior executive begins warming up. The trend is no longer to discuss a per square foot price, especially when it comes to luxury apartments. And the apartment we are sitting in is not being sold as is—the buyer gets just four walls, the 'box', which can then be designed according to the buyer's specifications. Want a very big living room with just three bedrooms? Your architect is free to do it. Want a bigger kitchen? Sure, why not. Everything from the paint on the walls to the walls themselves can be custom-made for the buyer, at the buyer's cost.

The price for this empty shell will be a modest ₹67 crore, or approximately $9 million, which makes it the most expensive address in the city. It becomes difficult to keep a straight face and not show shock and awe. Sensing that she needs to soften this blow, the executive says, 'Of course, we can talk about the price and see what can be done, if you are serious.'

There's more. Interior civil work and decoration—per the customer's needs—will come to approximately ₹5,000 per square foot, which would amount to another ₹2 crore, and legal costs—registration, stamp duty, etc.—would be about ₹7 crore ($1 million, which by itself would buy, even in expensive Mumbai, a pretty smart apartment.) The whole deal goes well over $10 million.

Sixty per cent of the apartments have already been sold, we are told. We promise to think about it and head out. On the way, we are shown the 'servants' room', which is outside the lift area, on the other side of the apartment. It consists of a tiny room with a bed and a small bathroom, just about enough for one person to squeeze in.

In the lobby, we get a small gift bag for having visited the site and a thick book about the project. The valet has already brought around the car. We drive off and immediately feel the heat and the dust. We are back to earth.

Mumbai has always been an expensive city for property, and the price of an average one-bedroom apartment in Mumbai municipal limits was calculated in 2018 to be ₹1.47 crore. This is a very rough estimate done by some analysts who used official records of registration to work out the number.

The Indian real estate business is anything but transparent. Nothing about it is what it seems; builders routinely give false promises, almost always break the laws and regulations, construct shoddy apartments and overcharge. Cash transactions, in 'black' or unaccounted money, are par for the course and they come in various guises; one parking slot is supposed to be handed over as part of the deal, but the builders want money off the books for it. At every point, the customer is short-changed and even cheated, and in the end, the dream property turns out to be a never-ending nightmare, requiring repairs and maintenance.

'The real estate business is like the Wild West; anything goes, and no laws are applicable,' said Vishal Bhargava, a market analyst who has been studying the sector for over a decade and often writes about it. 'It changed somewhat from 2017, and the industry was a little more regulated, but essentially it remains opaque.'

Sometime in the early 2000s, a real estate boom began and everyone—builders, investors, financiers, banks, buyers—got carried away by the momentum. This was happening all over the country, but in Mumbai, another factor played a big role—a serious paucity of buildable land. There was no hinterland, and while the satellite 'bedroom' suburbs did offer lucrative opportunities, it was Mumbai that was the golden goose.

Every bit of available land was open for grabs. From the 1990s onwards, when 600 acres of erstwhile mill land became available for exploitation, builders, with the help of the government's policies, bought out old apartment buildings, redeveloped slums, and even lobbied for buying land owned by government-owned public services, such as bus depots. The government was only too happy to help, disposing of family jewels for cash. After all, the land was lying idle—was its argument.

One big victory for the builders was to persuade the authorities to increase the floor space index and create a mechanism called the Transfer Development Rights (TDR), which allowed them to give up land elsewhere to utilize its benefits and zoning rights in a more lucrative area. Thus, a plot of land in a distant suburb that could not be commercially exploited was handed over to the government, and this gave the builder a free pass to add extra floors to an expensive project in say, Bandra, the hottest market in Mumbai. The TDR was a tradeable instrument, leading to hectic bidding among developers. The consequences were obvious—taller and taller buildings were built, adding to density in an already dense city. 'There are buildings of twenty-five storeys and above on plots that are very small; outside the buildings, the streets are narrow and cannot handle the additional people and the cars they own; one can imagine what happens at rush hour,' says Pankaj Joshi, an architect who heads the think tank Urban Design Research Institute.

Within a decade, Mumbai's landscape transformed, and tall buildings began springing up where earlier, much smaller, human-scale blocks had stood. Often, the older residents—not just slum dwellers but also middle-class families, all of whom had lived there for decades—were paid off to surrender their properties. Those who lived in slums in any case had no rights, and they were simply bought out.

In a Mumbai slum in the western suburbs, where 200-square-foot rooms are often inhabited by four to six members of a family, a local who calls himself a social worker and gives his name as Mahesh, explains how it works. 'Builders buy out the area from the original owner of the plot, who is only too happy to get money for the land, which was encroached upon by slums years ago. He has no other way of making money out of it.

'The builder's men come here and look around for those with some *vaat* (clout) here. You know, dadas, social workers, political party members. We have *vaat* either all over or a part of the property. I help locals get documents from government offices, help to get their children in school. I talk to the locals, persuade them that they can get money, even a small *kholi* somewhere.'

But some projects have to ensure that the old residents are accommodated in situ; they cannot just be paid off and expected to disappear. Their entire life is based in the neighbourhood—schools, jobs, friends, memories. They want to continue living there. The builder has no option but to agree and build apartments for them right there, next to his luxury condo, in a way that it does not disturb the new residents who will buy flats in the tower.

In one project in Tardeo in Central Mumbai, two high walls were built in a way that the slum buildings were completely hidden from view of not just the condo residents but also the visitors.

This building was constructed on a plot where a slum stood. By Mumbai standards, it was a small slum colony, but in a prime location. Three small buildings were constructed for the erstwhile slum dwellers, and each family was given a one-room flat, with a kitchen and a bathroom. The buildings are drab and grey and look stunted next to the magnificent tower. Hardly any light reaches there.

From the luxurious twentieth-floor apartment of this high-rise in a central part of Mumbai, the city ceases to exist except as distant, firefly-like lights. As the sun finally disappears into the sea, the sights, sounds and most of all, the smells of Mumbai vanish. This is a self-enclosed world in more ways than one—it is hermetically sealed from reality not just physically but also emotionally. There is simply no connection with Mumbai and no need for any. Every engagement with the world bypasses the city, except for travelling on its roads and drawing upon its resources—electricity, water and human beings.

On a weekend evening, the gathering here comprises people who experience Mumbai more or less the same way. They are global citizens, not just familiar with what the world has to offer, but also literally passport holders of another country, one where taxes are more manageable, travel does not involve sending your passport to get a visa stamp (including, horror of horrors, standing in line at the local consulate of a Western nation) and the lifestyle is better.

It's called Plan B, and this evening, a suave financier type, who is now a citizen of a European country, is explaining the concept and the process to a somewhat anxious young fund manager. 'There are many places on offer—Canada, Australia, New Zealand, and even the US. But those come with many limitations. It's more expensive and the passport takes years to acquire; you remain a resident.'

His preference? Malta. 'Portugal is good, and so is Cyprus, but Malta offers a more international lifestyle and what is more, understands money.'

Money is the key word—there are several ways to buy a Maltese passport, but each requires some kind of investment that can go up to ₹5 crores, which, for most people in the room, is not particularly difficult. Residency is one of the conditions too. At the end of it, the coveted passport becomes available, after which travelling anywhere in Europe and a large number of other countries is a smooth affair.

The liquor at the party is top class—though the wine is indifferent—and the food catered by a young and upcoming chef who is making a name for himself. The setting is a bit old fashioned—furniture from the old family home was shifted because the owner— my host—was much too sentimentally attached to it. He did not want to get an interior designer in to create a 'new, minimalistic aesthetic'.

He has requested me not to mention his name or identify the building in any way; but this anonymity is actually helpful in the circumstances. In this comfortable, self-enclosed world, there is not much curiosity about a new face.

The women here are no less accomplished and powerful; one runs a successful online business, another is part of the senior management of a head-hunting agency. College admission season is here, and they are fretting over the choices kids have to make—'She's got into Columbia, but is waiting to hear from her first choice, Princeton.' The old ways of parking your child in the family firm won't do. A smart foreign education is de rigueur now. The best, and most expensive, education consultant in the city is signed up three years before the child actually has to join college. Cost is immaterial. Think of the bragging rights.

My host's family moved here reluctantly. He had lived in a low-rise for at least two generations, and after he got married, his wife had moved in and had loved it, but the owner of the building sold it to a property developer. The tenants got a tidy sum, which helped him buy in this swanky building, but his heart wasn't in it. He had grown up stepping out on the street outside his old home, playing with the children in the neighbourhood, including those of the domestics who worked in the area. Life was connected with the outside world.

'Now my children don't know too many people here, and kids are not allowed to play in the building compound, only in designated areas like the small park or the club. As for setting out for a walk on the street—impossible. The slums, the horrendous traffic, the noise, everything is off-putting.' He compensates by going to his old club, but that still confines him, and he sees the same people over and over again.

'Most others here are happy. They feel insulated and secure. They don't want to engage with anyone outside their own small universe. Everyone tells me how lucky I am to live at this tony address.'

These kinds of buildings also impose rules and regulations—visitors cannot enter till the flat-resident permits them to on an app, and domestic help is checked before leaving to ensure they don't walk away with something from the apartment, he tells me. 'I was shocked to discover this—in my previous building, things were so much more informal, so much more human,' he says.

The skyscraper is now the signature typology of Mumbai, just like the mill chimney was till the 1980s. The landscape of chimneys belching smoke in parts of Central Bombay signified the working-class origins of the city, as if to say, cotton made it what it became and never should we forget that. The skyscrapers represent money and privilege, and only a remote connection with the rest of the city not just because of their height but also the architectural idiom. Seen from the Sea Link—where two-wheelers are not allowed and public buses don't ply—the view is no different from what it would be in any mid-sized American city, or Dubai, Hong Kong or Shanghai, except that the rest of the creaky infrastructure of Mumbai remains vastly different—shoddy and barely holding on.

Those who live in these skyscrapers cannot escape the realities of the city when they set out on their daily drive to work. Nor are they fully immune to the cheating ways of some developers. Almost everybody has a story or two to share about how painful it was to acquire the apartment and having done so, how they felt short-changed.

There are other investors whose investments are stuck, caught in either a welter of litigation almost impossible to unravel, or because the builder simply ran out of fashion. Thousands of buyers, lured by glossy brochures and sales pitches, are facing the same problem, their life's savings stuck in a project with little chance of getting either the apartment or their investment back; for the buyer of a luxury apartment, the stakes are simply higher.

Mr A, an investment adviser, finds himself in a real fix. Along with a few of his friends, he had put down big money for an apartment in Palais Royale, which was pitched as the tallest building not just in Mumbai but in all of India. Construction began in 2008 and customers made a beeline for what was on offer.

'It was a very attractive proposition—five acres in Central Mumbai, with a clear title and designed by Talati and Panthaky, the most respected architectural firm in the city; I was quite taken up by it, as were my friends,' A said.

The building was coming up on the site of the old Shriram Mills, which had shut down, and the former owner was the builder. The 300-metre-tall building was to have 120 apartments. The smallest would be 8,000 square feet, and the largest, a sprawling 14,000 square feet. Residents could enjoy a cinema theatre, a spa and enough space to play cricket, football and badminton. Three swimming pools were promised. 'The way it was designed, each resident would have a sweeping view of three sides of the city.' The project was worth almost half a billion dollars.

He invested only in 2015, by which time the entire structure was ready, and the builder was promising delivery in two years. 'I paid up 70 per cent of the price; a few put down 100 per cent.' He is coy about the exact sum, but considering that a flat there, if completed, would in 2020 be priced at ₹40 crores—close to $6 million—it couldn't have been a small sum.

'There was a case filed by an NGO about some violations, but the builder assured us that would be cleared soon.' In business circles, there was also talk of a deal with a rival builder gone wrong and that this would slow down progress. Meanwhile, the municipal corporation stepped in, saying some other infractions had taken place. New investment from buyers slowed down as they watched fearfully the growing problems facing the project. A big funder of the project, India Bulls, then sued to get back its dues and got possession of the property. It was finally auctioned in 2019 in its half-done state and sold for ₹705 crore, a bargain given the potential of the sale of around fifty apartments on the top thirteen floors.

'Our money is still stuck, but we are all hoping that things will move and one day we will get to move into the dream house,' A says.

Mumbai is dotted with half-finished buildings, with the workers and the cranes long gone—it is a testimony to not just greed, but a casual disregard for zoning laws. A few extra floors or enclosing more space than is permissible are more the norm than the exception. A is emphatic—'Builders are cheats, some more than the others, but one way or the other, the customer is the one who suffers. Don't think the big buyers are exempt.'

For Mr Sharma—again a nom de plume because he said he didn't want to 'lose friends'—his dream house was all he had wanted. The advertisements for the property had shown a young woman, her hair flying, staring out at an uninterrupted view of the Worli Bay, with its famous Haji Ali Mosque in the sea. In the foreground was the vast Mahalaxmi racecourse, with its magnificent horses. The builder's marketing had emphasized that buying in the building was 'by invitation only'. People with a certain profile would be chosen, not mere financial status—the idea was to keep out those who were not a cultural fit.

It was to be one of the most prestigious and expensive buildings in the city, and the builder had promised unprecedented amenities and luxuries. 'We were told, everything, barring the inbuilt cupboards and the furniture, would be given. The kitchen would come fitted with German equipment—all we had to do was to bring our gas cylinders and start cooking.'

A private lift for the exclusive use of residents who could only access it by an electronic card would take the person to their floor, opening right inside the apartment. Outside, the residents had the full use of cricket and football grounds, a club and a garden. 'It was the ultimate in luxury at the time.'

The building was completed in 2013, a year later than promised, but the residents could live with that, especially since it met all their expectations. 'They had delivered on all their promises—the kitchen was truly amazing,' says Sharma. Sharma is on a higher floor in the forty-eight-storey tower, and the view on the western side was spectacular, covering the full span of the Haji Ali Bay, the mosque glittering in the water.

But within months of moving in, the residents saw some activity in the slums near the railway tracks abutting the building. It was preparation for construction, and by the looks of it, it was to be a major job. Their fears turned out to be right—a new building was going to come up almost within shouting distance of their own towers.

This project was by another builder who planned to erect an equally tall residential building that would completely block their view of the bay. No one knew this would happen. 'The marketing agent who had brought us to see this place had emphatically told us that no other building would ever come up outside ours—it would be too close to the railway tracks. That had reassured me,' Sharma recalls.

Construction continued at full speed and in less than a year, the new tower had reached over half its height, completely blocking the vista and curtailing sunlight and the breeze that would flow in from the bay. Sharma and the other residents were in shock. They tried to find out more, even see if they could stall the project, but that was impossible—the other builder had all the permissions in order. The new tower became a reality and the dreams of forever living with a panoramic view were shattered.

The impact was swift. Property prices in the prestigious project where Sharma lived began stagnating, even falling. 'We are about 30 per cent less than a similar project a mile or so away, which also started around the time we first invested here. In fact, I had debated which one I should purchase, but finally decided to come here; it was the view that clinched it for me.'

Buyers still come here, attracted by the facilities and the lifestyle—plus the price is relatively attractive compared to similar complexes. The neighbourhood outside is insalubrious to say the least—traffic jams, honking cars and dusty streets; it is part of the old mill district, with its low-rise housing and small shops—but inside the gated complex, with its many layers of security and the open spaces and the club, it is a world apart, quiet, peaceful and unconnected with the grime of daily Mumbai reality. 'The right kind of people are here—CEOs, company presidents, big names. Barring this one problem, it is a great place to live,' Sharma says.

The desire to live in a big building is not limited to the upper middle classes, but it is they who can most afford it. For the salaried middle class, and especially those living in older residences, moving to a new, tall building entails not just a change in lifestyle, but also in expenses—monthly maintenance costs being the biggest. The expenses are never-ending—the upkeep of elevators, gardens and the general environs, security and government taxes.

Yet, high-rises are coming up all over Central Mumbai and the suburbs, especially where land is relatively cheaper and easier to access. Old, abandoned factories, land that the government wants to monetize and even one-time famous film studios, such as Raj Kapoor's R.K. Studios, have all got clear titles and hardly any constraints, such as slum settlements, to bother about—they all make for elegant and expensive gated complexes. And they all find buyers, as much for the surrounding ambience as for the elevation.

Despite much research and commentary worldwide about the human cost of living in a skyscraper—alienation, distance from the street and therefore reality, and even health—those tall buildings represent aspiration and success. They are new, with gleaming, high-ceilinged lobbies, and they offer facilities that the common citizen cannot get in his daily life—a neighbourhood park or clean and paved streets or indeed, peace and quiet. The residents of the gated community want to escape from the everyday life that lies beyond the well-guarded gate. They have stretched themselves and taken a hefty mortgage to get inside. They have effectively seceded from hardship by building their own little bubble.

Builders understand these needs and have constructed enclaves that offer a life where almost everything is available. In one 'vertical masterpiece' which offers an 'imperial lifestyle' in a seventy-three-storey tower, the buyer would get a 'spacious and luxurious home with a signature-class royal community living experience, a mesmerising view' and many other amenities such as an air-conditioned lobby, alarm systems, CCTV and a manned security surveillance system and, perhaps best of all, a Jain temple within the complex. All this for prices starting from ₹6.75 crores

Real estate developers have discovered that prospective buyers want not only well-designed apartments, but also an ambience that makes them feel good and facilities that are convenient. A club, a gym with the best equipment, parks and security are now the minimum that they expect, and they also want a lobby that makes them feel grand. A flat that is smaller than promised or even of shoddy construction can be painful, but the rest of what is offered makes up for it.

The trend of high-rises is not limited to Mumbai, it's the signature typology of other major cities, from Shanghai to Dubai to San Francisco to Sao Paulo—the skyscraper rising to meet the sky is a global trend. Mumbai can therefore feel part of the global community. But there is a difference, and a crucial one—in most cities, the skyscrapers tend to be in the downtown and business districts, while the residents choose to live in smaller, more human-scale housing. Barring a Hong Kong, where the tall blocks of flat, mostly featureless housing structures are the only way to pack in so many people, or a New York, where the rich like to stay far from the madding crowd, the ultra-tall buildings accommodate offices, which clear out in the evening. Business districts are buzzing in the daytime and go quiet at night. In Mumbai, the tall buildings are residential, adding to the density of already cramped neighbourhoods, putting additional pressure on the narrow roads. It reflects a warped sense of priorities.

An ambitious land grab by the political class and the builders, if successful, will see more such neo-brutalist towers in other parts of the city, especially on the seafront. Already, zoning laws and environmental regulations have been changed to allow construction on the seafront; with a long coastline that runs the length of the city, the lucrative possibilities of creating a waterfront playground for the rich are unending.

11

THE HIDDEN CITY

R.K. Studios in Chembur, in the eastern suburbs of Mumbai, is a landmark in the area. It was founded in 1948, and a big shooting lot was constructed in the 1950s. This is where Raj Kapoor, often described as a 'showman', shot his big films, this is where he lived and where he held his famous Holi parties with the biggest names in the film industry in attendance.

By the early part of the 2000s, fewer and fewer producers were hiring it—Chembur was now just too far to go to, and film-makers preferred the western Mumbai studios, which had better facilities and were near to where many stars lived. In 2017, R.K. Studios was gutted in a fire, losing all its memorabilia and became unusable. Rebuilding it was simply not worth it, and two years later it was bought over by the Godrej Properties group to construct luxury towers on its 2.2 acres—the legacy of the studio added a premium to the flat prices.

Chembur was once a leafy, sylvan suburb, far from the crowds and dirt of the rest of the city. But then, several big industries came up there—petroleum refining, fertilizer and chemical plants—generating air pollution. The city's garbage was dumped there with little or no treatment for decades—the Deonar dumping ground was set up in 1927, when the area was far from Bombay—and in 1970, an abattoir was constructed; the stink and the pollution gave it a new name: 'Gas Chamber'.

The Deonar garbage dump of Mumbai is a fetid hillock of trash, replenished every day, with a small *bastee* in its shadow. These small clusters of homes are illegal of course, and no one in their right mind would ever want to live or even survive there, but it is still a space to set up some sort of home and earn a bit of money. The locals pick at the mound for anything that may be worth something—a pair of shoes that may still be wearable, pieces of metal or rubber that can be sold as scrap, bits of plastic that can be recycled by small workshops. There is a parallel economy for such items, which then get sold on to low-income groups, both in Mumbai and in other rural areas. One collector once said that he found a serviceable watch, which got him a good deal. All day long, the scrap collectors, which include women and children, lugging sacks on their backs, walk around among the refuse, picking up stuff that they then sell off to dealers.

With all these hazards, though there are pockets of land available, no one wants to build on them. The government and other city authorities saw Chembur and its neighbouring suburbs, Deonar and Mankhurd, as the perfect place to set up cheap housing for those who had to be accommodated, but removed from areas much more lucrative, and dump them there. This is where slum dwellers who were categorized as 'Project Affected Persons' (PAPs)—bureaucratese for those whose land was needed for projects such as widening a road or building a flyover or laying a water pipe—were brought and given their meagre rooms. After that, they were left on their own. A report by an NGO, the Centre for Enquiry into Health and Allied Themes, called it 'involuntary resettlement', which gave the slum dwellers no choice at all—either shift or you will be left without a roof over your head.

This shift was presented as the government's largesse but in truth it was because of the rules mandated by the World Bank, which often financed the big projects, and had insisted that the slum dwellers be given alternative accommodation, so land had to be found at a suitably distant place, which nobody else wanted.

As an incentive to the person who owned the property that was needed, the government gave over Transfer Development Rights (TDR), a fungible and tradeable instrument created by the state administration that allowed builders to construct housing for the poor in return for permission to build taller luxury apartments elsewhere. It sounded fair but eventually was loaded in the favour of property owners, because the TDR was transferable and could be sold to anyone. Developers were only too willing to step in and build housing for the poor PAPs and use the rights to develop towers in other, in-demand suburbs. The land parcels in M Ward—where Deonar falls—were ideally located geographically; lucrative markets such as Juhu and Powai happened to be due north, and that made the TDR very attractive.

The authorities projected the scheme as a win for all the stakeholders—the Mumbai Metropolitan Region Development Authority (MMRDA) got unoccupied land for its large projects, the builders could now construct tall towers in hot markets with abandon and the slum dwellers got free homes, which was usually one room with a kitchen and toilet. These wretched souls had lived for years, maybe decades, in ramshackle slums open to the elements, and an entire community had only a few stinking toilets to use. Except that these former slum dwellers were not grateful at this largesse (of free homes)—they were unhappy and upset.

A short, ten-minute car ride from R.K. Studios takes us to one such housing project in Lallubhai Compound, named after the former property owner. Both R.K. Studios, which is soon to be converted into a gated community of tall, luxury towers, a club for residents and landscaped gardens, and Lallubhai Compound come within the administrative area called 'M East Ward'.

Leaving this promised paradise that will come up on the studio land for the exclusive use of a chosen few, we now enter a surreal, dystopic world tucked away in a corner of the city, where no one goes simply because no one needs to. It is a pocket that is conveniently hidden because it could be upsetting to behold.

Lallubhai Compound is built on land that was owned by Lallubhai Steel and sold to the MMRDA in 2000 using TDR.

It was never advertised when it was being built, no glossy brochures highlighting its many charms—like clubhouses, high-ceilinged lobbies, spectacular views and so on—were printed and no prospective buyers rushed there. Yet, the buildings were constructed by the very same builders who are household names—Hiranandani and Shah among them.

It is a densely packed cluster of 124 five-storey buildings, with an estimation of 10,000 people living in the complex.

The tenements made by the two builders are markedly different, Shah's buildings have dark, interior corridors with 225-square-feet flats on both sides; while Hiranandani placed the corridors in the front, like the traditional chawls, which allows much more light and breeze to get in.

All of these buildings look like a vertical slum, a brutalist creation like council estates elsewhere. Add to it the fact that it is in the back of beyond, and the sense of alienation and exclusion is complete.

'The M(E) Ward in Mumbai is a microcosm of the city: it is an extreme example of skewed development in the metropolis, with virtually all indicators showing an urgent need for action that is multi-dimensional, comprehensive and strategic to serve its burgeoning population. It has been the most neglected ward from the point of view of infrastructure and human development,' wrote Purva Dewoolkar in her master's thesis for her architecture degree. She now works for the M Ward project run by the Tata Institute of Social Sciences, a much-respected institution situated not far from Lallubhai.[1]

She is a regular here and moves around easily, and I have come with her to help me navigate the complex maze of the compound and its physical and social dynamic.

It is a working weekday, but the streets are busy: loud music plays at a makeshift kiosk (a pandal) with large, framed portraits of Dr B.R. Ambedkar, architect of the Indian Constitution and widely admired for his critiques of the caste-based hierarchy of Hinduism and for raising the political and social consciousness of Dalits, giving them a sense of dignity and power. He is revered by the Dalits, many of whom converted to Buddhism after he gave a call to reject the shackles imposed by the Hindu upper castes.

The music marks the carving out of space by the Dalit residents of Lallubhai Compound, though the pandal is a small setup and doesn't disturb in any way. Around it and beyond are vegetable vendors, who bring crucial supplies to the Compound, which has no market close by. Nor does it have easy access to public transport, or to a school or hospital. It is an island, marooned from the rest of the city, left to its own devices. These small entrepreneurs are a lifeline for locals, and business is brisk. It presents the look of any suburban scene in Mumbai, with all its hustle and bustle, except that there is no traffic, no stores lining the roads and no leafy trees.

Turning into a small pathway between two rows of buildings, we head towards the office of an NGO located in one of them further down. The path is barely wide enough for a car to drive on, except that there is no car anywhere around, just pedestrians and two-wheelers, which manoeuvre expertly between the vendors and passers-by who vie for space.

Only about three metres separate each building, and most of these spaces are strewn with rotting garbage thrown by the residents. With hardly any garbage collection, sanitary habits are primitive. A fetid stench rises in places.

In 2018, studies found that there was an extremely high incidence of tuberculosis (TB) in the complex and two other state-built colonies in the general area, Natwar Parekh compound and Ambedkar Nagar.[2]

The numbers were startling—1 in 10 households in the complexes, especially in buildings with poor ventilation and sunlight, had patients who suffered from the disease, and the percentage of cases per lakh local population was over three times the national average. Ironically, Lallubhai Compound had better results than the other two, giving us an idea of how poor the layout in the other two compounds was.

The onus is on the locals to make their lives as liveable as possible. In Lallubhai, two neighbouring buildings show that while access to sunlight may not always be possible, cleanliness and hygiene is. The path between the two is gated, with a prominently placed CCTV camera pointed on the road and a notice announcing that fact. It is clean, well-kept and is used for parking scooters and motorcycles. This is not allowed, since it is not private land, but who is to complain? The residents of both buildings must have taken this decision jointly, that they needed to guard their privacy and safety and keep the area clean—they want to live better than they did in their earlier circumstances and upgrade their lives.

The gates and the CCTV mimic the many upper middle-class enclaves in the city, and here they signify not just aspiration but a desire for security for their families and possessions. It becomes an exclusive enclave in a location that is otherwise public and open.

In a room on the ground floor of one of the buildings is a play centre for the local children. Colourful posters adorn the walls, and a few children are playing, waiting for permission to use the lone computer in the room. Husna, who runs this recreation centre, set up by YUVA (Youth for Unity and Voluntary Action), an NGO that works among marginalized communities, says that in the evenings and on weekends, the centre is full. Parents send their kids there, secure in the knowledge that they will be safe. Crimes against children and adolescents is an endemic problem in the compound.

Purva and I walk back to the main road. No school was built here, she says. On the ground floor of one building a private entrepreneur has set up a kindergarten of sorts, but it is no substitute. Children are ferried to a municipal school some distance away in a pooling arrangement by the parents. Some NGOs that are active in the education segment had plans to set up operations here but couldn't.

When the complex was set up, whole clusters of slum dwellers were shifted here. The bureaucrats who handled the operation planned such that each floor was populated with people from different parts of the city. Thus, a family from Colaba found that its neighbours were complete strangers, from Borivali or Ghatkopar. This bit of social engineering was to ensure that people, because they did not know each other, were less likely to gang up, but what it did was to break old support systems and networks. Fights broke out, and the new residents were wary of and hostile to each other.

Slums are mostly congregations of those with old ties, either from their village or to a linguistic group or even a caste. There are Muslim-dominated slums as much as there are those composed largely of, say, Marathi- or Telugu-speaking residents. In such densely packed environments, one family's business is everyone's business, and everyone knows what everyone else is doing all the time, sometimes stiflingly so. This is not a romantic view of slum community life, which is hard and cruel, and where each one guards their scarce resources zealously, but when the system fails to provide protection and is downright hostile, such mutual reliance is the only way to survive.

Lallubhai Compound upended that completely. The spatial changes in the living arrangements—a self-contained flat whose door was closed all the time rather than a flimsy shack that was wide open during the day—alienated the next-door neighbour. 'A scream from inside one, even if it could be heard outside, was ignored. It was not anyone's concern. Domestic abuse, for example, did not attract anyone's attention, much less intervention,' says Purva.

Living in a fully owned, self-contained flat brought with it rules and obligations that were totally alien. Each resident had to pay a monthly maintenance of ₹300, which the new property owners couldn't or wouldn't pay. For those earning say ₹8,000, with the costs of commuting long distances, school fees, food, electricity, etc., this outgo was an additional burden. Buildings began to look shabby. The lifts wouldn't work because the annual maintenance wasn't paid, corridor lights remained broken and garbage collection suffered. There were stories, probably apocryphal, about how senior citizens were stuck on the ground floor for two days waiting for the lifts to be repaired. The external paint of most buildings has peeled off, and the mounting garbage everywhere is a health hazard.

On the wide main road, two rows of buildings stand across each other. At the end of one 'arm' is a tall, mostly empty tower, waiting for a new batch of residents. 'The unoccupied flats are used by drug addicts, and there have been cases of assault on young girls and boys,' a YUVA representative tells me. Statistics of crime are difficult to come by since the lone police outpost will not release them, though one NGO did some research and found that 345 complaints of rape were filed in the local police station between 2014 and 2019.

Husna says the official numbers will never tell the whole story, but adds that fewer instances are being reported now as people have become more careful.

A few months later, I visit the Compound again. Marina Joseph, also from YUVA, and Husna accompany me. It is a Saturday and not a very hot day. The street market is busy. Autos wait for passengers, but business is slow because it is the afternoon.

We head to a spanking new sixteen-floor tower that was constructed much after the others were and is still largely unoccupied. It's the kind of building that could fit in any middle-class housing society. Several families, especially those who lived in pucca houses rather than slums, refused to move to the older buildings. These were termed, in bureaucratese, R and R (Relief and Rehabilitation) allotees—people whose buildings collapsed or their homes were destroyed in a fire. The new towers, which are taller, better looking (at least for now) and with larger apartments (500 square feet), were constructed for such families.

An old security guard mans a makeshift gate made of rusted tin. Three towers stand and there is a proper compound that runs around the three buildings, where a sedan is parked, the first car I have seen in Lallubhai.

Three men are hanging around and refuse to let us go inside to see a typical apartment. It is not clear what their official status is. A young man approaches us, a bit edgy and shifty, and asks us if we are looking to rent a place. He starts his sales patter, quickly telling us that he can get us a place on rent in the building. How so, given that it is still officially unoccupied? He is vague about the details but promises us that for ₹7,000 or ₹7,500 a month he can get the paperwork done. Apartments are selling for ₹17 lakh, and he has a great bargain on the first floor that is being offered for ₹25 lakh, because the owner has appropriated some extra space.

'You are not from MMRDA or the police, are you?' he asks the two women with me. He has been talking mostly to them, he does not look at me. My one question about the documentation for a rental seems to have put him off.

He looks like a novice real estate broker, hustling for a quick buck. Such deals are illegal, since the MMRDA has a rule that those given apartments cannot rent or sell them for ten years, but it is an open secret that transactions happen all the time. It is a complex arrangement, involving power of attorneys and much else, but if the original owner and the tenant are caught by the authorities, they can be prosecuted. It requires a broker experienced in managing the grey areas of the law to work it all out. This man is certainly not one of them.

He soon warms up and then starts telling us his story. He was working for a franchisee of a holiday home company and got a salary of ₹25,000 plus allowances for his mobile and for travel. Then the franchisee sold out, and the new owner offered him ₹10,000 for the same job. He couldn't take that 'insult' so he left; an uncle of his who was working as a broker in Lallubhai Compound asked him to join his business, and when they sold a flat and earned ₹1.5 lakh, he was hooked. That sounds somewhat implausible, since that would imply a sale price of ₹1.5 crore, but he seems unconcerned at this. 'We sold for ₹9.5 lakh and gave the client only ₹8 lakh.'

He intersperses his chat with stories about his own life. 'A tower is coming up in place of my old house in Bandra east and then I will move back there with my wife and two kids. This is just temporary.'

He lives in one of the Lallubhai Compound buildings but it is clear he doesn't feel he belongs there, among the residents. 'I don't talk to anyone. This is not a good place. I can get you a flat in this tower if you want.'

He says he finds his new occupation humiliating because 'In English, it sounds okay—agent, or broker. In Hindi the word is "*dalal*", and I cannot bear that.' It begins to make sense when he says he is from the north, where the word dalal is used derisively, to mean a wheeler-dealer middleman. 'That is why I haven't got a card made, but you can take my number.'

'What's your name?' I ask him. He finally looks at me. 'Mika, like the singer. I am from Gurgaon. I have a house and a life there. If this doesn't work out, I will go back. But a tower is being built in Bandra, and I think I can get a good job in Mumbai with all my experience—I even have a reference letter from there.'

Across the road, back in one of the older buildings, we go to the home of the Dongres, who were among the first families to be moved to Lallubhai. They used to live near St. George Hospital in south Mumbai. All the residents of the slum there were shifted en masse to Lallubhai Compound. They were all accommodated in four buildings with almost the same neighbours—the mix and match policy hadn't been introduced. It made for a sense of kinship, especially since the Dongres, like many from their village and district, had come to Bombay in 1972 escaping a severe drought.

Rahul Dongre was in class 5 when they moved here. He used to study in a municipal school near his slum and was proving to be quite a good student. There was no school in Lallubhai, so he had to be sent to one a little distance away—it was very difficult, his mother interjects softly. She is preparing lunch. The NGO Akanksha had begun classes for children in Lallubhai Compound and he was one of their best students. When he finished his board exams with a 73 per cent score, the elated boy applied for admission to St. Xavier's College, which is in south Mumbai. In the meantime, he had developed an interest in cricket and joined YUVA's child protection group.

He got in, but two years later, he did poorly in the next board exams, and did not get readmitted. So, he shifted to the government-run Elphinstone College. When we met him, he was cramming for exams and was confident that he would get a good degree in history, which he was studying.

'I want to appear for the state civil services examination, which is competitive, and want to become a government officer—regular income, security, and I can do something good,' he says confidently, his books spread out before him on the floor.

His mother is praying for him because his taxi-driver father's income is no longer sufficient. 'Let's see, if Rahul gets a job then we can move to a bigger place.'

He lives in this 220-square-foot flat with his parents, two brothers and one sister. It is a secure place, better than a slum, but the costs are heavy. And the room is not large enough. His grandparents, who lived with them, have passed away.

The house has linoleum flooring and tiles on the walls, an upgrade done by the family. There is a fridge and a flat-screen television, which the family doesn't watch for the moment to help Rahul concentrate on his studies. The aspiration in his eyes to move beyond his current life is unmissable—the whole family's dreams are riding on him.

We don't want to disturb him, so we leave.

Lallubhai Compound, dark as it is, is not the only colony for displacing and placing slum dwellers in M Ward. Yet another such project is Vashi Naka, another R and R colony, which is even more congested, the buildings closer to each other and each floor with four tightly packed apartments. Two of the residents are sitting in the YUVA office on the ground floor of a building. They complain about how the water quality and levels are poor and the buildings are in bad shape. This portion is known as RNA Nagar and was built by RNA Builders. They made many such buildings for R and R families, but in the centre of the entire project, also constructed a new building for middle-class buyers. It seems fully occupied.

Not too far away is Mahul, a similar project, which is in the vicinity of no less than six chemical plants. Technically, Mahul is in the M West Ward, created when the larger M Ward was split for administrative reasons, but that is only a nominal change—both wings were found suitable for 'rehabilitation' purposes. The buildings in Mahul are newer, but its problems run deeper—residents say that the chemical plants have caused them deep health distress.

Most of those given accommodation here were slum dwellers living cheek by jowl with water pipelines in nearby Ghatkopar, and the courts ordered in 2011 that they be shifted. The municipal corporation complied, and they were given apartments in Mahul.

Since then, the residents have complained that they have been dumped in a hazardous area, and the round-the-clock fumes have severely affected their health and quality of life. When I visit, the grouses come thick and fast. There is a pungent smell in the air, and even a visitor can sense something is wrong. The locals also say there is no public transport to get to the nearest railway station and water supply is erratic, but the pollution tops the list of their problems. They show me their skin, talk about growing asthma and stinging eyes. 'My old father is constantly wheezing, and if there is an emergency there is no hospital within miles,' says one resident.

The Mahul flats get more air and light, built as they are around atrium-like spaces that are open to the sky. But what use is that if the very air we breathe is so dangerous, is the refrain.

None of these localities are familiar to a vast majority of Mumbai residents. They remain distant, dark places that no one has heard of, and no one goes to. No one wants to know about them either—occasionally, they make the news, such as when Mahul residents went to the courts to immediately get them shifted. The courts have been sympathetic, but things have moved very slowly—Mahul, with all its original residents, continues to exist.[3]

A city like Mumbai, with its severe and endemic housing issues, will always have takers for a free flat, or even one where the rents are affordable—it is far better than a slum. Mumbai's commercial instincts ensure that there are always middlemen and dealmakers who will provide any service at a price. Relying on the official machinery, which is slow and cumbersome as well as distant and officious, does not always work.

Lallubhai Compound, Vashi Naka and Mahul are not just stark symbols of the official interpretation of 'rehabilitation', they also suggest that governments have begun to think of slums as not just a housing problem but also an aesthetic one. A slum in an upper middle-class neighbourhood is an ugly sight and an economic loss—it could be 'developed' and turned into luxury apartments. But political promises about providing slum dwellers free housing and pressure from international funding agencies make it incumbent to give alternative—and built-up—accommodation to those who live in slums on government land.

The government and its various agencies don't have the money, so the optimum solution is to give incentives to builders to construct buildings in faraway locations and offer them free to those who live in slums. This way they are out of sight, and, as it always turns out, out of mind. The builders are happy, the government is satisfied that it fulfilled its obligations and the privileged now don't have slums in their eyeline. And international visitors to Mumbai can see how attractive the city is.

Yet Mumbai needs its domestics, its drivers, its cabbies and its delivery boys, and they live in slums and in the R and R colonies. They need to be within reach, so the remote locations are still within the city's municipal limits. The white-collar workers, the former mill labour and the middle classes leave their old inner-city homes and move to the northern suburbs. And the rest, mainly consisting of the professional classes and the rich, get the attractive coastal areas and the central parts where they create gated companies. The city originally began growing when seven islands were forged together and the colonial administration actively invited outsiders to come and settle here. Now, not just migrants, but also inconvenient locals, with long histories in Mumbai, to which they contributed their blood and sweat like any other citizen, are being actively discouraged to set up home. New islands are emerging all the time—islands that are exclusionary and impossible to breach. Like other major metropolises around the world—New York, London, Paris—Mumbai is fast getting segmented on grounds of economic status.

This scenario is going to play out once more in Dharavi. For years the government has looked for solutions to 'develop' it, but nothing worked till the Adani Group stepped in. The state government found their proposal tenable and accepted their terms; but at its core this is the same old idea of giving new homes to the older residents in tall buildings and using all the surplus land to construct shiny new residential and office blocks. Dharavi sits on prime land, which is right next to the commercial district of BKC and, therefore, will command top dollar prices.

The developer also asked for extra land to accommodate tens of thousands of Dharavi residents in far-flung places—some in what was previously garbage dump land, which will need to be flattened, and the rest on salt pan lands—a request which the government swiftly accepted. In the end, its the same old Mumbai story of banishing the most vulnerable far away, out of sight and giving them the barest minimum.

The abiding image of this New Mumbai is the skyscrapers, the glittering new offices, the luxury apartments that sell for stratospheric prices—no different from any other metropolis in the world. But what it hides are the vast numbers of those who can't afford this glossy version of the city they have lived in all their lives. Mumbai is finally fulfilling its fantasies of becoming an international city, but at a human cost.

ACKNOWLEDGEMENTS

The idea of writing this book—about how Mumbai was changing rapidly—was with me for a long time. Mumbai is a moveable feast, constantly shedding its old skin, but in recent years—specifically from the 1990s—the pace has become turbocharged. The rapid construction of ever higher towers was only the most visible manifestation of this.

I could sense it, but was finding it difficult to pin it down. I needed help and advice from those who were closer to the ground, who could help me decipher them and were monitoring the human cost of this monumental transformation.

Mapping and recording this change, present in my subconscious mind, began to take shape. The story of a mutating city had to be told, but it couldn't just be a top-down version—it had to reflect the voices of all segments that make the city of Mumbai what it is.

Unseen and unheard by most, Mumbai's large network of NGOs silently work for and among its marginalized citizens, often in the most difficult of circumstances. When I reached out to them, they not only helped me, but put me in touch with other people—it was like one link led to another. This book just would not have been possible without them. They helped me reach those whose stories rarely get recorded.

Thank you to Sitaram Shelar of Pani Haq Samiti, for showing me how the politics of water functioned. And for introducing me to the feisty Shanti Ravi, who was born and still lives in the Darukhana slum where she takes up the cause of the entire community to ensure that the longtime residents don't get left behind.

To T.V. Shah, a retired chief hydraulic engineer of the Municipal Corporation, who knows all there is to know about how Mumbai's water supply works.

To Shweta Damle, housing activist who then worked out of a room in a Bandra (East) building, for her good cheer, no matter how tough and depressing things look, and for helping me get into Behrampada slum, with its dark and dingy mazes that even a regular could get lost in.

To Marina Joseph of YUVA, an NGO that has been working in Mumbai and elsewhere for over forty years, for taking me to Lallubhai compound, in the back of beyond, where many slum and pavement dwellers were given one room tenements and then left to their own devices.

There are many others who helped be along this journey. Prof. Amita Bhide, whose work on Mumbai is well known to all those who have studied the city deeply. A professor at the Tata Institute of Social Sciences, Amita set up a team to study the M ward of Mumbai, which includes not only Lallubhai compound, but many other areas and buildings in the vast area.

To Purva Dewoolkar, part of Prof. Bhide's team and an expert on sanitation and water supply, who was a great resource, accompanying me to various M ward areas and explaining the complex issues involved.

To Nauzer Bharucha, Mumbai's best reporter on housing, who helped me understand how the industry works—and often doesn't work—at least for the customer, including the upscale buyer of 'luxury' apartments.

To Prof. Hemant Burde, IIT and Pankaj Joshi of the Urban Development and Research Institute who explained to me how housing works for the marginalized.

To Firdaus Kawas Antia, who guided me to the community that has lived on the terrace of Queen's Mansion in Fort for years. It was an indication how the people of this city will make a home wherever they can get some space.

To Arjun Appadurai, Atul Kumar, P.K. Das and Rashna Poncha, all of whom who contributed in a big way to my understanding of what made Bombay of the past and the Mumbai of today.

To photographer Sudharak Olwe, who knows parts of Mumbai that many others don't, and was generous with his time and experience.

To Abigail McGowan, professor at the University of Vermont, who shares my love and interest in the period when the city was developing its western shores and when its Art Deco precinct was born.

To Abdullah Jam, journalist and map maker and expert on the backstreets of Mohammed Ali Road; Ashar Damani, who gave a walking tour of Dongri and Shaikh Ayaz, who accompanied me. They all were invaluable in helping me comprehend an area that often remains ignored and misunderstood.

To Murtaza Sadriwala, of the Saifee Burhani Upliftment Trust (SBUT), who showed me around Bhendi Bazar, an old precinct which was being transformed by the Trust.

To Shireen Dalvi, who was a great help in the Muslim-dominated township of Mumbra, just on the outskirts of Mumbai.

To Mustansir Dalvi, professor of architecture and poet, and Atul Kumar, both of whom experts on the Art Deco period, which brought twentieth century modernity to Mumbai. There are many more Mumbai-people who I cannot name, but you know who you are, thank you very much.

To Rahul Mehrotra, Shabana Azmi and James Crabtree, for their warm endorsements. And to Sumantro Ghoshal for his translation of the Kaifi Azmi nazm that Shabana Azmi so generously shared.

To Mita Kapur, my ever-patient agent and friend, whose reminders to finish were always delivered politely. And the equally patient Udayan Mitra, executive publisher at HarperCollins India, who showed faith in the book throughout its gestation period. The book's editor Shreya Dhawan, whose vigilant eye caught many mistakes that I had simply not noticed, and Shreya Mukherjee who guided me through the last stages of the book with her editing.

A big thanks to my family, who constantly chivvied me to get moving on the book even during the lockdown period, when stepping out of the home was simply impossible.

To my colleagues at *The Wire*, who allowed me the leeway to concentrate on the book when I should have been doing my day job.

Most of all, I want to thank the many people of Mumbai, who allowed me into their lives and shared their stories with me, sans inhibition. It helped me construct a picture of a city in transition from a point of view, which is not visible to us otherwise. Without them, this book would not have been possible.

NOTES

1. Introduction

1. PTI, 'Atal Setu sees average daily traffic of 22,689 vehicles in 1 year, below initial estimates', *Economic Times*, 14 January 2025, https://economictimes.indiatimes.com/news/economy/ infrastructure/atal-setu-sees-average-daily-traffic-of-22689-vehicles-in-1-year-below-initial-estimates/articleshow/117220635. cms?from=mdr.
2. Rahul Mehrotra and Sharada Dwiwedi, *Bombay: The Cities Within* (Mumbai: Eminence Designs, 2001).
3. Ibid.
4. Wife of British government official, she is known for laying down the foundation stone for All Saint's Church, Malabar Hills in Mumbai.
5. Mariam Dossal, *Theatre of Conflict, City of Hope-Mumbai 1660 to Present Times* (Delhi: Oxford University Press, 2010), p.163.
6. Ibid.
7. G. Owen W. Dunn, M. Inst.C.E., 'Housing question in Bombay', Journal of the Royal Society of Arts; London Vol. 58, (Nov 19, 1909): 393.
8. W.R. Davidge, 'Development of Bombay', Town Planning Review, 1924, 10/4: 275-79. Jan 2007, https://archive.org/details/davidge-1924-development-of-bombay.
9. UN Habitat, 'Chapter Sharpening the Global Agenda', 2003, p.1.

10. Varsha Kusnur, 'Dharavi: The New Hub of Minting Money', Reader's Blog, *The Times of India*, 27 February 2023, https:// timesofindia.indiatimes.com/readersblog/ppsijc-musings/dharavi- the-new-hub-of-minting-money-50956/.
11. Adarkar, Neera (ed.), *The Chawls of Mumbai: Galleries of Life* (Mumbai: ImprintOne, 2011).
12. *The Times of India*, 'Big chunk of 800 city high-rises sprang up in the mill belt in 16 years', fhttps://timesofindia.indiatimes.com/city/mumbai/big-chunk- of-800 -city-highrises-sprang-up-in-mill-belt-in-16 -yrs/articleshow/113773087.cms.
13. Mansee Dave and Sarmeeli Mullick, 'Buy Vs Rent: Why are Mumbaikars choosing to rent a house over buying?', *ET Now*, 5 March 2023, https://www.timesnownews.com/business-economy/ real-estate/buy-vs-rent-why-are-mumbaikars-choosing-to-rent-a- house-over-buying-article-98424560.
14. Anulekha Ray, 'Mumbai property rates in 2024: Check residential property price, rent in Mumbai, Thane, other areas of MMR in Q3', *Economic Times*, 26 October 2024, https://economictimes.indiatimes.com/wealth/real-estate/mumbai-property-rates-in-2024-check-residential-property-price-rent-in-mumbai-thane-other-areas-of-mmr-in-q3/articleshow/114623048.cms?from=mdr.
15. Knight Frank, 'India Real Estate', 2023, https://content.knightfrank.com/research/2802/documents/en/india-real-estate-residential-and-office-market-h2-2023-10856.pdf.
16. Express News Services, 'Bajaj Auto chairman Niraj Bajaj buys Rs 252.5 crore apartment in South Mumbai', *Indian Express*, March 2023, https://indianexpress.com/article/cities/mumbai/bajaj-auto-chairman-niraj-bajaj-buys-rs-252-5-crore-apartment-in-south-mumbai-8499072/.
17. Linah Baliga, 'Theme park, garden planned on 120-acre racecourse land', *The Hindustan Times*, 6 January 2024, https:// www.hindustantimes.com/cities/mumbai-news/theme-park- garden-planned-on-120-acre-racecourse-land-101704483027343. html#google_vignette.

2. A Home Is a Home

1. Samuel T. Sheppard, *Bombay Place-names And Street-names: an Excursion Into the By-ways of the History of Bombay* City (Bombay: Times Press, 1917).
2. John Fryer, John, *A new account of East India and Persia in eight letters: being nine years travels, begun and finished 1681*. (Delhi: Periodical Experts Book Agency, 1985). Link: https://www.loc.gov/item/85901416/.
3. Reginald Heber, *Narrative of a Journey through the Upper Provinces of India, from Calcutta to Bombay, 1824–1825*, 10.1017/CBO9780511995965.

4. Marienne Postans, *Western India in 1838* (London: Saunders and Otley, Conduit Street. 1839).

3. A Pandemic Hits the City

1. J.K. Condon, 'The Bombay Plague: Being a History of the Progress of Plague in the Bombay Presidency from September 1896 to June 1899', Printed at the Education Society's Steam Press, 1900, https:// books.google.co.in/books?id=MvA2AQAAMAAJ.
2. P. Robbeditor, 19841807438, English, Miscellaneous, UK, 0-7007-0161-3, London, Rural India. Land, power and society under British rule., (viii + 314pp.), Curzon Press, Rural India. Land, power and society under British rule, (1983).
3. Atikh Rashid, 'How oppressive containment measures during Poona plague led to assassination of British officer', *Indian Express*, 9 June 2020, https://web.archive.org/web/20200609143341/https:// indianexpress.com/article/research/how-oppressive-containment- measures-during-poona-plague-led-to-assassination-of-british- officer-6450775/.
4. Sidney Low, *A Vision of India* (New York: E. P. Dutton; London: Smith, Elder, 1907).
5. 'The Bombay Plague', Condon.
6. M. Ramanna, *Healthcare in Bombay Presidency 1896-1930* (Delhi: Primus Books, 2012).

4. Bombay Turns Westward

1. Sadat Hasan Manto, *Stars from Another Sky: The Bombay Film World of the 1940s* (Delhi: Penguin Books, 2000)
2. The Development of Bombay, Davidge, W. R.
3. Sharada Dwivedi and Rahul Mehrotra, *Bombay Deco* (Mumbai: Eminence Designs, 2008).
4. Building Development Supplement, *The Times of India*, February 28, 1940, Page 14.
5. Building Development Supplement, *The Times of India*, February 28, 1940, Page 19.
6. Interview with author.

5. Dinner, Dance, but No Drinks

1. Interview with author.
2. Interview with author.
3. Breckenridge, Carol A., *Consuming Modernity: Public Culture in a South Asian World*. NED-New edition. University of Minnesota Press, 1995. http://www.jstor.org/stable/10.5749/j.ctttt4v5.

4. Bromfield, Louis. *Night in Bombay*. (London: Harper & Brothers, 1940)

6. Mills Become Malls

1. M.L. Dantwala, *A Hundred Years of Indian Raw* Cotton (Bombay: East India Cotton Association, 1947).
2. Madhoo Pavaskar, *Saga of the Cotton Exchange*, (Bombay: East India Cotton Exchange, 1985).
3. Ardeshir Godrej, *Final Victory: The Life and Death of Naval Godrej*, (Delhi: Penguin Viking, 2000).
4. Rajnarayan Chandavarkar, 'Neighbourhood to Nation: TH Rise and Fall of the Left in Bombay's Girangaon in the Twentieth Century', Tata Institute of Social Sciences, http://millmumbai.tiss.edu/wp-content/uploads/2015/03/From-Neighbourhood-To-Nation.pdf.

7. Ghettos, Old and New

1. Hussain Zaidi, *Dongri to Dubai: Six Decades of the Mumbai Mafia* (Delhi: Roli Books, 2012).

8. Ship-Breaking and Slums

1. J. Gerson da Cunha, *The Origin of Bombay* (Bombay: Society's library, 1900).

9. The Red Light Fades

1. *Bombay Place-Names and Street-Names*, Sheppard.
2. Pages 58. 59 of By-Ways of Bombay, D B Taraporevala and Sons and Co. Bombay, 1912 Edwardes, S. M. (Stephen Meredyth). By-ways of Bombay. Bombay: D.B. Taraporevala Sons & Co., 1912
3. S. Bharat, P. Aggleton and P. Tyrer, 'India: HIV and AIDS-Related Discrimination, Stigmatization, and Denial', UNAIDS, https://www.unaids.org/sites/default/files/media_asset/jc316-uganda-india_en_0.pdf

11. The Hidden City

1. P. Dewoolkar, 'Understanding the Marginalized Landscape, Case M (East) Ward Mumbai', Masters dissertation, Kamla Raheja Vidyanidhi Institute for Architecture.
2. MMR-EIS, 'Final TB report', 2018, https://www.mmreis.org.in/images/research/Final_TB_report_ submitted.pdf
3. 'A Struggle For The Right To The City: The Case Of Mahul', https://www.cps.iitb.ac.in/a-struggle-for-the-right-to-the-city-the-case-of-mahul/

INDEX

ABOUT THE AUTHOR

Sidharth Bhatia is a Mumbai-born journalist and writer. He has been in the media, print and electronic, for over four decades. He is a founding editor of *The Wire* and was part of the original team that launched the Mumbai-based English daily *DNA*. He has written three books—*Cinema Modern: The Navketan Story* (2011), *'Amar Akbar Anthony': Masala, Madness, Manmohan Desai* (2013) and *India Psychedelic: The Story of a Rocking Generation* (2014). This is his fourth book. He tweets at @bombaywallah.

HarperCollins *Publishers* India

At HarperCollins India, we believe in telling the best stories and finding the widest readership for our books in every format possible. We started publishing in 1992; a great deal has changed since then, but what has remained constant is the passion with which our authors write their books, the love with which readers receive them, and the sheer joy and excitement that we as publishers feel in being a part of the publishing process.

Over the years, we've had the pleasure of publishing some of the finest writing from the subcontinent and around the world, including several award-winning titles and some of the biggest bestsellers in India's publishing history. But nothing has meant more to us than the fact that millions of people have read the books we published, and that somewhere, a book of ours might have made a difference.

As we look to the future, we go back to that one word—a word which has been a driving force for us all these years.

Read.